DramaContemporary

LATIN AMERICA

THE DRAMACONTEMPORARY SERIES

DramaContemporary is a series specializing in the publication of new foreign plays in translation, organized by country or region. The series developed in response to the increasing internationalism of our age that now links world societies more closely, not only economically, but culturally as well. The last twenty years, in particular, is characterized by cross-cultural references in writing and performance, East and West and throughout the Americas. The new drama series is designed to partake of this movement in world patterns of culture, specifically in the area of our specialty, theatre.

Each volume of DramaContemporary features a selection of recent plays that reflects current social, cultural, and artistic values in individual countries. Plays are chosen for their significance in the larger perspective of a culture, as a measure of the concerns of its artists and public. At times, these plays may find their way into the American theatrical repertoire; in other instances, this may not be possible. Nevertheless, at all times the American public can have the opportunity to learn about other cultures—the speech, gestures, rhythms and attitudes that shape a society—in the dramatic life of their plays.

The Publishers

IN PRINT:

DramaContemporary: Czechoslovakia
DramaContemporary: Spain
DramaContemporary: France
DramaContemporary: Latin America

IN PREPARATION:

DramaContemporary: Hungary
DramaContemporary: Poland
DramaContemporary: Germany

DRAMA CONTEMPORARY

LATIN AMERICA

plays by

Manuel Puig
Antonio Skármeta
Mario Vargas Llosa
Carlos Fuentes

Edited, with an Introduction, by
George W. Woodyard & Marion Peter Holt

PAJ Publications
(A Division of Performing Arts Journal, Inc.)
New York

Library of Congress Cataloging in Publication Data
DramaContemporary: Latin America
CONTENTS: *The Kiss of the Spider Woman, Burning Patience, Kathie and the Hippopotamus, Orchids in the Moonlight*
Library of Congress Catalog Card No.: 86-62157
ISBN: 1-55554-004-X (cloth)
ISBN: 1-55554-005-8 (paper)

Printed in the United States of America

Publication of this book has been made possible in part by a grant from the National Endowment for the Arts, Washington, D.C., a federal agency, and public funds received from the New York State Council on the Arts. Additional funds were provided by the AT&T Foundation.

General Editors of the DramaContemporary Series:
    Bonnie Marranca and Gautam Dasgupta

Contents

Introduction

George W. Woodyard
and
Marion Peter Holt

NOVELIST-PLAYWRIGHTS

The contemporary Latin American novel has, over a period of almost two decades, enjoyed an ever-increasing popularity in the United States and Europe, inspiring and determining a new world-view of the cultures to the south. Even before the current fiction "boom" the Chilean poets Gabriela Mistral and Pablo Neruda had achieved a degree of international attention as recipients of the Nobel Prize for Literature, but the theatre of the vast area we know as "Latin America" is only beginning to be translated and performed abroad—despite a large existing repertoire of viable plays and the remarkable number of new ones that appear each year.

Some of the Latin American plays that have been staged in recent years outside the countries of their origin are by writers who are already known through their novels, and the focus of the present collection is on four such novelist-playwrights who have successfully bridged the genre gap. Examples of novelists who also qualify as dramatists can, of course, be found in many literatures. (Some obvious names would be Wilder and Saroyan in the United States, Sartre and Camus in France, and Graham Greene in England.) The plays of Mario Vargas Llosa, Carlos Fuentes, and Antonio Skármeta have now been seen on three continents, and those of Manuel Puig in both South America and Europe. Their productions have demonstrated that Latin American theatre can be as accessible as Latin American fiction, whether strongly reflecting the culture and ambience of the author's homeland (like Skármeta's *Burning Patience*) or displaying a more cosmopolitan sensibility (as do Fuentes's *Orchids in the Moonlight* and Vargas Llosa's *Kathie and the Hippopotamus*).

No collection of four plays, representing such diverse nations as Argentina, Chile, Peru, and Mexico can claim to be totally illustrative of the wide spectrum of dramatic styles and thematic interests visible today in the Latin

American countries. These distinctively individualistic plays do, however, provide a partial introduction to a larger multinational upsurge in theatrical activity and suggest the vitality of Latin American drama in the 1980s. They may also provoke a rethinking of the literary parameters of four major writers who defy simplistic categorizing.

LATIN AMERICA: YEARS OF FERMENT, YEARS OF CHANGE

Just as the publication of Garcia Márquez's *One Hundred Years of Solitude* in 1967 marks the beginning of the novelistic boom in Latin America, 1968 is a critical year in the trajectory of Latin American theatre. Since its colonial beginnings—and we note that theatre existed in the New World before the Spanish arrived nearly 500 years ago—the lines of cultural communication between Europe remained especially strong. Later contacts emphasized the importance of British and North American theatre, particularly in the twentieth century. The missing factor was a sense of identification among the theatre movements in the Latin American countries themselves. As an indicator of change, the year 1968 was significant on a global scale. The Tet Offensive signaled a turning point in the United States's bloody involvement in Vietnam, the student protests in Paris were an important prelude to countless strikes and demonstrations throughout the world, including Tlatelolco in Mexico the same year and Kent State two years later. Elections in Chicago were marked by violence, and even Cuba, in spite of its relative isolation, experienced the infamous Padilla affair which caught one of its major playwrights, Antón Arrufat, in the backlash.

In the midst of great political turmoil, in a world never far removed from the threat of nuclear annihilation, several theatrical events in Latin America struck a positive note in favor of cultural understanding: Peru celebrated its first festival of university theatre, the Café La Mama opened a branch in Bogotá, the initial Central American cultural festival opened in San José, Costa Rica, and in conjunction with the Olympic activities in Mexico, a festival of "new" Latin American theatre took place in the Teatro Reforma. One event was of special international significance: the first Latin American festival of university theatre brought participating groups from seven countries to the provincial city of Manizales, Columbia, and its impressive Teatro Fundadores, where a distinguished panel of judges included Jack Lang (later French minister of Culture) and Chilean poet Pablo Neruda. Guatemalan novelist and Nobel Laureate Miguel Angel Asturias served as honorary president. This festival was instrumental in establishing a pattern of inter- and intracontinental festivals, symposia, and conferences that have continued to the present. These events have served to promote the theatre throughout Latin America and have brought a new and heightened awareness of aspirations and stagecraft to the participants at all levels, whether actors, directors, playwrights or critics.

In the 1950s and 1960s, Latin American dramatists often employed realistic techniques to examine questions of psychological identity, metaphysical or ontological concerns, and socio-political issues inherent in society. In his existentialist play, *Las manos de Dios* (Mexico, 1956), Carlos Solórzano dealt with a set of complex relationships between church and state, focusing on oppression and freedom. René Marqués's *Los soles truncos* (Puerto Rico, 1958) offered a penetrating look at three aristocratic sisters who have decided to close themselves off from society by negating time. Jorge Díaz, known for his early humorous absurdist plays such as *El cepillo de dientes* (Chile, 1961), chose socio-economic backgrounds that refuted bourgeois values. Egon Wolff warned of an impending class struggle between haves and have-nots in *Los invasores* (Chile, 1962), a play using dream techniques and cyclical action. In a variety of stage works, Latin American writers sought to spell out in theatrical terms the problems within their countries in which military dictatorships spawned repression, the church encouraged obedience to tradition, and the social system offered a disproportionate share of the national wealth to a privileged few.

The new theatre that came to the fore in Latin America in the late 1960s is often designated as "popular theatre." As class struggle became more pronounced in the aftermath of the Cuban Revolution, playwrights began to seek new methods and operational styles to express the same socio-political concerns that earlier plays had set forth in more traditional ways. The Brechtian principles of epic theatre were discovered and adapted by various groups looking to transform society from within. Old notions of theatrical hierarchies that assume an author's text is performed by actors under the control of a director for the benefit of an audience are suddenly inverted, so that involvement elevates the public from the traditional role of spectator to participant in the action. Working collectively, groups developed their own texts—allegedly in the absence of plays suitable to their objectives. In the process, psychologically motivated characters gave way to character types who lent themselves to quick interchanging of roles; popular music provided integrated commentary or background; episodic structure allowed greater flexibility than conventional cause-and-effect sequencing; and signs or placards complemented simple stylized costumes and sets. Brecht's V-effect, integrated through various techniques, maintained the public awareness of an ideological, dialectical position.

The Aleph Group in Chile, Libre Teatro Libre in Córdoba, Argentina, Teatro Arena in São Paulo, and the long-established Colombian Experimental Theatre of Cali (the TEC, directed by theoretician Enrique Buenaventura) were all collectives instrumental in conceptualizing and disseminating throughout Latin America the principles of a new social order of theatre. In Cuba the Teatro Escambray, formed in 1968, became one of that nation's most accomplished popular theatre groups by working closely with people in the provinces to express their concerns about generational conflicts, the role of women, and a variety of issues in the new revolutionary society. The group spent months interviewing teachers, parents, and local officials, collecting 400 hours of taped materials, before staging Roberto Orihuela's *Los novios*, an examination of values and personal relationships from a revolutionary perspective. During the same period, Augusto Boal, Brazilian theorist, playwright, and director, was engaged in developing a series of theatrical innovations ranging from journalistic and invisible theatre to what he defined as "theatre of the oppressed."

Although certain groups broke totally with the traditional concepts of director, playwright, actor, and technical crew to work in an egalitarian framework of interchangeable roles, others maintained the division of functions while still attempting to revolutionize their theatrical processes, commonly along Marxist lines. The positive results were to bring theatre artists, especially authors and directors, into a closer working relationship in order to harmonize all aspects of theatrical production. Some would observe, however, that the negative corollary was often to discredit the importance of the dramatic text while emphasizing theatrical process.

This alternative theatre has rarely produced transcendent aesthetics, but the methods address the ideological needs of groups intent on using theatre to bring about social change. In Colombia, La Candelaria, under the direction of Santiago Garcia, has had notable success with *Guadalupe, años sin cuenta*, a chronicle of the years of violence in that area. The Teatro Popular de Bogotá staged *I Took Panama* (original title in English), a play that documents American intervention in the Panama Canal issue during the presidency of Theodore Roosevelt. Chile's Teatro Popular Ictus has collaborated regularly with Chilean writers José Donoso (*Sueños de mala muerte*), David Benavente (*Pedro, Juan y Diego*), Sergio Vodanovic (*¿Cuántos años tiene un día?*), and others in staging committed experimental plays before, during, and after the Allende period.

Documentary drama, whether the product of collective creation or of a single playwright, characterizes much of recent Latin American theatre. Dramatizing particular events, historical episodes, or even incidents of less moment, permits the re-examination of present attitudes and values through an historical paradigm. Vicente Leñero, in Mexico, has used the technique to good effect in *Pueblo rechazado, El juicio*, and in his recent *Martirio de Morelos*. José Rial, a dramatist of Spanish birth living in Venezuela, has created vivid antinaturalistic visions of historical events in *La muerte de Garcia Lorca* and *Bolívar* (the latter performed by the Rajatabla Company at New York's Public Theatre in 1985). Antonio Skármeta's *Ardiente paciencia* represents still another approach to the dramatization of historical events by integrating excerpts from Pablo Neruda's writings and his acceptance speech for the Nobel Prize into the framework of a play about the poet-diplomat's relationship with three ordinary Chilean citizens.

Within the Latin American nations, actual theatrical production is affected by conditions peculiar to each. In Mexico City, which benefits from a long theatrical tradition, as well as decades of political stability, theatre tends to resemble its counterparts in other world capitals, with an obvious dichotomy between commercial offerings that are rarely challenging and those of the experimental groups and the activist playwright. Similarly, in Buenos Aires, South America's most important center of theatrical production, dramatic fare covers the spectrum of commercial plays, avant-garde drama, cabaret satire, and opera. Where the theatrical tradition is less strong or nonexistent, the new activist theatre may well provide the only contact with live performances. Except in countries (such as Cuba) which subsidize the arts, writers, directors, actors, and other theatre artisans must survive by devoting some portion of their lives and talents to other professions. As for the audiences, the theatre may well be an expendable luxury; even though tickets are inexpensive by current standards in the United States, they remain beyond the reach of much of the population.

Censorship continues to be a threat to freedom of artistic expression in some Latin American countries—though formerly taboo themes (criticism of church and state, for example) are generally tolerated even in a tightly controlled system like Chile's. However, José Agustín's *Círculo vicioso*, censored in Mexico in 1972, and Marco Antonio de la Parra's *Lo crudo, lo cocido y lo podrido*, canceled one day before opening in Chile in 1978, are reminders of the enduring possibility of governmental interference.

Political events, or the search for a more congenial creative environment, have produced cycles of exile and return, dispersal and reintegration, as well as permanent changes of citizenship. In many instances the first productions of works by Latin American dramatists have taken place abroad (Europe, the United States, or a Latin American country other than the writer's homeland), where the political or artistic climate was more favorable. During the period of repression in Argentina in the 1970s, a number of Argentinean theatre artists found outlets for their talents in a liberalized Spain which had recently abolished governmental censorship. Borges, Vargas Llosa, Fuentes, Puig, and Jorge Díaz have all spent some of their creative years abroad. At present, Antonio Skármeta finds a receptive German-speaking audience for his work in West Germany, far from the military rule in Chile. Maria Irene Fornes, Cuban by birth but a U.S. citizen by adoption, has forged a notable career in the English-speaking theatre and is rightly considered an "American" playwright.

In spite of a certain xenophobic attitude toward foreign drama in general, Latin American plays are being performed with some frequency in the United States in the 1980s—not only by the pioneering Hispanic companies, such as the Puerto Rican Traveling Theatre and INTAR, but by enterprising professional regional theatres as well. Fuentes's *Orchids in the Moonlight* was staged by the American Repertory Theatre in Cambridge in 1982; the same year, Milwaukee Repertory Company produced *The Government Man* by the rising

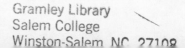

young Mexican playwright, Felipe Santander; and Alonso Alegría's *Crossing Niagara* has had productions on both the east and west coasts. Since 1984, grants from Theatre Communication Group's Hispanic Translation Project have made possible a number of translations of viable Latin American plays, providing the impetus for productions (to date) of Vargas Llosa'a *Kathie and the Hippotamus* at the Hippodrome State Theatre (Gainesville, Florida), Uslar Pietri's *The Mythweavers* (*Chuo Gil y las tejedoras*) at Seattle's Intiman Theatre, and Virgilio Pinera's *A Cold Air* by INTAR in New York.

THE KISS OF THE SPIDER WOMAN

The versatility of Latin American writers is nowhere more apparent than in the career of Manuel Puig. To date his works have included novels, plays, and screenplays (some published but unfilmed). Puig published *The Kiss of the Spider Woman* as a novel in 1976; he then adapted it for the stage, and its premiere in Valencia, Spain, in April 1981 was followed by an extended run in Madrid. It has since been performed in South America. The most recent treatment of the work is, of course, the motion picture version filmed in Brazil by the Argentinean director Hector Barbenco, with a screenplay by Leonard Schrader.

As in Vargas Llosa's *Kathie and the Hippopotamus*, the basis of the dramatic action in Puig's play is the process of storytelling, though the motivations and outcome are quite different. In this instance, two men share a prison cell where they are serving sentences for crimes against society—one for terrorist activities, the other for seducing minors. Throughout the two acts of the play, divided into nine scenes, Molina, the homosexual, narrates to Valentin, the revolutionary, the story and scenic effects of *Cat People*, a favorite film of his childhood. As Molina continues to distract Valentin like a male Scheherazade, he gains his confidence in order to extract information for the authorities about his group's terrorist activities.

The play challenges conceptions of stereotypical behavior through the interaction of two presumably dissimilar characters whose relationship grows to the point of physical union. Conventional notions of strength and weakness, domination and submission, male and female roles and, ultimately, physical courage vis-à-vis sentimentality are all put to test in a closely encapsulated dramatic encounter. The technique of pre-taped voices preserves the simplicity of the two-character play while providing the external element necessary to advance the action, and the unconventional forward retrospective at the end satisfies our curiosity about events beyond the final leave-taking on stage.

Since *The Kiss of the Spider Woman* began as a prose work that rejected traditional narrative techniques in favor of a fundamental element of drama (dialogue), it is hardly surprising that the reduction for the stage was achieved with little departure in form and spirit from the original. Puig's experiment with the novel in dialogue has, to be sure, notable antecedents. One of the classics of

Hispanic literature is Fernando de Roja's fifteenth-century dialogued novel, *La Celestina*, which has inspired several stage reductions and has even been performed recently in Spain in its entirety. *Spider Woman* differs from the more expansive *La Celestina* in its narrow focus on two characters and action confined to a claustrophobic prison cell (except for brief segments). Here the only escape for reader (or spectator), as well as the characters themselves, is Molina's recreation of a remembered film.

Puig's decision to limit Molina's basic narration to the well-known *Cat People* (1943) rather than including segments of the other five films (two real and three inventions of Puig's), which also figure conspicuously in the novel, made possible an aesthetic dimension that is missing in Barbenco's cinematic version. By using the familiar, classic movie rather than an obscure one, the metafictional allusions are easily accessible, providing a special level of audience association for the play. *Cat People* endures because of its frequently noted use of suggestion and its capacity for manipulating the imagination, and it serves as an ideal complement to Puig's own evocative skills.

In all three versions of *The Kiss of the Spider Woman* — novel, play, and film — we find an intermingling of genres (or media). Molina's narrations are in a sense "novelistic" treatments of stories pre-existing in cinematic form. The structure of the novel itself is dialogic, as it remains in play and film, without narrative connectives that describe physical surroundings and character traits or that permit the direct insertion of the author's point of view. In the motion picture version, the narrations are once again transmuted into cinematic form to open up the action beyond the confines of the prison. In the process, however, much less is required of the re-creative powers of the audience. Still, it remains for the most part self-reflective in its conscious use of the film-within-the-film and thus essentially true to its source.

BURNING PATIENCE

The poetry of Chile's Nobel Laureate Pablo Neruda ranged from epic works to elemental odes and has been translated into many of the world's languages. His ambassadorial posts and his devotion to communist causes made him a highly acclaimed and controversial figure; his death only a few days after the military coup that resulted in Salvador Allende's assassination and General Pinochet's assumption of power seemed particularly ironic.

Neruda himself wrote one play, *Fulgor y muerte de Joaquin Murieta* (1966), about a bandit of the California Gold Rush days. It was a work that later inspired Chile's leading playwright, Jorge Diaz, to write a committed play dealing with the last four months of Neruda's life. For the younger Antonio Skármeta, the poet is a national hero, and his *Burning Patience* pays tribute both to Neruda the spokesman for Chilean culture and to a Neruda who was very much aware of his own role as a continuer of Western poetic traditions (as suggested by his use of the line from Rimbaud that gives the play its title).

After the military coup in Chile, Skármeta took up residence in West Berlin, where he has written novels and screenplays as well as *Burning Patience*. Although his prose works have brought him the most critical attention to date, he has also had extensive firsthand experience in the theatre. Before leaving his homeland, he worked closely as an actor and director with an experimental group at the University of Chile, translating and staging works by Albee, Saroyan, and others. In Europe he has collaborated in the staging of his own play and directed a film version which won him awards at both the Biarritz and Huelva film festivals in 1984.

Burning Patience gives a tender and intimate view of Pablo Neruda from the perspective of the young postman, Mario Jiménez, who delivers mail to his home in Isla Negra. Neruda's role in Mario's incipient love affair with Beatriz, daughter of the local innkeeper, demythifies the poet and paints him as a warm and humorous individual genuinely concerned with those around him. In the early scenes the play concentrates on the personal aspects of human relationships, and the inclusion of Neruda poems establishes his poetic concerns with sensual love and with the manifestations of natural forces in Isla Negra. The tension builds as the later scenes of Mario (now married and a father) and his family receiving nostalgic greetings from Neruda in Paris and listening to the poet's acceptance speech at the Nobel presentation are followed by news of the assassination of Allende's aide-de-camp. After a moving reunion between Mario and the dying Neruda, the play's final scene strikes an ominous note about fascist governments as Mario is taken off for questioning by two policemen.

Skármeta's fascination with sounds, music, and verbal effect give *Burning Patience* a lyrical quality that counterbalances its political thrust. In the first version of the play (1982), sounds and lights were designated as "characters" in the cast list, and although these designations were deleted during revisions, the functions remain essentially the same. The sounds of the ocean and bells that Mario records on tape to send to the Paris-based Neruda reinforce metonymically the human dimensions and are reminders of the source of Neruda's own inspiration. The language is always under careful control, as Skármeta interweaves authentic passages from Neruda's memoirs to carry forward the action or punctuate a key scene. Skármeta's concern for the right phrase and sound is an influence not only from Neruda but also from his other idol, Shakespeare, as the intercalation of Mercutio's dying words into Neruda's death scene suggests.

Although Mario, his wife-to-be Beatriz, and the redoubtable mother-in-law Rosa González are simple citizens of Isla Negra who sometimes speak with an earthy directness, they are not, strictly speaking, naturalistic characters, nor are the scenes in which they appear intended as a literal recreation of a slice of Chilean life. Rather these characters are seen through Neruda's prism and heard via the poetic sensibilities of the playwright. Their remarkable (and frequently amusing) susceptibility to poetic metaphor exceeds the ordinary as Skármeta transforms them into archtypical Chileans (with views that do not always parallel those of Neruda). For all its political implications and forceful denunciation of authoritarianism, *Burning Patience* is, above all, a celebration of humanity and of nature's recurring cycles in which return and rebirth follow destruction.

KATHIE AND THE HIPPOPOTAMUS

Mario Vargas Llosa's first work for the stage, *The Young Lady from Tacna* (1980), dealt with the restructuring of memory through the application of artistic imagination, and its narrator was a novelist called Belisario. His second play, *Kathie and the Hippopotamus* (1983), though vastly different in mood and setting, also deals with the transformation of memory and fantasy into fiction or drama. In this instance the instigator is a well-to-do young Peruvian woman who hires a male "ghost writer" to record and, in practice, enact with her a series of scenes that either evolve from their imaginations or represent the exploration of realities that might have been under different circumstances. These fantasies require the introduction of two additional actors to appear as remembered or invented characters in the plays-within-the-play. The results are experiments in both drama and fiction carried on within the framework of a play.

Vargas Llosa goes beyond the memory technique employed in his earlier play to a more overtly metatheatrical approach that involves characters who are consciously calling attention to their own theatricality. Even the setting itself has been preconceived by a character as a setting, for in order to establish a proper environment for dictating her novel, Kathie, the banker's wife, has furnished a studio in Lima to correspond to her idea of a Parisian garret, theatricalizing from the outset her unorthodox experiments in spontaneous creativity. In his essay on "The Theatre as Fiction" and his notes on "Set Design, Costumes and Effects" (both of which accompany the text of the play), Vargas Llosa explains in some detail his aesthetic intent, providing specific ideas (and cautions) about the setting and costumes he envisions. He notes that he set out to write "a comedy carried to the limits of the unreal" and that only during the writing process did he come to realize that the deeper theme was the relationship between life and fiction.

While the play may indeed qualify as a comedy, its farcical elements are not on a surface level but rather, as the author tells us, in its subtext, "the invisible root of what is said and done on stage." Even when we are amused by Kathie's extravagant adventure fantasies, we are reminded of the underlying seriousness of the play by those episodes (real or invented) that reflect her own life and that of her collaborator Santiago outside the security of the "Paris loft." Although the conclusion is never directly stated within the context of the play itself, the implication is that a deliberate recreation of reality alongside other possible "realities" may prove the most effective approach to self-realization, and a life barren of a degree of fictional embellishment can only prove stultifying.

Techniques of mingling theatre and fictional narration or recall, and the transformation of memory into dramatic recreations, have produced some of the classics of modern drama. They have been used to advantage by a wide range of playwrights that includes Tennessee Williams and Thornton Wilder in the United States. As with the plays of Puig and Skármeta, the conscious break with the more conventional limits of genre in *Kathie and the Hippopotamus* is fundamental to its theatrical efficacy, providing the very qualities that lift the play above the ordinary. Although there may be a variety of subtle modern influences on Vargas Llosa's work, it is essentially in the long Spanish tradition of incorporating calculated playacting into a larger fictional or dramatic frame (*Don Quixote* and *Life is a Dream* being familiar prototypic illustrations) and of exploring the endless interrelationships between illusion and reality.

ORCHIDS IN THE MOONLIGHT

At an early age the bilingual, bicultural Carlos Fuentes made a conscious decision to write in Spanish in order to enhance Mexico's literature, since he considered the United States to be already rich in novelists. His prose works have normally been translated immediately into English, and in some cases (such as *Terra nostra*) were translated as they were being written. *Orchids in the Moonlight*, however, represents yet another level of creativity, since it was written simultaneously by Fuentes himself in both Spanish and English — a process that caused him to modify the coexisting versions during their evolution because of the distinct operative and linguistic codes.

Fuentes's third play follows patterns established in his two earlier stage works. Both had responded to the author's concern about the Mexican national heritage and character, whether expressed in the historical and symbolic figures of Moctezuma, Marina, and Hernán Cortés in *Todos los gatos son pardos* (1970) or in the metaphorical and quasi-religious struggle between domination and free will of *El tuerto es rey* (1970). *Orchids in the Moonlight* continues the examination of cultural and attitudinal values within the national patrimony. Echoing Puig's interest in the cinema, Fuentes singles out two film stars of Mexican heritage, Dolores del Rio and Maria Felix, and places them in an improbable ménage in Venice, California (quite different from the other fabled Venice that Dolores imagines). Their fixation of remembered glory is not unlike that of Norma Desmond in *Sunset Boulevard*, and it is clear, even in the opening lines of dialogue, that their present identities are meaningless in the world outside their curious sanctuary. When the Fan, a mysterious and unidentified admirer, appears at the door — possibly in response to Dolores's phone call—the action takes a bizarre course, accelerating in intensity as it threatens the modus vivendi of the aging stars.

With its constant referral, both visually and verbally, to specific details of films in which Del Rio and Felix starred, *Orchids in the Moonlight* shows decided similarities to Puig's *Kiss of the Spider Woman*, which in its first incarnation as a novel offered more extensive cinematic recreations than the terser stage version. Similarly, the dramatic structure is based on a series of metatheatrical self-dramatizations that have parallels in the more extended plays-within-the play that are the focus of Vargas Llosa's *Kathie and the Hippopotamus*. But unlike these plays, where fantasies are developed within a basically realistic framework, Fuentes's drama unfolds in an atmosphere of unreality and culminates in a surrealistic, ritualistic recitation of titles of films in which the two actresses appeared. In the initial character descriptions, Fuentes established the nonliteralness of the play as well as its metatheatrical essence when he offers a variety of conceivable casting possibilities: both roles portrayed by the actresses who inspired them; the two actresses reversing their roles; a perverse type of casting against reality with two plump blondes in the parts; and, finally, the possibility of the female roles being played by men.

The two stars on whom the characters are based were strong female figures who created their own myths and daringly asserted new standards for their times within the predominantly *machista* culture. The similarities and differences between the two are key to the play's development, as is the relationship to "Mummy," the unseen figure who lives upstairs. But *Orchids in the Moonlight* is more than a feminist statement about positive action within a male-oriented society. Fuentes has created in the work, just as in his novels, archetypal figures who transcend their immediate circumstances to make statements about life and death, domination and submission, identity and oblivion. He also raises provocative questions about the distortion of historical perspective in a film-oriented society through the persistent remolding of cinematic biography to fit the persona of a star. That the action of the play takes place on "the day Orson Welles died"—a premature and fictional event at the time Fuentes was writing—is particularly ironic. Even before the actual death of Welles, who directed Del Rio in *Journey into Fear*, the reading of the invented obituary recounting his thwarted career proved one of the most trenchant scenes for its comment on a living figure who had died long before as far as Hollywood was concerned.

ABOUT THE TRANSLATIONS

The English version of Puig's *The Kiss of the Spider Woman* is translator-critic Michael Feingold's revision of his earlier adaptation of the play. In one key scene, where the stage directions of the English version offer a staging alternative significantly different from Puig's original and from the production in

Spain in 1981, a note has been provided by the editors. The translation of *Burning Patience* is based on Skármeta's final, approved version of the play which eliminates some of the specific directions for the integration of sounds, lighting, and scenic effects in his earlier script. The present version of Vargas Llosa's *Kathie and the Hippopotamus* is a revision by Kerry McKenney and Anthony Oliver-Smith of the translation they completed under a grant from Theatre Communication Group's Hispanic Theatre Translation Project for the Hippodrome State Theatre (Gainesville, Florida), where it was staged for the first time in English in 1983 as *Sweet Tango of Lies*. The original Spanish version contains a number of English names and expressions (darling, nice, sorry, cheek to cheek, etc.) which provide social commentary or have humorous implications in the Spanish context. These words have been placed in quotation marks in the translation. For the Hippodrome production, the play was somewhat restructured; the present version returns to Vargas Llosa's original sequence of scenes.

Orchids in the Moonlight is not a translation at all, since it was written originally in both Spanish and English. This published version is Carlos Fuentes's revision of the script used for the play's first production in English by the American Repertory Theatre (Cambridge) in 1982.

The Kiss of the Spider Woman

a play based on Puig's novel of the same name

Manuel Puig

THE KISS OF THE SPIDER WOMAN
From the film version
Directed by Hector Babenco

CHARACTERS

Molina
Valentin

SETTING

A small cell in the Villa Devoto prison, Buenos Aires. Upstage, slanted corridors lined with wire mesh lead to other parts of the prison. The cell door is barred. Three kinds of lighting should be used to represent the different times of day: yellow for daylight, orange for electric lights after sunset; blue for late night, when the prison lights are turned off. The light on the actors should be mostly white and sharp, in contrast with the muted colors of the light on the upstage areas.

ACT ONE

SCENE 1

(*Total darkness. White light suddenly picks out the heads of Molina and Valentin, sitting on the floor, facing in opposite directions.*)

MOLINA: . . . and right away you notice there's something strange about her, she's not like other women. She's fairly young, her face is . . . more round than oval, with a little pointy chin like a cat's face.

VALENTIN: And her eyes?

MOLINA: They might be green. She's sketching at the zoo and she stares at the black panther lying in its cage. Then when she rattles her sketch pad, the panther notices her.

VALENTIN: Wouldn't it smell her first?

MOLINA: Then suddenly someone's standing behind her, trying to light a cigarette, but the wind blows out the match.

VALENTIN: Who is it?

MOLINA: Wait. She jumps up. It's a man, not a handsome movie-star type, but a nice-looking guy, with his hat pulled down low on his forehead. He raises it and smiles at her, and says her drawing is terrific. And she kind of touches up her hair-do.

VALENTIN: Go on.

MOLINA: He hears her accent and asks if she's a foreigner, and she explains that she came to New York when the War broke out. He asks if she misses Bucharest, and it's like a cloud comes over her face, and she tells him she's from up in the mountains, from Transylvania.

VALENTIN: Just like Dracula.

MOLINA: Anyway, he's an architect, and the next day you see him at the office with his colleagues, one of them's a girl, and when it's three o'clock he just feels like throwing away his slide-rule and compasses and running across the street to the zoo. And the girl architect asks him what he's so happy about, you can see she's really in love with him, even though she tries to hide it.

VALENTIN: I bet she's a real dog.

MOLINA: No, nothing special, but kind of cute, brown hair. But he can't forget the one down at the zoo, whose name is Irena, and she's disappeared. Days go by and he can't get her out of his mind, then he's walking down a street with a lot of expensive shops and sees something in the window of an art gallery. It's the work of somebody who never draws anything but . . . panthers. So he goes in, and there's Irena being congratulated by this whole crowd of people. And I can't remember what happens next.

VALENTIN: Try and think . . .

MOLINA: Wait a minute . . . Okay, he goes up and congratulates her too. And she ditches all the art critics and goes off with him. He tells her he just happened to be passing by, he was really on his way to buy somebody a present.

VALENTIN: The architect girl.

MOLINA: What he's trying to figure out is if he's got enough cash to buy two identical presents. And he stops at a pet shop, she looks perturbed, they specialize in birds, all kinds of birds in cages, taking sips of fresh water.

VALENTIN: Wait a second . . . Is there water in the pitcher?

MOLINA: Yeah, I filled it when they let us out to go to the john. (*The white light has now come up full so that we see both men for the first time; simultaneously, the blue light has come up on the prison corridors.*)

VALENTIN: Good.

MOLINA: You want some? It's nice and cool.

VALENTIN: No, I just wanted to make sure we had some for tea tomorrow. Go on.

MOLINA: It's no problem, there's enough to last all day.

VALENTIN: Don't get me into bad habits. I forgot to get some when they let us out to shower. If it hadn't been for you we'd be out of water.

MOLINA: I told you, there's plenty. (*Pause.*) Anyway, when they go into the pet shop it's like all hell broke loose. The birds go crazy, they start flying against the bars of their cages, trying to get out, they bruise their wings. And she grabs his hand real fast and pulls him out of there, and immediately the birds calm down. Then she says she has to be going, so he makes a date with her for the next night. Then he goes back into the shop alone, and this time the birds don't react at all, they just go on singing their little songs. So he buys one for the girl in his office. And then . . . well, I don't remember what happens next, I'm tired.

VALENTIN: Come on, just a little more.

MOLINA: No, I forget things when I'm tired. Over tea tomorrow.

VALENTIN: No, it's better at night. I don't want this nonsense to distract me during the day. I have more important things to think about. (*Molina shrugs.*) Don't get me wrong. It's just that when I'm not reading, I'm thinking.

MOLINA: (*A little sarcastic, piqued by Valentin's remarks.*) Don't worry, I won't bother you.

VALENTIN: I'm glad you understand. Good night. (*Valentin stretches out to go to sleep.*)

MOLINA: Good night, pleasant dreams of Irena. (*Molina stretches out too, but stays half sitting up, pensive.*)
VALENTIN: I like the architect girl better.
MOLINA: I knew it.

(*Lights.*)

SCENE 2

(*Molina and Valentin are still sitting, not looking at each other, but in a different position than in Scene 1. Only their heads are lit; gradually the blue light on the corridors comes back up.*)

MOLINA: So they keep seeing each other and they start to fall in love. She caresses him and she cuddles in his arms, but when he tries to hold her tight and kiss her, she slips away. She asks him not to kiss her, but to let her kiss him, and then she kisses him very gently, with her soft full lips all puckered up tight, like a baby's, and she keeps her mouth closed . . . (*Valentine starts to comment but Molina keeps going.*) Anyway, next thing we see them at a quaint little restaurant. He tells her she's looking better than ever, in that stunning black top. But she's totally lost her appetite, she won't touch her food, so they get up and go. It's snowing outside and there's dead silence all over the city. In the distance you hear animals roaring, they're not far from the park where the zoo is. And she whispers to him that she's afraid to go home and spend the night by herself. So they get a cab and go to his place. (*Molina slowly becomes more engrossed in the story.*) It's a nice apartment, in an elegant old brownstone, there's a huge hand-carved staircase, with a palm tree in a magnificent antique pot, I think it has a Chinese design. You can hardly hear their footsteps, the carpet is so thick, like the snow outside. It's a big, roomy apartment, full of old turn-of-the-century furniture that belonged to the guy's mother.
VALENTIN: And what does he do?
MOLINA: Nothing, he lights his pipe and just looks at her in this nice way, like he always does.
VALENTIN: I'd love to know how you picture his mother.
MOLINA: (*Not joking.*) Why? So you can make fun of her too?
VALENTIN: I won't, I promise.
MOLINA: I don't know . . . a really charming woman. Always did her best to make her husband happy, and her kids. Always beautifully dressed.
VALENTIN: Do you see her scrubbing the floors?
MOLINA: No, she's always impeccable, a beautiful high-necked dress, with a fancy lace collar so you can't see the age lines around her neck.

VALENTIN: Impeccable, sure, she had servants, she exploits people who have no choice but to wait on her for pennies. And her husband exploits her in his turn, keeping her locked in the house like a slave, waiting on him, so, sure, she makes him happy . . .

MOLINA: Hold on . . .

VALENTIN: . . . waiting for him every night, to get back from the law office or the clinic. She accepted the system, she internalized all that crap and raised his son to live by it, and now *he* ends up with a panther woman. Serves him right.

MOLINA: (*Irritated.*) Dammit, you make me mad! Here I am telling you about the movie, and I've forgotten all about this rathole we're in, and now you have to bring all that up.

VALENTIN: I'd forgotten all about it too.

MOLINA: Then why break the spell?

VALENTIN: Let me explain . . .

MOLINA: Tomorrow. (*Pause.*) Why couldn't I have the panther woman's boyfriend for a cellmate instead of you?

VALENTIN: That's something else and I'm not interested.

MOLINA: Afraid to talk about it?

VALENTIN: It bores me, that's all. You don't have to explain anything, I know what you are.

MOLINA: Stop playing psychologist; I told you I was in here for corrupting the morals of a minor, that tells you everything.

VALENTIN: (*Trying to make light of it.*) I know why you like the panther woman's boyfriend—it's because he smokes a pipe, right?

MOLINA: No, because he's gentle and understanding.

VALENTIN: His mother castrated him, that's all.

MOLINA: Look, I like him, that's all there is to it. And you like the architect girl, I suppose you think she's some kind of guerrilla leader.

VALENTIN: Well, sure, I like her more than the panther woman. But I don't think the guy with the pipe is right for you.

MOLINA: Why not?

VALENTIN: What you have in mind isn't just talking, right?

MOLINA: Course not.

VALENTIN: Well, he likes Irena because she's frigid and he doesn't have to put the moves on her, that's why he can take her home to his mother, who's obviously there, even if she's dead.

MOLINA: (*Getting more and more infuriated.*) Go on.

VALENTIN: See, if he's kept the house just like it was when his mother was alive, it means he doesn't want to grow up, so instead of a woman he brings home another kid to play with.

MOLINA: That's all in your mind. I don't know if it's his mother's house, I just like the way it's decorated, and since it's all done with antiques I said it might be his mother's. For all I know he rents it furnished.

VALENTIN: In other words, you're making up half the movie.

MOLINA: I'm not, I swear. It's just that I have to, you know, get everything organized to make it clear, like the house. And don't forget, I'm a window dresser, that's almost like a decorator. (*Pause.*) Anyway, she finally starts to tell him her story, I don't remember exactly how it goes, but the main thing is that she comes from a little mountain village where there were these panther women a long time ago. And these stories used to terrify her when she was a kid.

VALENTIN: And the birds, why were they afraid of her?

MOLINA: That's what the guy asks her, and do you know what she answers? She doesn't answer at all! And the scene fades out on him in pajamas and a bathrobe, nice but not too fancy, solid color, watching her fall asleep on the sofa, while he sits in the bedroom, lights his pipe and thinks about her story.

VALENTIN: You know what I like about it? It's sort of an allegory, the woman's afraid to give herself to a man, because her sexuality makes her a bit of an animal, right?

MOLINA: (*Ignoring Valentin's comment, which he dislikes.*) She gets up, her day is dawning.

VALENTIN: She wakes up because she feels the cold, just like us.

MOLINA: (*Annoyed.*) I knew you'd say that. As a matter of fact, she's awakened by a canary singing in its cage. At first, she's afraid to go near it, but the bird keeps on singing and finally she comes right up to the cage. She gives a big sigh of relief because the bird's not afraid of her. Then she goes and makes toast, and cereal, and pancakes . . .

VALENTIN: Don't talk about food.

MOLINA: . . . pancakes, and . . .

VALENTIN: I'm not kidding. Just don't ever mention food or naked women.

MOLINA: Okay, so she wakes him up and he's delighted to see her making herself at home, and he asks her if she wants to marry him and stay there forever. She says with all her heart, and she looks round and sees the dark velvet window curtains, and they look so beautiful to her. (*Emphatically.*) And *that's* when you get to see all the gorgeous antique furniture. But Irena wants to wait a while before she becomes his wife for real, until she's sure her fears are over for good.

VALENTIN: And you know what happens to her, don't you?

MOLINA: Hold on. He agrees and they get married. And on their wedding night, she sleeps in the bed and he sleeps on the sofa.

VALENTIN: Taking care of Mommy's furniture. Tell the truth, it's your dream house, right?

MOLINA: Yes, dammit! And I suppose now I'll have to listen to you telling me what everybody tells me.

VALENTIN: Yeah? What's that?

MOLINA: Always the same, they all hand you the same line.

VALENTIN: What?

MOLINA: That I was pampered too much when I was a kid, and that's how I got this way, that I'm too tied to my mother's apron strings but it's never too late to change and all I need is a good woman because there's nothing better than a woman.

VALENTIN: They tell you that?

MOLINA: And here's what I tell them: Terrific! You're absolutely right! And if there's nothing better than a woman—then I want to be a woman! So thanks for the tip but forget it, because I know what I want and it's all perfectly clear to me.

VALENTIN: I'm sure it's not clear to me, at least not the way you explain it.

MOLINA: There's nothing to explain. If you want, I'll go on with the movie, and if not, I'll tell it to myself in a whisper and that's that, goodbye, *Arrivederci, Sparafucile!*

VALENTIN: Who's Sparafucile?

MOLINA: You don't know anything about opera. He's the hit-man in *Rigoletto*. (*Pause.*) So where were we?

VALENTIN: The wedding night, when he doesn't touch her.

MOLINA: I forgot to tell you: they made an arrangement that she would go to see a psychiatrist.

VALENTIN: What? Sorry . . . Look, don't let this upset you, but . . .

MOLINA: What?

VALENTIN: (*Gloomy, withdrawing.*) I can't concentrate on what you're saying.

MOLINA: Am I boring you?

VALENTIN: No, it's not that. I've got something on my mind. (*By now talking more to himself than to Molina.*) I need a little silence. You know that feeling you get when you're just on the verge of figuring something out, like you've got the tip of the thread and if you don't start pulling right away you'll lose it?

MOLINA: (*After a pause.*) How come you like the architect girl?

VALENTIN: Well, everybody has to like someone. (*Self-deprecating.*) I know it's a weakness.

MOLINA: It's not a weakness.

VALENTIN: (*Philosophically; not sentimental.*) It's funny how you can't avoid feeling affectionate about something or other . . . It's like the mind oozes emotion all the time . . .

MOLINA: You think?

VALENTIN: Like a leaky faucet. The drops have to land somewhere.

MOLINA: Where?

VALENTIN: Anywhere. You just can't stop it.

MOLINA: And you'd like to stop thinking about your girlfriend, right?

VALENTIN: (*Warily.*) How'd you know I have a girlfriend?

MOLINA: It's only normal.

VALENTIN: I can't avoid it . . . I become attached to anything that may resemble her. Well, I better get back to those other matters I told you about.

MOLINA: Pull the thread.

VALENTIN: You got it.

MOLINA: But be careful you don't get it tangled, Valentina, or you'll flunk Home Economics.

VALENTIN: That's enough.

MOLINA: Okay, I'll leave you to your thoughts.

VALENTIN: And don't call me Valentina, I'm not a woman.

MOLINA: I have no proof.

VALENTIN: Sorry, I don't give demonstrations.

MOLINA: I wasn't asking for one.

(*Lights.*)

SCENE 3

(*Night. Orange light that suggests the prison's electric light. Molina and Valentin are sitting on the floor, eating.*)

VALENTIN: (*Finishing his last bite.*) You're a good cook, Molina.

MOLINA: Thank you.

VALENTIN: But you're spoiling me. It'll be bad for me in the long run.

MOLINA: You're crazy! Live for today!

VALENTIN: I don't believe that live-for-today stuff. This isn't the garden of Eden.

MOLINA: Do you believe in Heaven and Hell?

VALENTIN: Hold on. If we're going to talk about something serious, then let's do it in an organized way. Let's not jump from one thing to another like high school kids.

MOLINA: I'm not jumping from one thing to another.

VALENTIN: Then let's set up an outline.

MOLINA: I'm listening.

VALENTIN: I can't live for today because my life is part of a political struggle, right? I put up with my life here, which is bad enough—although it's nothing if you compare it to the torture; you can't know what that's like.

MOLINA: I can imagine.

VALENTIN: It's beyond imagining. (*Pause.*) Anyway, I put up with it all, because there's a plan. The social revolution is the most important thing. Any kind of sensual pleasure is secondary. The real pleasure is to know you're serving a cause that's noble and . . . well, you see my ideas— (*The electric lights go off, leaving them in the blue light of nighttime.*) It's eight o'clock.

MOLINA: What about your ideas?

VALENTIN: I mean my ideology—Marxism. I can feel the pleasure of being a part of that anywhere, even in this cell, even under torture. And that's my strength.

MOLINA: And your girl?

VALENTIN: That's all secondary. It's secondary for her, too, because she knows there is something more important.

MOLINA: Hmmm.

VALENTIN: You're not convinced?

MOLINA: Never mind. I'm going to sleep.

VALENTIN: Now? You're crazy! What about the panther woman?

MOLINA: Tomorrow.

VALENTIN: What's got into you?

MOLINA: Look, that's how I am, I take things to heart. I mean, I cooked for you, with my rations. Even worse, I gave you half of my avocado, despite the fact that it's my favorite food and I could have saved it for tomorrow. And what do I get? You tell me I'm spoiling you and I shouldn't do it.

VALENTIN: Don't be so sensitive! You sound just like a— (*Stops himself.*)

MOLINA: Go on, say it.

VALENTIN: Say what?

MOLINA: Valentin, I know what you were going to say.

VALENTIN: Don't be a jerk.

MOLINA: You were going to say, "just like a woman."

VALENTIN: You're right.

MOLINA: Well, what's wrong with being soft like a woman? Why can't a man or whatever, a dog, or a faggot, why can't he be a little sensitive if he feels like it?

VALENTIN: It's like an excuse that keeps a man from doing things.

MOLINA: What things? Like torturing somebody?

VALENTIN: No, like fighting to get rid of the torturers.

MOLINA: If all men were soft and feminine there wouldn't be any torturers.

VALENTIN: And what would you do without men?

MOLINA: You're right—they're brutes, but I love them.

VALENTIN: (*Musing.*) If all men were soft and feminine there wouldn't be any torturers. You know, Molina, you've got a point at least. It's a weird point, but it's still a point.

MOLINA: The things you say! (*Imitating Valentin.*) "You've got a point at least."

VALENTIN: I'm sorry it bothered you.

MOLINA: It's all right, it's nothing.

VALENTIN: Okay, then cheer up and stop punishing me.

MOLINA: Should I go on with the movie?

VALENTIN: Well, sure, man.

MOLINA: Man? What man? Where's a man? Don't let him get away!

VALENTIN: (*Trying to conceal that he finds this funny.*) Go on with the story.

MOLINA: Okay. Irena goes to see the psychiatrist, who's a terrific looking guy, gorgeous.

VALENTIN: What kind of guy do you think of as gorgeous? I'm curious.

MOLINA: Well, actually, the one who plays the psychiatrist isn't my type.

VALENTIN: Who's the actor?

MOLINA: I don't remember, he's too thin for my taste. You know, the type that looks good in a double-breasted suit, but with a regular suit they have to wear a vest. It's a type women like a lot. With a little toothbrush mustache. But he's a phony—the minute you see him, you know there's something wrong. And Irena knows. She doesn't go to her second session, she lies to her husband and instead of going to the doctor she puts on her favorite coat, the black plushy one, and she goes to the zoo to watch the panther. And the keeper comes by and opens the door of the cage, he throws the meat in the cage and shuts the door again, but he forgets, because he's kind of absent-minded, to take the key out of the door. So Irena comes up close to the cage, surreptitiously. She puts her hand on the key and stands there, thinking for a couple of seconds.

VALENTIN: What does she do?

MOLINA: That's all for tonight. I'll go on tomorrow.

VALENTIN: Could I ask you just one question?

MOLINA: What is it?

VALENTIN: Who do you identify with? Irena or the architect girl?

MOLINA: Irena, of course. I always go with the leading lady.

VALENTIN: Go on.

MOLINA: What about you? You probably think the guy is just a jerk, so you lose, right?

VALENTIN: Don't laugh—I identify with the shrink. But I didn't say anything about your choice, so don't make jokes about mine. (*Pause.*) You know something? I'm finding it hard to concentrate.

MOLINA: What's wrong?

VALENTIN: Nothing.

MOLINA: Come on, a little communication.

VALENTIN: When you talked about the girl arriving in front of the panther cage, I felt it was my girl who was in danger.

MOLINA: I know what you mean.

VALENTIN: I'm sure that you've figured out that she's in the struggle too. Of course, I shouldn't be telling you this.

MOLINA: Don't worry.

VALENTIN: I mean I don't want to burden you with information that it's safer for you not to have.

MOLINA: With me it's not a woman, I mean, not a girlfriend, it's my mother. She has high blood pressure and kind of a weak heart.

VALENTIN: But people can last for years with something like that.

MOLINA: Sure, if you don't upset them. But imagine having a son in jail, and think why.

VALENTIN: At least she's been through the worst of it, right? She's not in any danger.

MOLINA: Except the danger she carries inside her, the weak heart.

VALENTIN: She'll wait for you, the eight years'll go by, you might get time off for good conduct and all that.

MOLINA: (*Trying not to seem nosy.*) Tell me about your girl, would you mind?

VALENTIN: I'd give anything to be with her, right now.

MOLINA: That day will come. You're not here for life.

VALENTIN: But what if something happens to her?

MOLINA: Write to her. Tell her she mustn't take risks, you need her.

VALENTIN: Never. If you think like that you'll never change anything in this world.

MOLINA: (*Not realizing he's mocking Valentin.*) Do you think you can really change the world?

VALENTIN: Yes, and you can laugh all you want, I know it sounds ridiculous, but the thing I have to do above all else is . . . change the world.

MOLINA: But you can't change it just like that, all by yourself.

VALENTIN: I'm not all by myself, that's the point! I'm with her and all the others who think like we do. That's the tip of the thread that sometimes gets away from me. I'm not locked away from my comrades! I'm with them! Whether I can see them or not!

MOLINA: (*Skeptically.*) If that makes you feel good, terrific.

VALENTIN: How dumb can you be!

MOLINA: The way you talk!

VALENTIN: Well, then don't get on my nerves. I'm not some asshole talking politics in a bar, and the proof is that I'm here.

MOLINA: Sorry.

VALENTIN: It's all right . . .

MOLINA: (*Trying not to sound too inquisitive.*) You were going to tell me something about your girl . . .

VALENTIN: It's better if we just drop the subject.

MOLINA: Whatever you want.

VALENTIN: Though I don't know why it gets me so upset.

MOLINA: Well, don't name her if it upsets you.

VALENTIN: The main thing is that I mustn't tell you her name.

MOLINA: What kind of girl is she?

VALENTIN: She's twenty-four, two years younger than me.

MOLINA: Thirteen years younger than me—no, that's a lie, seventeen.

VALENTIN: She's always been a revolutionary. The first thing was, well, I don't have to mince words with you, the first thing was sexual revolution.

MOLINA: (*Quite interested, with humor.*) Do go on.

VALENTIN: She comes from an upper-middle-class family, not very rich, but, you know, pretty well off. But all through her childhood and adolescence she watched her parents destroying each other, and she got fed up with it. The father was always cheating on the mother, you know what I mean.

MOLINA: No, I don't.

VALENTIN: He cheated by not telling her straight out that he needed other women. And the mother dedicated herself to being a victim. I don't believe in monogamy.

MOLINA: But it's beautiful when a couple is devoted to each other for life.

VALENTIN: Is that what you really want?

MOLINA: It's my dream.

VALENTIN: Then why do you like men?

MOLINA: What's wrong with that? I'd like to spend my whole life with one man.

VALENTIN: Deep down you're an ordinary bourgeois man.

MOLINA: A bourgeois lady, please.

VALENTIN: You wouldn't like it so much if you were a woman.

MOLINA: I'm in love with a marvelous man, and all I want is to live with him for the rest of my life.

VALENTIN: And that's impossible, because since he's a man, he wants a real woman, so you'll never lose your illusions.

MOLINA: I don't want to hear about myself. Tell me some more about your girlfriend.

VALENTIN: She was brought up to be the lady of the house. (*Starts to think better of telling him all this.*) You know, piano lessons, French, drawing . . . I have to think about something I was reading today.

MOLINA: You're just trying to get back at me.

VALENTIN: Don't be silly. And I'm tired, too.

MOLINA: That's funny, I'm not sleepy at all.

(*Lights.*)

SCENE 4

(*Night. Orange light, the prison's electric light. White light on both men. Valentin is studying, concentrating deeply. Molina, bored, is flipping through a magazine he's already read many times.*)

VALENTIN: (*Raising his head from the book which he puts aside.*) Why is our dinner so late? The next cell got theirs a long time ago.

MOLINA: (*Sarcastic.*) Is *that* all you're studying tonight? I'm not hungry, thank heavens.

VALENTIN: That's strange. Don't you feel well?

MOLINA: It's my nerves. They're on edge.

VALENTIN: (*Listening.*) Sounds like they're coming now.

MOLINA: Hide those magazines. Otherwise they'll steal them.

VALENTIN: I'm starved.

MOLINA: Valentin, please don't complain to the guard.

VALENTIN: I won't . . . (*Two bowls of porridge pass under the door; one portion is visibly larger than the other. Molina and Valentin look at each other. Pause. Unenthusiastically.*) Porridge . . .

MOLINA: Yeah. (*Valentin shrugs. Molina gives the bowl a strange look.*) Thanks.

VALENTIN: (*To Guard, supposedly in the corridor.*) How come this bowl has so much less? (*To Molina.*) For your sake I didn't start a fight with him. I should have thrown this shit back in his face, it looks like glue.

MOLINA: No use complaining.

VALENTIN: That son of a bitch must be crazy; this bowl has nearly twice as much as the other one.

MOLINA: It's okay, Valentin, I'll take the little one.

VALENTIN: No, you always eat the porridge.

MOLINA: Skip the compliments. You take it.

VALENTIN: I said no. Why should I have the bigger one?

MOLINA: Why should I?

VALENTIN: Because you like the stuff.

MOLINA: I told you I'm not hungry.

VALENTIN: Just start and you'll see how fast you finish. (*Starts to eat out of smaller bowl.*)

MOLINA: No.

VALENTIN: (*Eating.*) It's not that bad today.

MOLINA: I don't want any.

VALENTIN: You on a diet?

MOLINA: No . . .

VALENTIN: Then eat. The porridge à la rubber cement is edible for a change.

MOLINA: (*Against his will, starts to eat; talks longingly.*) Today's Thursday, ladies half-price at the movies. In my neighborhood, they always used to have a triple feature—all love stories.

VALENTIN: Is that where you saw the panther woman?

MOLINA: A little old movie house in Buenos Aires. In the German side of the neighborhood, streets of nice houses with gardens in front. I lived there, but in the crummy part of the neighborhood. On Mondays they showed German movies. During and after the war.

VALENTIN: Nazi propaganda movies.

MOLINA: Yeah, but the musical numbers were fabulous.

VALENTIN: You must be out of your mind. (*Valentin has emptied the small bowl.*) No use cracking a book, it'll be lights out soon. (*Puts his books away. Peremptorily, not realizing it sounds like an order.*) Go on with the movie, she was standing with the cage key in her hand.

MOLINA: (*In between laborious spoonfuls of porridge.*) Well, she finally takes it out of the cage lock and hands it to the keeper. And the old man is real grateful. Then Irena goes home and waits for her husband to get there, she really wants to kiss him, on the mouth.

VALENTIN: (*Fascinated.*) Uh-huh.

MOLINA: So Irena calls his office, it's late. And the architect girl answers. Irena hangs up. She's seething with jealousy. She paces up and down the room like a caged animal. She walks by the little bird cage and she sees the canary flapping its wings desperately, trying to get out. She can't resist the impulse, she sticks her hand in the cage and the canary falls over dead, like it's been struck by lightning, just from her hand being there. Irena runs out to look for her husband. And, of course, as she goes by the bar in the corner of the office building, she sees them. And she wants to tear the other woman to shreds. Irena always wears black. You remember the blouse he likes so much in the restaurant scene, the one with all the rhinestones, she never wears that again.

VALENTIN: What are rhinestones?

MOLINA: Don't you know? I can't believe it.

VALENTIN: Well, what are they?

MOLINA: Like diamonds, but worthless; little pieces of glass that shine. (*The electric light goes off; the blue light comes on. Valentin makes a gesture of impatience.*)

VALENTIN: I better go to sleep now. All this trivia is getting a bit out of hand.

MOLINA: (*Overreacting; very hurt.*) Well, I'm just grateful there's no light on, so I don't have to see your face.

(*Note: The production must establish that when the blue light is on—meaning night time—they cannot see each other, and so are free to express themselves as they like in gestures and body language.*)

MOLINA: Just don't talk to me ever again!

VALENTIN: I'm sorry. (*Molina sulks.*) I really am. I didn't mean to offend you.

MOLINA: Well, you did, because I really love this movie a lot. You don't understand, because you've never seen it. (*Molina is crying.*)

VALENTIN: Are you crazy? It's nothing to cry about.

MOLINA: If I . . . if I feel like crying, I'll cry.

VALENTIN: Whatever you want. I'm really sorry.

MOLINA: Don't think you're the one who's making me cry. It's that today is my mother's birthday, and I'm dying to be with her . . . and not with you. (*Pause.*) I don't feel well.

VALENTIN: What's wrong?

MOLINA: Ay! . . . Ay!

VALENTIN: What is it?

MOLINA: The girl's got it bad.

VALENTIN: What girl?

MOLINA: Me dummy. Oh, God, my stomach hurts.

VALENTIN: Do you want to throw up?

MOLINA: The pain's lower down, it's in my guts.

VALENTIN: I'll call the guard, okay?

MOLINA: No, don't, I think it's going away.

VALENTIN: The food didn't do anything to me.

MOLINA: I guess it's just my nerves. I was so on edge today. I think it's letting up.

VALENTIN: Try to relax. As much as you can. Loosen your arms and legs.

MOLINA: Yes, it seems to be letting up a little.

VALENTIN: You want to sleep?

MOLINA: I don't know . . . God, how awful . . .

VALENTIN: Maybe if we keep talking it'll help you forget the pain.

MOLINA: You mean the movie?

VALENTIN: Where were we?

MOLINA: What's the matter, you afraid I'll die before telling you the end?

VALENTIN: It'll be good for you. We stopped when they were at the corner bar.

MOLINA: Well, they finally get up to leave. Irena hides behind a tree so they won't see her. The architect girl takes a shortcut home, through an unlit park. See, at the bar the boy told her everything: that Irena doesn't sleep with him, that she has nightmares about the panther women. And the girl had given up any hope of getting him, but now she's hopeful again. Then you hear footsteps behind her. She looks back and sees a woman's silhouette. And the footsteps start to get faster. Anyway, the architect girl gets frightened, because you know what it's like when you've been talking about scary things. But she's only halfway across the park, and if she starts to run it'll get worse. Then suddenly you don't hear the human footsteps anymore . . . Ay! . . . Ay! it's still hurting me . . .

SCENE 5

(*Daytime. Yellow light. Valentin lying on his bed, Molina standing and looking down at him.*)

VALENTIN: (*Making a visible effort to conceal his stomach pains.*) You can't believe how much it hurts. The pain's just brutal.

MOLINA: Now you know how I felt day before yesterday.

VALENTIN: Molina, I think it's getting worse.

MOLINA: Maybe you should go to the infirmary.

VALENTIN: Don't be an asshole. I told you, I don't want to.

MOLINA: Let them give you a little seconal, it won't hurt you.

VALENTIN: You can get hooked on that stuff. A lot you know about it.

MOLINA: What don't I know?

VALENTIN: Never mind . . .

MOLINA: Come on, don't be like that, tell me.

VALENTIN: It happened to one of my companions, they got him hooked on it, they took away his will power. A political prisoner can never go to the infirmary, you hear me, never. Then you don't have any resistance when they interrogate you. Ay, ay . . . Fuck, it's like being stabbed over and over again . . . Oh, my stomach . . .

MOLINA: I told you not to gulp down your food that way.

VALENTIN: (*Getting up, with difficulty.*) You were right. I feel like I'm ready to explode.

MOLINA: Stretch out and relax a little.

VALENTIN: I don't want to sleep, I had nightmares all night and again this morning.

MOLINA: (*Relenting, like a middle-class mother.*) Well, I swore to myself I'd never tell you another movie. I'll probably go to hell for breaking my word.

VALENTIN: (*In pain.*) Oh! . . . Fuck . . . (*Molina hesitates.*) Go on, tell me, don't worry if I scream.

MOLINA: All right, I'll tell you a special one for tummy ache. You were asking me about those German movies, right?

VALENTIN: Hmm, to find out how their propaganda machine worked. But better continue with the panther. We stopped when the architect girl doesn't hear human footsteps anymore.

MOLINA: Well, so she starts to shake with fear, she's afraid if she looks back she might see the panther . . . She stops for a minute, just to see if she can hear the woman's heels again, but there's nothing, total silence, just the bushes rustling in the wind . . . or because something's hiding in them . . . (*Molina imitates the girl's reaction.*) And she turns around with a start.

VALENTIN: I think I have to go to the john again.

MOLINA: Should I call them to open the door?

VALENTIN: No, I'll hold it in . . .

MOLINA: It'll only get worse.

VALENTIN: They'll see that I'm sick.

MOLINA: They won't take you to the infirmary for diarrhea.

VALENTIN: It'll go away, tell me more.

MOLINA: (*Repeating the girl's reaction.*) So she turns around with a start.

VALENTIN: Oh! . . . Oh!, God, what pain!

MOLINA: (*Pauses reluctantly in mid-scene. Suddenly.*) Tell me something: How come your mother doesn't bring you food?

VALENTIN: She can be very . . . difficult, that's why I never talk about her. She's never approved of my ideas, she thinks she deserves everything she's got, her family has a certain social position, and so on.

MOLINA: Still, it's your fault if you didn't tell her to bring you food every week.

VALENTIN: If I'm here it's because I made my choice, she has nothing to do with it.

MOLINA: You know, my mother hasn't been coming because she's sick.

VALENTIN: You never told me.

MOLINA: She thinks she'll recover any minute, and in the meantime she's screwed me because she doesn't want anyone but herself to bring me food.

VALENTIN: And if you could get out of here and go home she'd recover, right?

MOLINA: You're reading my mind again. Well, to continue: (*Repeating the girl's reaction.*) She turns around with a start.

VALENTIN: Any . . . ay . . . sorry . . . what did I just do?

MOLINA: Wait, don't wipe it with the bedsheet, hold on . . .

VALENTIN: Oh, stop, don't use your shirt . . .

MOLINA: Yes, take it, wipe yourself, you need the sheet to keep you warm at night.

VALENTIN: But it's the only shirt you have.

MOLINA: Wait, lift up, so it won't go through; that's it, careful, wait, so it won't go through; that's it, careful, wait, so it doesn't get on the sheet.

VALENTIN: Did it go through?

MOLINA: No, just on your shorts. Take them off, come on, don't be shy.

VALENTIN: I'm so embarrassed . . .

MOLINA: That's it, careful, take your time . . . terrific. Now comes the bulky part: take the shirt and wipe yourself.

VALENTIN: It's embarrassing . . .

MOLINA: You said a man has to be tough, right? So what's all this embarrassment?

VALENTIN: Roll up my shorts, Molina, so they don't smell.

MOLINA: Don't worry, I know how to do these things. See? I wrapped them in the shirt—easier to wash than the sheet. Now take some toilet paper.

VALENTIN: No, it's yours, you won't have any left.

MOLINA: You never have any, come on, skip the heroics.

VALENTIN: Thank you.

MOLINA: It's nothing. Relax a little, you're shaking.

VALENTIN: I'm furious, I can't help it, I'm so mad at myself for letting them get to me like this.

MOLINA: Come on, just try to relax a little.

VALENTIN: (*Seeing Molina wrap the dirty shirt in newspaper.*) Ah . . . so it won't stink up the place.

MOLINA: Good idea, huh?

VALENTIN: I'm freezing.

MOLINA: (*Lighting kerosene stove and putting water on to boil.*) I'll fix you some tea. We've just got one little bag left.

VALENTIN: Don't bother, it'll go away.

MOLINA: You're nuts.

VALENTIN: I'm not nuts, you are, wasting all your supplies on me.

MOLINA: They'll bring me more.

VALENTIN: Your mother can't come, she's sick.

MOLINA: I'll manage. (*Ironically.*) So she turns around with a start. She opens her mouth to let out a long, desperate moan when . . . WHACK!!! the door of a bus opens up right by her, with a big whoosh. The driver saw her standing there, so he stopped. (*Pours hot water.*) Your tea's almost ready.

VALENTIN: You don't know how grateful I am. And I want to apologize . . . because I know I'm very curt sometimes, and . . . I hurt people without meaning to.

MOLINA: Forget it. (*Serves him the tea.*)

VALENTIN: No, forget about the movie, I'm going to tell you a true story. I lied to you about my girlfriend. I told you about another girl that I used to love, madly. But I didn't tell you the truth about my girl. And you'd like her, because she's a nice girl, simple and unassuming, but she's also very brave. (*Drinks tea.*)

MOLINA: Please, don't tell me. I don't want to know anything about your political affairs.

VALENTIN: Don't be silly, who's going to question you about my actions?

MOLINA: They might interrogate me.

VALENTIN: You confide in me, don't you?

MOLINA: Yes . . .

VALENTIN: Then don't pull back when I want to do the same thing; share and share alike.

MOLINA: It's not that . . .

VALENTIN: There's nothing worse than feeling guilty because you hurt someone. And I did, I hurt her, I forced her into the movement when she wasn't quite ready for it, she's just an ordinary kid. Quite . . . simple.

MOLINA: Well, don't tell me now, I do the telling for the time being. Where was it we had stopped? (*There is no answer. Molina looks at Valentin and finds out that he has fallen asleep.*) At what point were we? (*Molina is proud of having helped his companion.*)

SCENE 6

(*Daytime. Yellow light. Molina and Valentin lying on their cots, each wrapped in his own private melancholy. We hear a bolero tune in the distance.*)

MOLINA: (*Half-singing along.*) "So here I am, my dear, writing to you again . . . The silence of the night is urging me to say what's in my heart, And darling, I can only hope that you remember when . . . our strange ill-fated passion had its start . . . "

VALENTIN: What the hell is that?

MOLINA: It's a hit tune, a bolero, "My Love Letter."

VALENTIN: Only you could come up with that.

MOLINA: So what's wrong with it?

VALENTIN: It's cornball romantic crap; you're crazy.

MOLINA: Excuse me for picking the wrong time.

VALENTIN: What do you mean?

MOLINA: You're all depressed from that letter you got, and here I am singing about 'Dear John' letters.

VALENTIN: Well, it was bad news. You can read it if you want.

MOLINA: I better not.

VALENTIN: Don't start that again, nobody's going to interrogate you. Besides, they read it when it came in. (*Valentin opens the letter and reads it over.*)

MOLINA: (*Looking over his shoulder.*) Her handwriting looks like chicken tracks.

VALENTIN: She hasn't had much of an education . . . It's in code. She's telling me a guy died, one of our companions, and now she's in charge of our group.

MOLINA: Ah . . .

VALENTIN: And she says she's doing what I told her to, having relations with another companion.

MOLINA: Relations?

VALENTIN: She was missing me too much. We all take this vow not to get too attached to anybody, because it might paralyze you when it's time to act.

MOLINA: Act how?

VALENTIN: Act, take action, risk your life . . . If we start to think, "Somebody wants me alive," it makes you fear death—well, maybe not fear dying, but, you know, regret dying, you think about someone suffering because you're gone, and so forth. Anyway, she has another friend now.

MOLINA: But you said your girlfriend was not as you had told me . . .

VALENTIN: Shit, just looking at the letter made me dizzy again.

MOLINA: You're still weak.

VALENTIN: I feel a little nauseous, and I've got chills. (*He pulls the blanket over himself.*)

MOLINA: I warned you not to eat.

VALENTIN: I was so goddam hungry. (*Molina tucks him in.*)

MOLINA: Yesterday you felt better, so you ate and got your system screwed up again, and today you did the same thing. Promise me you won't touch one bite tomorrow.

VALENTIN: The other chick I told you about, the high-class one, she did finally join the movement, but she copped out. And she tried a million times to get me to go with her.

MOLINA: Why?

VALENTIN: She liked her life too much, being with me made her happy. And that was that. So we had to split up.

MOLINA: Because you loved each other too much?

VALENTIN: Sounds like one of your boleros.

MOLINA: The truth is you make fun of those songs because they're too close to you. You only laugh to keep from crying. There's a bolero that goes something like that—or maybe it's a tango.

VALENTIN: When I was hiding out I stayed for a while in the same apartment with this poor guy who was killed, and his wife and their kid. I changed the baby's diapers more than once . . . But you don't know the worst, it's that I can't write to them, 'cause it would be . . . like denouncing them.

MOLINA: And you can't write to your girlfriend either?

VALENTIN: (*Fighting back tears.*) Oh, God . . . it's so awful . . .

MOLINA: What can you do . . .

VALENTIN: Take . . . take my arm out from . . . under the blanket.

MOLINA: What for?

VALENTIN: Hold . . . hold my hand, Molina. Please.

MOLINA: Hold tight.

VALENTIN: There's something else that's eating away at me. I don't like to think about it.

MOLINA: Say it, get it off your chest.

VALENTIN: The one I really want to hear from . . . to have next to me right now, holding me . . . it's not my girlfriend in the movement, it's the other one . . . Marta, that's her name.

MOLINA: If that's the way you feel . . . Oh, I almost forgot, if your stomach feels real empty there's some crackers left over, just plain ones that won't do you any harm. I had forgotten about them . . . totally . . . (*Not letting go of Valentin's hand, he reaches out and gets the packet of crackers with his other hand.*)

VALENTIN: (*Not listening.*) I talk a good game but deep down . . . what I still like is a high-class kind of woman, I'm just like all the reactionary sons-of-bitches that killed my comrade . . . just like one of them, all the way.

MOLINA: It's not true.

VALENTIN: And I think I don't even like Marta for herself, but because she's got class . . . I'm just like all the other class-conscious sons-of-bitches . . . in the world.

GUARD'S VOICE: (*On loudspeaker.*) Convict Luis Alberto Molina, visit in Locutory!

(*The cell door opens, Molina and Valentin let go of each other's hands as if they were caught in some shameful act. Molina goes out. The cell door closes. Then we hear Molina's voice in conversation with someone else. The Warden's voice is bluff, conventionally authoritarian.*

Meanwhile, Valentin shakily lifts his hand out from under the blanket, holding the packet of crackers. There are not too many left—no more than four. He toys with them before eating them, slowly, one by one, trying to resist temptation and leave them for later, and then giving in.)

WARDEN'S VOICE: Don't be afraid, sonny, we're not going to do anything to you.

MOLINA'S VOICE: It's not that, sir. I'm shaking because I've been sick in the stomach. But I'm over it now.

WARDEN: Well, don't be afraid. We've arranged it to look like you had visitors. Your cellmate won't know a thing.

MOLINA: No, he doesn't suspect.

WARDEN: Your protector came home for dinner last night. He had some good news for you. Ever since this prospect of paroling you came up, your mother's been feeling much better.

MOLINA: Really . . .

WARDEN: What's wrong? Stop trembling like that . . . You should be smiling: if this works out, we'll be letting you off. . . . So, what have you got to tell us? Any information yet? Is he starting to open up, is he telling you things?

MOLINA: Not yet, sir, but you know, these things take time.

WARDEN: Did it help when we weakened him physically?

MOLINA: Well, the first special portion you fixed I had to eat myself.

WARDEN: You were quite wrong.

MOLINA: See, he doesn't like the porridge, and one bowl had a lot more than the other . . . so he insisted on my taking the bigger one. If I'd refused, he would have suspected something. I mean, you told me the fixed food would come in a new tin plate, but they were wrong to overload it.

WARDEN: Fine, well, I'm sorry for the mistake.

MOLINA: Now it's probably better for you to let him get well.

WARDEN: (*Annoyed.*) That's for us to decide. We know what we're doing here. All right, when you go back to your cell, you can say your mother came to see you, that'll explain why you're so excited.

MOLINA: No, it's impossible, she always comes with a bagful of food.

WARDEN: Well, we could send out for some supplies. That'll make up for you having to eat the bad porridge. Poor Molina!

MOLINA: Thank you, warden.

(*Valentin has now eaten the last cracker. He arranges the packet so it looks full, and stares at it.*)

WARDEN: Give me a list of what your mother usually brings.
MOLINA: Give you a list?
WARDEN: Yes, and make it quick, I've got a lot to do.
MOLINA: (*As lights fade or curtain falls, very slowly.*) Chocolate fudge, peach halves in syrup . . . two roast chickens . . . a big bag of sugar, two packets of tea leaves, one china black, one chamomile . . . Condensed milk, bath soap, the large size, and, just let me think a second, my mind's a blank . . .

ACT TWO

SCENE 7

(*Orange light; the electric lights are on. The cell door opens and Molina comes in, carrying a large bag of groceries.*)

MOLINA: Look what I've got!

VALENTIN: (*Pleasantly surprised.*) No! . . . You mean your mother . . .

MOLINA: Right!!!

VALENTIN: So she's better . . . ?

MOLINA: A little better, yeah . . . And look what she brought me. Sorry. I mean look what she brought *us.*

VALENTIN: (*Secretly pleased.*) Come on, man, what are you saying? She brought it for you.

MOLINA: No back talk, you're a sick man. And the roast chicken is all for you, so you can get well fast.

VALENTIN: I won't let you do this.

MOLINA: It's no sacrifice, I'll do without the chicken if it means—I can spare myself the odor you give off . . . Seriously, you've got to stop eating the junk they feed you here. At least for a couple of days.

VALENTIN: You think so?

MOLINA: And then when you're all better . . . close your eyes. (*Valentin closes his eyes and Molina puts a foil-wrapped package in his hand.*) Guess.

VALENTIN: (*Enjoying the game.*) How can I tell? (*Molina puts a similar package in his other hand.*)

MOLINA: You can tell by the weight . . .

VALENTIN: They're heavy . . . I give up.

MOLINA: Open your eyes.

VALENTIN: Chocolate fudge!

MOLINA: But not until you're better, and yes, you can bet that's for both of us.

VALENTIN: Great.

MOLINA: First of all . . . I'm going to have some chamomile tea, because my nerves are shot, and you have some chicken . . . or, no, it's only five . . . You'd better just have some tea and some of these new crackers, they're better for your stomach than the other kind.

VALENTIN: Can't I have some just now? Just a taste? Please?

MOLINA: (*Giving him crackers.*) Okay, but just a little! It's a good thing all this other stuff she brought is easy to digest; except for the fudge, there's nothing you can't have right away.

VALENTIN: (*Eating.*) I'm so hungry I could eat a horse. What about that chicken leg right now?

MOLINA: (*After a beat.*) Here . . .

VALENTIN: (*Grabbing it and devouring it.*) And I was really feeling lousy. Thanks . . .

MOLINA: It's all right . . .

VALENTIN: (*Mouth full.*) And there's just one thing missing to make this a full program.

MOLINA: Wait a minute, I'm supposed to be the pervert here.

VALENTIN: Stop fooling around. What we need is a movie . . .

MOLINA: Oh . . . Okay . . . (*While putting the packages away.*) Let's see, now comes a scene where Irena's wearing a totally different hair-do.

VALENTIN: I'm starting to feel dizzy again.

MOLINA: Are you sure?

VALENTIN: I'm a little nauseous, just like before.

MOLINA: It couldn't be the chicken. It's probably all in your mind.

VALENTIN: I just felt so full all of a sudden.

MOLINA: I saw the way you gobbled up that chicken, you hardly even stopped to chew.

VALENTIN: And this itch is driving me nuts. I haven't washed for four days.

MOLINA: Don't even think about it. That freezing cold water, in your sickly state? Anyway, she looks really gorgeous here, it's raining and you see her reflected in the window with drops of rain coming down, her beautiful hair pulled back in an upsweep. I should explain what that is . . .

VALENTIN: (*Interrupting Molina.*) It's pulled back! Never mind all these silly details.

MOLINA: Silly, my foot. She winds it up in a braid, and decorates it with rhinestone flowers.

VALENTIN: (*Nervous from his itch and conscious of an increasing tension with Molina.*) I know what rhinestones are, you don't have to explain!

MOLINA: Ooh, you are nervous!

VALENTIN: Look I have to tell you something.

MOLINA: Okay.

VALENTIN: I really feel all screwed up—you know, confused—would you mind writing a letter for me? I know if I try to focus my eyes, I'll get dizzy again.

MOLINA: Let me get a pencil.

VALENTIN: It's kind of you to do this.

MOLINA: I'll just take some scratch paper for the rough draft.

VALENTIN: Take my pen.

MOLINA: Wait, I'm sharpening my pencil.

VALENTIN: (*Very nervous.*) I said, you can use my pen!

MOLINA: Okay, calm down.

VALENTIN: Sorry, it's just everything's starting to go black.

MOLINA: Okay, shoot.

VALENTIN: (*Very sad.*) Dearest . . . Marta: You may find it strange . . . to get this letter. I know I won't put you in danger. I'm just . . . so lonely, I need you, I want . . . to be near you somehow, I want you to give me . . . a word of encouragement . . .

MOLINA: . . . "of encouragement" . . .

VALENTIN: . . . at a time when I'm so weak, I'd be ashamed to face my companions . . . I'm all bruised inside, I need somebody to rub some balm into my wounds . . . And you're the only one who can understand because you were brought up like me, raised in a nice comfortable house to enjoy life, and Marta, I'm not ready to be a martyr, I get furious at the thought . . . or else, maybe . . . I can see this more clearly because I'm sick . . . I'm terribly afraid of dying . . . and because this is all I have, because my life has been reduced to this little bit of nothing, I can't help thinking I don't deserve it, I never exploited anybody, I never hurt anybody . . . I just fought, because I could see what was happening . . . fought against the exploitation of others . . . of my brothers and sisters . . .

MOLINA: Go on.

VALENTIN: Where was I?

MOLINA: . . . "the exploitation of others, my brothers and sisters"

VALENTIN: . . . because I want to be alive and out on the street again one day, I don't want to die. And sometimes I think I may never, never touch a woman again, and I can't bear the thought . . . and when I think of women . . . all I can think of is you, and what a relief it would be to think that right now, while I'm writing this letter, you're thinking of me . . . and you're running your hands over that beautiful body that I remember so well . . .

MOLINA: Hold on, don't go so fast.

VALENTIN: . . . your body that I remember so well, and you start to think it's my hands . . . that would be like touching you myself, my love . . . because part of me has stayed inside you, hasn't it? Just the way your scent has stayed in my nostrils . . . and I feel your soft skin under my fingertips . . . now I've memorized it, do you see? Of course, it's not a question of seeing . . . it's a question of believing, sometimes I'm sure a part of you is with me . . . that I'll never lose, and sometimes it's gone, I feel there's no one in this cell but me, all alone . . .

MOLINA: (*Concealing his humiliation.*) ". . . but me, all alone." Go on.

VALENTIN: . . . that there's no trace of you left, and my good luck at having been so happy with you, spending all those nights, and afternoons, and mornings, of pure joy, is no good to me at all, in fact, it only makes things worse for me . . . because I miss you like crazy, and all I can feel is the torture of my loneliness, and all I have in my nostrils is the digusting stench of this cell and of my body . . . which I can't wash because I'm so sick and weak, and the cold water might give me pneumonia, and what I feel under my fingertips isn't your skin but the chill of my fear of death, I can feel it freezing my bones . . . It's a terrible thing to lose hope, and that's what's happened to me . . .

MOLINA: I'm sorry to interrupt you . . .

VALENTIN: What?

MOLINA: When you're through with the letter I want to tell you something.

VALENTIN: (Upset by the interruption.) Well, what is it?

MOLINA: I mean, I know if you go under that shower it'll kill you . . .

VALENTIN: (Practically hysterical.) Well, so what? Tell me, goddammit!

MOLINA: I could help you wash. Look, I already had this water hot for boiling potatoes, I've got two towels, I'll put soap on one so you can soap yourself up in front and I'll do the back, and then I'll put the other one in water to wash off the soap.

VALENTIN: So at least my skin won't itch anymore?

MOLINA: Right! We can go bit by bit, so you don't catch cold.

VALENTIN: Would you really help me?

MOLINA: Of course.

VALENTIN: When?

MOLINA: Right now. The water's boiling, so we'll mix it with cold. (He starts doing this.)

VALENTIN: (Unbelievably happy.) No itching! Will I be able to sleep in peace!

MOLINA: Take off your shirt. Meantime we'll heat some more water. (He mixes hot and cold water.)

VALENTIN: But it's your kerosene, you'll run out.

MOLINA: Doesn't matter.

VALENTIN: Molina . . .

MOLINA: What?

VALENTIN: Give me the letter.

MOLINA: What for?

VALENTIN: Just give it to me.

MOLINA: Here. (Molina gives the letter to Valentin, who tears it up.) What are you doing?

VALENTIN: This. (He folds the pieces and tears them in half again.) Let's not talk about it again.

MOLINA: If you like . . .

VALENTIN: It's bad to let yourself give in to despair . . .

MOLINA: But it's good to let it all out. You said that to me once.

VALENTIN: But it's bad for me. I've got to learn to handle it. (*Molina is silent.*) Look, one day I'll be able to thank you for this, I mean it. (*Molina puts more water on to boil.*) You need that much water?

MOLINA: At least . . . and don't be silly, there's nothing to thank me for. (*Molina motions to Valentin to turn over; he obeys.*)

VALENTIN: Just tell me one thing: how does the film end? Just the last scene.

MOLINA: (*Starting to wash Valentin's back.*) It's either all or nothing.

VALENTIN: Why so?

MOLINA: Because of the details. The upsweep is very important! See, women wear it, or anyway they used to, to show that they were at a turning point, because the upsweep, where you leave the neck bare, gives the woman's face a kind of nobility. (*Valentin, despite his exhaustion, rests his head in his hands and smiles, amused.*) Why that vicious little smile? (*Without irony.*) I'm talking seriously.

VALENTIN: My back doesn't itch anymore.

SCENE 8

(*Daytime. Molina is tidying things up, very quietly so as not to disturb the sleeping Valentin, who wakes up anyhow. They both seem more energetic; the dialogue starts casually but soon becomes tense and accelerated.*)

VALENTIN: Morning . . .

MOLINA: Good morning.

VALENTIN: What time is it?

MOLINA: Ten after ten. Like my momma. I mean I sometimes call her "ten after ten" because she walks with her feet pointing out like that.

VALENTIN: It's so late.

MOLINA: When they brought in our coffee, you just rolled over and went back to sleep.

VALENTIN: What'd you say about your old lady?

MOLINA: Look who's still asleep. Never mind. Did you sleep well?

VALENTIN: I feel a lot better.

MOLINA: Any dizziness?

VALENTIN: Not sitting up in bed.

MOLINA: Terrific! In that case, why not try walking?

VALENTIN: No, I can't yet, you'll laugh.

MOLINA: At what?

VALENTIN: It's something that happens to a normal man when he wakes up in the morning with excess energy.

MOLINA: (*In all innocence, glad that Valentin's recovered.*) You've got a hard-on? . . . Fabulous!

VALENTIN: Look the other way, will you? I kind of feel . . . (*He gets up to wash his face with water from the pitcher.*)

MOLINA: (*Turning away, eyes closed.*) My eyes are closed, tell me when.

VALENTIN: I'm a little shaky on my legs, but I don't feel dizzy. Thanks to you and your food. Okay, you can look now. (*Getting back into bed.*) I'm going to lie down a while longer.

MOLINA: (*Being bossy.*) I'll heat up some water for tea.

VALENTIN: Just heat up the coffee, that's all.

MOLINA: Oh, I threw it away when I went to the john. You've got to eat right if you want to get well.

VALENTIN: But I feel lousy using up all your tea and everything. I'm all better now.

MOLINA: Be quiet, a lot you know.

VALENTIN: Listen to that—

MOLINA: (*Cutting him off.*) Listen nothing, there's no problem, momma's bringing me more stuff from home.

VALENTIN: Okay, thank you, but not after today. (*Starts to look for his books.*)

MOLINA: And no reading, you have to rest! While we're waiting for the tea, I'll start a new movie.

VALENTIN: I'd better try to study, at least just to see if I can yet. (*He starts reading.*)

MOLINA: Won't it be too much of an effort?

VALENTIN: We'll see.

MOLINA: You're such a fanatic.

VALENTIN: (*Throwing down the book, getting increasingly nervous.*) It's no use . . . everthing's a blur.

MOLINA: I told you so. Feeling dizzy?

VALENTIN: Only when I read.

MOLINA: You know what it is? You're always weaker in the morning. Have some nice bread and ham, and it'll go away.

VALENTIN: You think?

MOLINA: Then later, after lunch, you'll take a little nap and then you'll be able to study, I promise.

VALENTIN: I feel so fatigued, I'm going to lie down.

MOLINA: (*Schoolmistressy.*) No, staying in bed'll just weaken you, it's better if you stand or at least sit up. (*Hands Valentin a cup of tea.*)

VALENTIN: This is the last day I'll accept this.

MOLINA: (*Mistress of the situation.*) Ha-ha, fooled you! I told the guard not to bring morning coffee anymore.

VALENTIN: (*Annoyed.*) Look, you can do what you want for yourself, but I want that coffee even if it is piss.

MOLINA: You know nothing about a proper diet.

VALENTIN: (*Trying to keep calm.*) Look, really, I don't want anyone else running my life.

MOLINA: (*Counting on his fingers.*) Today's Wednesday . . . Monday I'm seeing my lawyer, and everything depends on what he says. I don't believe in appeals and all that, but if he can pull some strings, like he promised, then I've got something to hope for.

VALENTIN: (*Not paying much attention.*) Why not?

MOLINA: (*Subtly, while fixing another cup of tea.*) If they let me out . . . who knows what you'll get for a cellmate.

VALENTIN: Didn't you have breakfast yet?

MOLINA: You were sleeping, I didn't want to make noise. (*Takes Valentin's cup to refill it.*) And now you can join me in a second cup.

VALENTIN: Not at all.

MOLINA: (*Opening another package, not letting Valentin see it.*) What are you going to study after your nap?

VALENTIN: What're you doing?

MOLINA: It's a surprise. Tell me what you're reading.

VALENTIN: Nothing . . .

MOLINA: Oh, how uncommunicative. All right, then . . . we open the surprise package . . . it's got something special inside . . . that I've been saving . . . to go with tea . . . Fruitcake!

VALENTIN: Oh, no thanks . . .

MOLINA: What do you mean, no thanks? The water's already boiling. Oh, I get it! You have to go to the john! Well, for goodness sake, ask the guard to let you out and hurry right back!

VALENTIN: Please don't tell me what to do.

MOLINA: (*Chucking Valentin under the chin, jokingly.*) Oh, come on, let me mother you a little.

VALENTIN: Goddammit, that's enough!

MOLINA: (*Affectionate, as with a pet.*) Why not? What's wrong with that?

VALENTIN: (*Throwing teacup and plate violently against the heater.*) Just shut the fuck up!

MOLINA: The cake . . . (*Valentin sulks.*) Look what you've done . . . (*Molina scurries about picking things up.*) We'll be done for without heat. And you broke the saucer . . . (*Silence from Valentin.*) And the tea . . .

VALENTIN: (*With difficulty.*) I'm sorry. (*Molina tidying up ignores him.*) I got out of control. Look, I'm very sorry. I mean it. (*No response from Molina.*) Look, the kerosene spilled, but the heater didn't break. (*No response.*) Molina, I'm sorry I blew up. (*Molina sits on the edge of his bed, head down.*) I'm sorry, I really am. Please forgive me.

MOLINA: (*Deeply hurt.*) There's nothing to forgive.

VALENTIN: There is. When I got sick if it hadn't been for you, God knows where I'd be now.

MOLINA: There's nothing to thank me for.

VALENTIN: There is, a lot.

MOLINA: Forget it all. Nothing happened.

VALENTIN: It did, and I'm dying with shame . . . I'm a bastard . . . Look, I'll call the guard, so I can get some water, we're almost out . . . Please look at me. Raise your head. (*Molina doesn't react.*)

GUARD'S VOICE: (*On loudspeaker.*) Convict Luis Alberto Molina, visit in locutory. (*The cell door opens, Molina goes out. Valentin tries to clean up the mess he has made.*)

WARDEN'S VOICE: Well, Molina, it's Monday. What news have you got for me?

MOLINA'S VOICE: I'm sorry to say, sir, not much.

WARDEN: I see.

MOLINA: But he's confiding in me more and more.

WARDEN: Well, but you know, Molina, the bad part is, I'm under a lot of pressure from above, and I mean from the President's office. They want to interrogate this prisoner. And give him the works, if you know what I mean.

MOLINA: Oh, no, sir, he's so weak now he'd never make it through, and what good would that do them?

WARDEN: That's what I keep telling them, but it doesn't do any good.

MOLINA: Please, warden, just one more week . . . I've got an idea.

WARDEN: Let's hear it.

MOLINA: He's real tough, but he has a sentimental streak.

WARDEN: Yes . . .

MOLINA: So . . . if a guard comes and says that next week I'm being moved to a different cell block because, you know, with the appeal and all, I'm now in a different category, well, he'll probably soften up a lot more.

WARDEN: Is that it?

MOLINA: Yes, sir, that's all there is to it, honest. I have this hunch that if he thinks I'm leaving he'll want to open up totally with me. You know, sir, that's what prisoners are like . . . take away their cellmate and they feel more helpless than ever.

(*At this moment Molina, carrying the grocery bag, reenters the cell. He takes the groceries out of the bag as the Warden's Voice enumerates them. Valentin looks at Molina, deeply embarrassed and apologetic.*)

WARDEN'S VOICE: Sergeant, note this down: Two roast chickens, four baked apples, a carton of potato salad, half a pound of fresh ham, half a pound of smoked ham, four loaves of French bread, four large pieces of glazed fruit, a jar of orange marmalade, two fruitcakes . . .

(*Taped voice fades out.*)

MOLINA: (*Calm and very sad; he was really hurt by Valentin's outburst.*) Here's the smoked ham, and here's the fresh. I'm going to make myself a sandwich before the bread goes stale. You can have one if you want.

VALENTIN: (*Deeply ashamed of himself.*) Thank you.

MOLINA: (*Calm, distant.*) I'll just have this little bit, a slice of the bread, a dab of butter, and some smoked ham. And a baked apple.

VALENTIN: It sounds good.

MOLINA: If you want some of the chicken while it's still hot, feel free.

VALENTIN: Thank you, Molina.

MOLINA: We'll each make our own meals, so I won't be pestering you.

VALENTIN: Whatever you say.

MOLINA: There's some glazed fruit, too. Just leave me the pumpkin, that's all I ask.

VALENTIN: (*Having a hard time apologizing.*) I'm still so ashamed . . . of the way I lost my temper. (*Molina is silent.*) I guess it made me nervous that you were . . . so generous to me . . . because I didn't want to be . . . the same way with you.

MOLINA: Look, I've been thinking too, and I remembered something you said . . . that when you're fighting a battle like yours . . . it's not, well, convenient to get too fond of anybody. Well, "fond" is maybe the wrong word, I mean, you know, close to somebody like a friend.

VALENTIN: It's kind of you to see it that way.

MOLINA: You see, sometimes I do understand what you're saying.

VALENTIN: But to think the world has us so hemmed in that we can't act like human beings, not even for a minute . . . Is the enemy outside that powerful?

MOLINA: I'm not sure I follow you.

VALENTIN: Our oppressors are outside this cell, not in it. What's got me so upset is the idea that . . . I've been so worn down, or brainwashed, I can't believe somebody wants to treat me well, without asking for something in exchange.

MOLINA: I don't know about that . . .

VALENTIN: About What?

MOLINA: Don't take this the wrong way, but, if I treat you well, it's because I want you to be my friend and, well, why not say it . . . I want you to like me. Just like I treat my momma well because she's a good person and I want her to love me. And you're a good person, too, you're an idealist, you're risking your life for something that, I mean, I don't totally understand but I know it's not just for yourself . . . Please don't turn away, am I embarrassing you?

VALENTIN: (*Looking straight at Molina.*) A little.

MOLINA: That's why I respect you, and I feel good about you, and I want you to feel good about me, too. See, my momma's affection is the only good feeling I've ever had in my life, because she loves me . . . just the way I am.

VALENTIN: (*Pointing to the chunk of bread Molina has broken off for his sandwich.*) Can I cut that for you?

MOLINA: Sure.

VALENTIN: (*Slicing bread.*) Didn't you ever have close friends who were important to you?

MOLINA: My friends were always . . . silly faggots like me, and we never—how can I put this?—we never really trusted each other, we were all such sissies. We were always looking for friendship, or whatever, with somebody more serious, with a real man, of course. And that just never comes true, because what a real man wants is a woman.

VALENTIN: (*Picking up a slice of ham for Molina's sandwich.*) Are all homosexuals like that?

MOLINA: Well, there are some that fall in love with each other. But me and my friends, we're *girls*. We don't go for all those pervert games. We're normal women, we go to bed with men.

VALENTIN: (*Too interested to see the humor of this.*) Butter?

MOLINA: Please. There's something I have to tell you.

VALENTIN: Of course, the new movie.

MOLINA: (*A little nervous at putting his scheme into effect.*) My lawyer says things are moving along.

VALENTIN: What a rat I am, I didn't even ask.

MOLINA: And when they start considering your appeal, they move you to another cell block. I might be out of here by the end of the week.

VALENTIN: (*Very upset by this and trying to conceal it.*) That's great . . . you should be real happy.

MOLINA: I don't want to think about it too much, get my hopes up. Have some potato salad.

VALENTIN: Should I?

MOLINA: It's very good.

VALENTIN: (*Getting up.*) Your good news made me lose my appetite.

MOLINA: Pretend I didn't say anything, we don't know for sure.

VALENTIN: No, the prospects are good, we've got to be happy.

MOLINA: Where does it hurt? Stomach?

VALENTIN: No, it's my head. I'm all confused.

MOLINA: About what?

VALENTIN: Let me rest for a while.

(*He sits down, his head in his hands; the light changes from yellow to orange to indicate a passage of time; both men stay in the same position; there is a great deal of nervous tension in the air.*)

MOLINA: The boy is totally confused, he doesn't know what to do with this weird wife of his. She comes in, sees him there looking very serious, goes into the bathroom to take off her shoes—they're all covered with mud—and meanwhile he tells her he's upset because he went to pick her up at the shrink's and found out she hadn't been showing up. So she starts crying and says her life is ruined, she is what she was always afraid of becoming, she's insane and has hallucinations, or what's worse, she may be a panther woman. So he softens up and takes her in his arms, and you were right when you said he treats her like a child, because when he sees her looking so helpless and lost, he realizes again how much he loves her, and he tells her everything's going to be all right . . . (*A deep sigh.*)

VALENTIN: What a sigh!

MOLINA: Life is so difficult . . .

VALENTIN: What's wrong?

MOLINA: I don't know, I'm worried that I might build up all these dreams about getting out of here . . . and find myself stuck in some other cell somewhere, with who knows what kind of creep.

VALENTIN: Think about something else. Your mother's getting well and that's important, right?

MOLINA: Right . . .

VALENTIN: So just think about that, okay?

MOLINA: (*His restraint giving way.*) I don't want to think about that! (*Starts sobbing.*)

VALENTIN: Hey . . . what's all this?

MOLINA: It's nothing!

VALENTIN: Come on, don't hide in your pillow . . . Is there something you haven't told me?

MOLINA: (*Crying.*) It's . . . it's . . .

VALENTIN: It's what? When you get out of here you'll be free, you could even go political if you want and join a group.

MOLINA: You're crazy. They wouldn't trust a faggot.

VALENTIN: But I can tell you who to talk to . . .

MOLINA: (*Suddenly sitting up, very forcefully.*) Swear to me, by whatever you love most, that you'll never, and I mean never, you hear, tell me anything about your comrades.

VALENTIN: But who would ever think you were seeing them?

MOLINA: They could interrogate me, whatever, who knows? If I don't know anything I can't tell them anything, it's safer that way.

VALENTIN: Anyway, there's all kinds of political groups, even some that just talk. When you're outside things'll be different.

MOLINA: (*Crying out again.*) No, that's what's so terrible, nothing will be different!

VALENTIN: How many times have I seen you cry already? (*Humorously, to cheer him up.*) Come on, all these tears are making me nervous. You want to start a flood?

MOLINA: I just can't take it anymore . . . always . . . such rotten luck . . .

(*The orange light goes off; they are left in the blue lights and can no longer see one another.*)

VALENTIN: (*Firmly.*) Lights out already? Listen, when you get out join a group first thing, you mustn't be so alone.

MOLINA: I don't understand all that stuff. I don't believe in it much either.

VALENTIN: Then shut up and don't complain.

MOLINA: (*Still crying a little.*) Let's not talk about it anymore . . .

VALENTIN: (*Friendly.*) Oh, come on . . . don't be like that. (*Pats him on the shoulder.*)

MOLINA: Please don't touch me . . .

VALENTIN: Can't a friend pat you on the back?

MOLINA: That makes it worse . . .

VALENTIN: Why? What's wrong with you?

MOLINA: (*Intensely.*) I'm so tired, Valentin. I'm tired of suffering. I ache all over inside.

VALENTIN: Where does it hurt?

MOLINA: In my chest, in my throat . . . Why is it that when you're miserable you always feel it there? Like a knot? Choking you?

VALENTIN: It's true, that's where you feel it. Is it very tight?

MOLINA: Yes.

VALENTIN: Is this where it hurts?

MOLINA: Yes . . .

VALENTIN: Want me to stroke it?

MOLINA: Yes . . .

VALENTIN: (*After a pause.*) What a relief . . .

MOLINA: Why is it a relief?

VALENTIN: Not thinking about my problems for a change. I guess because you need me, and I feel like I'm helping you.

MOLINA: You're so crazy . . . always trying to explain things.

VALENTIN: I don't like things to run away with me. I want to know why they're happening.

MOLINA: Can I touch you?

VALENTIN: Yes . . .

MOLINA: I want to touch that mole . . . the little round one, over your eyebrow. (*He does. Valentin is silent.*) You're very kind.

VALENTIN: No, you're the one who's kind.

MOLINA: If you want, you can do what you want with me . . . because I want it, I do. (*Valentin is silent.*) If it doesn't disgust you.

VALENTIN: Don't say that. It's better to be quiet.

(*The following stage directions are only a suggestion to the director. The important thing is to find a stage convention that will serve as an equivalent for the sexual act—impossible to perform on stage for more than one reason—and stress for the audience how it intensifies the relationship of Molina and Valentin.*

Both men get up and come downstage, in bright light, their arms around each other's shoulders; they speak the following dialogue looking straight out at eye level.)*

VALENTIN: Move a little toward the wall.

MOLINA: (*After a pause.*) It's so dark I can't see a thing. (*Pause.*) Go slow . . . (*Pause.*) Not like that, it hurts. (Pause.) Easy, easy . . . (*Pause.*) Yes, like that . . . (*Long pause.*) Thank you.

VALENTIN: Thank you. How do you feel now?

MOLINA: Good . . ᐟ And you, Valentin?

VALENTIN: Don't ask me . . . I don't know what . . .

MOLINA: Oh, so nice . . .

VALENTIN: Let's not talk for a minute . . .

MOLINA: I just feel so strange . . . For no reason I put my hand over my eyebrow, looking for that mole.

VALENTIN: You don't have a mole there, I do.

MOLINA: I know, but I put my hand up there . . . to touch the mole . . . I don't have.

VALENTIN: Shhh, let's not talk for just a minute.

MOLINA: You know what else I felt, just for one second . . . ?

VALENTIN: Tell me, but don't move, hold still.

MOLINA: For just one second, I felt like I wasn't here . . . not in here, or outside. (*Valentin is silent.*) I felt like I wasn't here, you were here alone. (*Valentin is silent.*) Or that it wasn't me. That now . . . I was you.

SCENE 9

(*Daylight. Each in his own bed.*)

VALENTIN: (*The usual greeting, but now with a clearly different tone.*) Good morning.

MOLINA: Good morning, Valentin.

VALENTIN: Did you sleep well?

MOLINA: Yes. (*Calmly, trying not to impose.*) Would you like coffee or tea?

VALENTIN: Coffee, so I can wake up and study. Till I get back into the swing of things . . . Is your bad mood over?

---

*There is no break in the realism of the scene in the Spanish version. The sexual encounter was enacted realistically in the first production in Valencia and Madrid but in deep shadow, upstage from the audience.

MOLINA: Yes, but I'm dazed. My mind's gone, I can't think of anything.

VALENTIN: Me neither. I'm just going to study. That'll save me.

MOLINA: From what? Feeling guilty about what happened?

VALENTIN: I'm more and more convinced that sex is innocence itself.

MOLINA: Can I ask you a favor? Let's not try to analyze anything today.

VALENTIN: Whatever you want.

MOLINA: I feel . . . good, and I don't want anything to make me stop feeling that way. I haven't felt this good since I was a kid, and my momma bought me a toy.

VALENTIN: Do you remember which toy you liked best?

MOLINA: A doll, with long blond hair.

VALENTIN: (*Breaking up with laughter.*) Ay!

MOLINA: Why are you laughing?

VALENTIN: Well, there goes my career as a psychologist.

MOLINA: What?

VALENTIN: . . . Nothing . . . I just wanted to see if there was a link between your favorite toy . . . and me.

MOLINA: (*Playing along.*) You deserve it for asking.

VALENTIN: You're sure it wasn't a boy doll?

MOLINA: (*Laughing, completely relaxed.*) No, a pretty little girl doll, with braids, in a little Austrian peasant dress.

VALENTIN: (*Using the occasion to raise a question that's much on his mind.*) Tell me something . . . Physically, you're as much a man as I am.

MOLINA: Uh-huh . . .

VALENTIN: Why don't you ever think of . . . acting like a man? I don't mean with women, if they don't attract you, but with another man.

MOLINA: I don't like it. I only enjoy myself this way.

VALENTIN: Well, if you like being a woman . . . you shouldn't feel less of a person because of that. (*Molina is silent.*) I mean that you shouldn't feel that you have to pay, or do favors for someone, because that's what you like. You shouldn't have to . . . subjugate yourself.

MOLINA: But if a man is my husband . . . he has to give the orders, to feel good, that's natural.

VALENTIN: No, the man and the woman have to have an equal share in things. Otherwise it's exploitation.

MOLINA: But that way there's no kick to it.

VALENTIN: What?

MOLINA: If you really want to know . . . what gives it a kick is that, when a man puts his arms around you, you're a little frightened.

VALENTIN: That's so screwed up. Who put that idea into your head?

MOLINA: That's the way I feel.

VALENTIN: You didn't always feel that way, they taught you to feel like that. Just to be a woman doesn't mean . . . you have to be . . . a martyr. If I didn't think it would hurt like hell, I'd ask you to do it to me, just to show you that being macho doesn't give you any rights over anyone else.

MOLINA: (*Upset.*) This talk is not getting us anywhere.

VALENTIN: Yes it is, and I think we should talk about it.

MOLINA: But I don't, and that's that. Please, I beg you.

GUARD'S VOICE: Convict Luis Alberto Molina, visit in locutory.

(*The door opens, Molina goes out as the warden's voice is heard on tape; Valentin relishes going back to his books.*)

WARDEN'S VOICE: Hello, dear, can you please put me through to your chief . . . How are you? What's new over there? Here? Nothing . . . Yes, that's why I called. I'm seeing him in a few minutes . . . Yes, I understand. You need the data before you begin your big counteroffensive . . . What if Molina still hasn't gotten us anything? What should I do with him? . . . Really? . . . Let him out today? . . . Why so soon? Right, there's no time to lose. I see, if the other one gives him a message, Molina will lead us right to where his pals are hiding . . . I see, giving them some minutes alone so the other one has time to work something out . . . We'd better be careful Molina doesn't know he's being shadowed . . . You can't always predict the way these degenerates will react.

(*Molina comes back into the cell; he is totally crushed.*)

MOLINA: Poor Valentin, you're looking at my hands.

VALENTIN: I didn't mean to.

MOLINA: Poor darling, your eyes gave you away . . .

VALENTIN: Such language.

MOLINA: There was no package for me. I'm sorry. Ay, Valentin . . .

VALENTIN: What's wrong?

MOLINA: Ay, you don't know . . .

VALENTIN: What happened? Say it!!

MOLINA: Today I'm out.

VALENTIN: Of this cell? What a drag . . .

MOLINA: No, I'm out, I'm free.

VALENTIN: No . . .

MOLINA: They're letting me out on parole.

VALENTIN: (*An unexpected burst of joy.*) But that's fabulous . . .

MOLINA: (*Confused by it all, not least Valentin's reaction.*) I don't know . . .

VALENTIN: But it's incredible . . . It's the best thing that could have happened!

MOLINA: (Totally bewildered by this.) I'm glad you're so happy for me.

VALENTIN: For you and also for a different reason, this is terrific! And I promise you there won't be any risk in it either.

MOLINA: What are you talking about?

VALENTIN: Look . . . I've thought of a wonderful plan for action, and I've been dying with frustration because I can't pass it on to my people. I was racking my brains trying to find a way . . . and you serve it up on a silver platter.

MOLINA: (*Shocked.*) I can't do it, you're crazy.

VALENTIN: You can memorize it in ten seconds. That's how easy it is.

MOLINA: I'll be on parole, something like this and they'll shut me back in forever.

VALENTIN: I swear to you, there's no risk.

MOLINA: Please, I don't want to hear a single word. Not who they are, not where they are, nothing.

VALENTIN: Don't you want me to get out one day too?

MOLINA: Out of here?

VALENTIN: Yes, and be free.

MOLINA: There's nothing I'd like better. But I'm telling you, for your own good . . . I can't do this, if they caught me I'd talk.

VALENTIN: My companions are my responsibility, not yours. Look, you just have to wait a few days after getting out, and then call somebody from a phone booth. And you arrange to meet them in a fake place.

MOLINA: A fake place?

VALENTIN: The place names are in code, for instance, if you say the Palace Movie Theatre that means a specific bench in a certain square.

MOLINA: I'm frightened.

VALENTIN: You won't be after I've explained it all.

MOLINA: But what if the phone's tapped? I'm done for!

VALENTIN: No, you use a public phone, and you disguise your voice, it's the easiest thing in the world, I'll show you. There are a thousand ways, with a piece of candy in your mouth, with a toothpick under your tongue . . .

MOLINA: No.

VALENTIN: We'll talk about it later.

MOLINA: No!

VALENTIN: Whatever you say. (*Molina throws himself on his bed, exhausted, and buries his head in the pillow.*) Look at me, please.

MOLINA: (*Not looking at him.*) I made a promise, I don't know to whom, to God, I guess, not that I believe that much.

VALENTIN: And . . .

MOLINA: And I swore that if I got out of here I would devote my life to taking care of momma. And I would sacrifice everything to do it. And I've got my wish.

VALENTIN: Very generous, thinking of someone else first.

MOLINA: But is it fair? I always end up with nothing . . .

VALENTIN: You have your mother, she's your responsibility, you have to take care of her.

MOLINA: Listen, my mother's had her life, she's lived, she had a husband, a son . . . she's old, her life is already over.

VALENTIN: But she's still alive.

MOLINA: And so am I . . . But when will my life start? When is it my turn to have something?

VALENTIN: Out there you can start all over again.

MOLINA: The only thing I want is to stay with you. (*Valentin is silent.*) Does it embarrass you, my saying that?

VALENTIN: No . . . well, yes. Yes, it does embarrass me a little.

MOLINA: If I carry that message you'll be out sooner?

VALENTIN: It's a way of helping the cause.

MOLINA: But you don't mean they'll let you out any faster. You think it'll help the revolution happen sooner.

VALENTIN: Yes, Molina . . . Don't worry about it, we'll discuss it later.

MOLINA: There's no time to discuss anything.

VALENTIN: (*Trying to be funny.*) Besides, I want to hear the end of the panther movie.

MOLINA: It's a sad ending.

VALENTIN: Why?

MOLINA: She's a very flawed woman. (*With his usual irony.*) All of us flawed women come to sad endings.

VALENTIN: (*Laughing.*) And the psychiatrist? Does he get her in the end?

MOLINA: No, she gets him! But good! . . . No, it's not what you think.

VALENTIN: And does she kill me?

MOLINA: In the movie yes. In real life no.

VALENTIN: Go on.

MOLINA: That's all. Irena gets worse and worse, she's insanely jealous of the other girl, and tries to kill her. But the other one's lucky and gets away. Then one day, the husband, in desperation, invites the shrink over to their house while she's not there. But things get mixed up and when the shrink comes Irena's home alone. So he tries to take advantage of her and grabs her and kisses her. And right then she turns into a panther. By the time the husband gets there the guy's already bled to death. Meantime Irena's gone to the zoo, it's night and she's alone there, and she heads for the panther's cage. That afternoon she got the key when the old zookeeper left it in the lock by mistake. She walks toward the cage, it's like she's in another world. And the husband's coming, with the police, at top speed. Irena opens the panther's cage, and the beast jumps on her and kills her with one blow. Then it hears the police sirens and gets frightened and runs out into the street, and a car runs it over and kills it.

VALENTIN: Molinita, I'm going to miss you.

MOLINA: My movies, anyway.

VALENTIN: Anyway.

MOLINA: I wanted to ask you for a goodbye present. Something we never did, even though we did worse things.

VALENTIN: What?

MOLINA: A kiss.

VALENTIN: It's true, we never did.

MOLINA: But just before I leave.

VALENTIN: Okay.

MOLINA: Why didn't you ever kiss me? . . . Did the thought disgust you?

VALENTIN: Um . . . Maybe I was afraid you'd turn into a panther.

MOLINA: I'm no panther woman.

VALENTIN: That's for sure.

MOLINA: It's sad to be a panther woman, no one can kiss you. Or anything else.

VALENTIN: You're the spider woman, you trap men in your web.

MOLINA: (Flattered.) How nice! I like that.

VALENTIN: And now you have to promise me something: That you'll make people respect you, that you won't let anybody treat you bad, or exploit you . . . Promise me that you won't let anyone put you down.

GUARD'S VOICE: Convict Luis Alberto Molina, ready with your belongings.

MOLINA: Valentin . . .

VALENTIN: What?

MOLINA: Nothing . . . Nothing . . . (Pause.) Valentin . . .

VALENTIN: What is it?

MOLINA: Nothing, just nonsense . . .

VALENTIN: Was it what you asked me about before?

MOLINA: What?

VALENTIN: The kiss.

MOLINA: No, it was something else.

VALENTIN: Don't you want me to kiss you now?

MOLINA: Yes, if it won't disgust you.

VALENTIN: Don't get me mad. (He goes to Molina and kisses him on the mouth, timidly.)

MOLINA: Thank you.

VALENTIN: Thank you. (Long pause.)

MOLINA: Valentin . . .

VALENTIN: What is it?

MOLINA: Tell me everything you want to say to your companions.

VALENTIN: Whatever you want.

MOLINA: And you have to tell me everything I'm supposed to do.

VALENTIN: (Holding him.) All right. Was that what you wanted to say before?

MOLINA: Yes.

VALENTIN: (Holding him tighter.) You don't know how happy you've made me The number is 323-1025.

(*Bolero music starts, it chokes Valentin's voice as he gives his instructions. Molina and Valentin separate slowly, Molina puts all his belongings in a duffel bag. They are now openly broken-hearted; Molina can hardly keep his mind on what he's doing, Valentin looks at him in total helplessness. Their taped voices are heard as all this takes place.*)

MOLINA'S VOICE: Valentin, what happened to me when I got out of here?

VALENTIN'S VOICE: The police watched you every minute, monitored your phone, everything. The first call you got was from an uncle, your godfather; he told you never to mess around with minors. You gave him the answer he deserved, to go fuck himself, because in jail you learned what dignity was. Your friends phoned, and you called each other Greta, Marlene, Marilyn; the police thought it might be a code. And every evening you looked out the window, in the same direction.

MOLINA: Which direction?

VALENTIN'S VOICE: Towards this prison. This was what you were looking at. And one day you met my comrades, but the police were tailing you and they arrested you. And from their getaway car my comrades shot you to death, the way you asked them to in case you were caught. And that's all . . . And me, Molina, what happened to me?

MOLINA'S VOICE: They tortured you, a lot . . . and your wounds got infected. A doctor felt sorry for you and secretly gave you morphine, and you had a dream.

VALENTIN'S VOICE: About what?

MOLINA'S VOICE: You dreamed that inside you, in your chest, you were carrying Marta, and that nothing would ever separate you again. And she asked you if you weren't sorry for what had happened to me, for my death, which she said was all your fault.

VALENTIN'S VOICE: And what did I tell her?

MOLINA'S VOICE: You told her I had died for a noble and unselfish ideal. And she said no, not at all, that I had sacrificed myself just so I could die like a movie heroine. And you told her I was the only one who would ever know that. And in your dream you broke out of jail, and afterwards you were very hungry, and you came to a savage island, and in the middle of the jungle you met a spider woman who gave you food. And she was so sad and lonely, out there alone in the jungle, but you had to go on with your struggle, and go back to your comrades now that your strength was renewed by the nourishing food the spider woman had given you.

VALENTIN'S VOICE: And at the end, did I get away from the police or did they catch up with me?

MOLINA'S VOICE: No, in the end you left the island, so glad to be joining your comrades in their struggle, because it was a short dream, but a very happy one . . .

(Molina has finished his packing, leaving behind the stove and the cookware. He holds out his hand to Valentin, who takes it and then embraces him tightly. Molina goes out.)

END

Burning Patience

Antonio Skármeta

BURNING PATIENCE
INTAR (New York)
Directed by Paul Zimet

CHARACTERS

Pablo Neruda, age 60.
Mario Jiménez, age 18.
Beatriz González, age 16.
Rosa (the widow González), age 40.
First Policeman
Second Policeman

SCENE 1

(*Neruda's Voice from offstage. Music.*)

PABLO: I've been spending almost all of 1969 in Isla Negra. From early morning the ocean begins its fantastic way of rising. It seems to be kneading an endless loaf of bread. The spilt foam is white as flour, pushed up by the cold leavening from the depths.

In winter the houses in Isla Negra live wrapped in the darkness of night. Only mine is aglow. At times I think there's someone in the house across the way. I see a lighted window. It's only an illusion. There's no one in the captain's house. It's only the light from my window reflected in his.

SCENE 2

(*On one side of the stage, the door of Pablo's house. On the other side, a public telephone. Pablo is tearing open an envelope. Mario is standing beside him.*)

MARIO: Where's it from?
PABLO: Sweden.
MARIO: Why are you opening it before the others?
PABLO: Because it's the one that interests me most.
MARIO: How do you know before you open it?
PABLO: Because it's from Sweden.
MARIO: And what's so special about Sweden—except all those blonds?

PABLO: The Nobel Prize for Literature, my boy.

MARIO: Are they going to give it to you?

PABLO: If they do, I'm not going to turn it down.

MARIO: How much money would you get?

PABLO: 125,000 dollars. (*Pause.*)

MARIO: Why do you get so many letters, Don Pablo?

PABLO: Are you getting tired of bringing them to me?

MARIO: Not at all. I like to. The fact is you're the only person on the island who gets mail. If you weren't here, I wouldn't have this job.

PABLO: Then I'll try to live forever, so you won't get laid off.

MARIO: I'd really like to get a letter someday. What's it like?

PABLO: That depends. If you're expecting a love letter . . . anxiety.

MARIO: Anxiety's like being on pins and needles. Right?

PABLO: Like being on pins and needles? Yes.

MARIO: What does the letter say?

PABLO: Mario, my friend, I can't read it if you keep on asking me questions.

MARIO: I'm sorry, Don Pablo. (*Pablo reads his letter.*)

MARIO: Well?

PABLO: Huh?

MARIO: Are they going to give you the prize?

PABLO: Maybe. But there are other candidates with a better chance.

MARIO: Why is that?

PABLO: Because they've written great books.

MARIO: What about the other letters?

PABLO: I'll read them later.

MARIO: Er . . . (*Pause.*)

PABLO: What's on your mind, Mario?

MARIO: The other letters . . . Do you think they're love letters?

PABLO: Look, I'm a married man. You know my wife Matilde!

MARIO: I'm sorry, Don Pablo.

PABLO: Well, here . . . go buy yourself something. (*He gives him a tip.*)

MARIO: Thanks.

PABLO: So long, now.

MARIO: So long. (*Pause.*)

PABLO: What's wrong with you?

MARIO: Don Pablo?

PABLO: You act like you're nailed to the floor.

MARIO: Like I was struck by a bolt of lightning?

PABLO: No, like a knot on a log.

MARIO: Like the cat who ate the mouse.

PABLO: (*Laughing.*) It sounds like you've taken up metaphors.

MARIO: Sir?

PABLO: Metaphors, my boy.

MARIO: What are they?

PABLO: Ways of describing a thing by comparing it with something else. Do you understand?

MARIO: Give me an example.

PABLO: Well, if you say the sky is weeping . . . what do you mean?

MARIO: That's easy. That it's raining, of course.

PABLO: Well, that's a metaphor.

MARIO: If it's so easy, why does it have such a long name?

PABLO: Because names have nothing to do with how simple or how difficult a thing is. According to your way of thinking, a tiny creature that flies shouldn't have a name as long as "butterfly." Think about "elephant," for example. It has one letter less than "butterfly," and it's so big it can't get off the ground. (*Pause.*) Now what's on your mind?

MARIO: I think I'd like to be a poet.

PABLO: My boy, everybody's a poet in Chile. It's more original to keep on being a postman. At least the exercise will keep you from getting fat. In Chile all the poets have potbellies.

MARIO: It's just that if I was a poet, I could say what I mean.

PABLO: And what would that be?

MARIO: Well, that's exactly the problem. Since I'm not a poet, I can't express it. (*Pause.*)

PABLO: Mario?

MARIO: Don Pablo.

PABLO: I'm going to say goodbye now and close the door.

MARIO: Yes, Don Pablo.

PABLO: I'll see you tomorrow.

MARIO: Till tomorrow.(*Pablo closes the door. Mario doesn't budge. Pablo opens the door again.*)

PABLO: I opened the door again because I suspected you were still here.

MARIO: I was thinking.

PABLO: Do you have to stand in one spot to think? If you want to be a poet, you can start by thinking while you walk. Right now you're going to walk along the beach to the post office, and as you watch the movement of the sea, you can invent metaphors.

MARIO: Give me an example.

PABLO: Here's a poem.
"Here on the island the sea,
and so vast a sea,
rises again and again
saying yes, and no, and no
and no, and no;
saying yes, in blue,
in foam, in a gallop.

Saying no, and no.
It can't keep still,
my name is sea, it shouts,
striking a rock,
trying to convince to no avail.
Then with seven green tongues
of seven green dogs,
of seven green tigers,
of seven green seas,
it explores, kisses, and moistens,
as it strikes its own breast,
repeating its name."
(*Pause.*) What do you think of it?

MARIO: It's strange.

PABLO: Strange? You've certainly become a harsh critic!

MARIO: I don't mean the poem's strange. Strange is how I feel when you say the words.

PABLO: Fine, Mario. Now let's see if you can get yourself together. I can't give up the whole morning to the pleasure of your conversation.

MARIO: Well, how can I explain it? When you were reciting the poem, the words were going back and forth.

PABLO: Like the ocean, or course!

MARIO: That's it! They were moving just like the ocean!

PABLO: It's called rhythm.

MARIO: And I felt funny. I got sort of . . . seasick from all that movement.

PABLO: You got seasick!

MARIO: You see, I was moving back and forth like a boat rocking on your words.

PABLO: "Like a boat rocking on my words."

MARIO: Right.

PABLO: Do you know what you've done?

MARIO: What?

PABLO: Created a metaphor.

MARIO: (*Laughing.*) But it doesn't count because it just came out by accident.

PABLO: There's no image that isn't pure chance, my boy. The world itself is one immense chance happening.

MARIO: Do you think that the world, I mean *the whole world*, with the wind, the oceans, trees, mountains, fire, animals, houses, deserts, rains . . .

PABLO: . . . now you can say "etcetera" . . .

MARIO: . . . etcetera! Do you think that the world is a metaphor for something? (*Pause.*) Don Pablo?

PABLO: Mario?

MARIO: Did that sound crazy to you?

PABLO: No, boy, no.

MARIO: But you got such a funny look on your face.

PABLO: No, it's just that . . . I started thinking.

MARIO: About what I said?

PABLO: Exactly. Look, Mario, let's make a deal. I'll go to the kitchen now, make myself an aspirin omelette to mull over your question, and tomorrow I'll give you my opinion.

MARIO: You mean it, Don Pablo?

PABLO: Yes, I do. I'll see you tomorrow. (*Pause.*)

MARIO: Aren't you going inside?

PABLO: Oh, no. This time I'm waiting for you to go.

MARIO: So long, Don Pablo.

PABLO: So long, Mario.

MARIO: (*From a distance.*) See you tomorrow, Don Pablo. (*Blackout.*)

SCENE 3

(*Neruda's voice from offstage.*)

PABLO: "Sonnet for Matilde"
You'll discover that I love you when I don't,
since life presents a double face.
A word can be a wing of silence,
fire can have its share of cold.

I love you to begin to love you
to start anew an endless course
that makes my love for you eternal:
and that is why I do not love you yet.

I love you and I don't as if I held
between my hands the keys to happiness
and to a sad uncharted future.

My love has two lives for loving you.
That's why I love you when I don't
and why I love you when I do.

SCENE 4

(*As the lights come up, Mario is ringing Pablo's doorbell insistently.*)

PABLO: (*From a distance.*) I'm coming. (*He opens the door.*) Oh, it's you.

MARIO: I was lucky. A telegram came for you!

PABLO: You had to get up awfully early.

MARIO: No problem for me. I was glad, because I needed to talk with you.

PABLO: It must be very important. You're panting like a horse.

MARIO: Don Pablo . . . (*Pause.*) I'm in love!

PABLO: Well, that's not such a serious disease. It can be cured.

MARIO: Cured? Don Pablo, I'd rather stay sick. I'm in love, hopelessly in love.

PABLO: Against who?

MARIO: I don't understand, Don Pablo.

PABLO: I'm sorry. I meant: who are you in love with?

MARIO: Her name's Beatriz.

PABLO: Shades of Dante!

MARIO: Sir?

PABLO: There was a poet who fell in love with a certain Beatriz. His name was Dante. Girls named Beatriz inspire great loves. What are you doing?

MARIO: I'm writing down the name of that poet. Dante.

PABLO: Dante Alighieri.

MARIO: Ali . . . what?

PABLO: Here, I'll write it for you. (*Sound of pencil on paper.*) There you are. (*Pause.*) Well?

MARIO: I'm in love!

PABLO: You've already said that. And what am I supposed to do?

MARIO: You've got to help me!

PABLO: At my age?

MARIO: You have to help me because I don't know what to say to her. The minute I see her in front of me, I'm speechless. Nothing comes out.

PABLO: You haven't talked with her?

MARIO: Almost not at all. Last night I took a walk on the beach like you told me. I looked at the ocean a long time and nothing came to me. Then I went to the Inn and bought a bottle of wine. With the tip you gave me. Well, *she* was the one who sold me the bottle.

PABLO: Beatriz.

MARIO: Beatriz. I just stood there with my eyes on her and fell in love.

PABLO: On the spot?

MARIO: No, it took maybe ten minutes.

PABLO: What did she do?

MARIO: She said: "What are you staring at? Is my face dirty?"

PABLO: And you?

MARIO: I couldn't think of anything to say.

PABLO: Nothing at all? You didn't say a word to her?

MARIO: Not nothing at all. I said . . . a total of five words, I guess.

PABLO: Which were? . . .

MARIO: What's your name?

PABLO: And she said?

MARIO: She said "Beatriz González."

PABLO: You asked her name, and that took three words. What were the other two?

MARIO: "Beatriz González."

PABLO: "Beatriz González."

MARIO: She said "Beatriz González" to me and then I repeated "Beatriz González."

PABLO: Son, you've brought me an urgent telegram, and if we go on talking about Beatriz González the news will go stale in my hand.

MARIO: All right, open it.

PABLO: As a postman, you should know better than anyone that mail is private.

MARIO: Don Pablo, I've never opened anybody's mail!

PABLO: I didn't say that. What I meant is that a person has the right to read his letters in peace, without spies or witnesses.

MARIO: Don Pablo, if it's not too much trouble, I'd like to ask you to write me a poem for her instead of giving me money.

PABLO: Mario, I don't even know her. A poet needs to know a person to be inspired. You can't just sit down and write something out of nothing.

MARIO: Then what can I say to her? You're the only person on this island who can help me. All the rest are fishermen who don't know how to talk.

PABLO: But those fishermen fell in love just like you and managed to find something to say to the girls that caught their eye.

MARIO: All those girls were dog faces.

PABLO: Well, somebody fell in love with them and married them. What does your father do?

MARIO: He's a fisherman.

PABLO: There you have it. He must have spoken to your mother sometime or other to convince her to marry him.

MARIO: Don Pablo, Beatriz González is prettier than my mother.

PABLO: Mario, my boy, I can't resist any longer my curiosity to see what this telegram has to say. May I?

MARIO: It's your house, Don Pablo.

PABLO: Thank you. (*He tears open the envelope.*) Let's see now.

MARIO: It's not from Sweden, is it?

PABLO: (*Distractedly.*) No, no.

MARIO: Do you think they'll give you the Nobel Prize this year?

PABLO: I've decided to stop worrying about that. It's beginning to irritate me seeing my name in the yearly competitions as if I were a race horse.

MARIO: Who's it from then?

PABLO: From the central committee of the Party. (*He reads.*) Good God!

MARIO: Bad news?

PABLO: The worst! They want me to be a candidate for president of the Republic.

MARIO: But Don Pablo, that's terrific.

PABLO: Terrific that they're making me a candidate, but what if I get elected?

MARIO: Of course you'll get elected. Everybody knows you. In my father's house there's only one book and it's by you.

PABLO: And what does that prove?

MARIO: What do you mean what does it prove? If my papa, who doesn't know how to read or write, has a book of yours, that means we'll win.

PABLO: *We'll* win?

MARIO: Of course. I'll certainly vote for you.

PABLO: I appreciate your support. Now I'll go with you to the Inn to meet the famous Beatriz González.

MARIO: Don Pablo, are you kidding me?

PABLO: I'm quite serious. We'll go up to the bar, sip a little wine, and take a look at your girlfriend.

MARIO: (*Excited.*) She's going to die when she sees us together. Pablo Neruda and Mario Jiménez, together having a drink at the Inn! She'll just die!

PABLO: That would be very unfortunate. Instead of writing a poem, I'd have to cook up an epitaph for her. Let's go. (*Pause.*) Now what's wrong?

MARIO: Don Pablo, if I marry Beatriz González . . . would you agree to be my best man at the wedding?

PABLO: After we have our wine at the Inn we can decide both questions.

MARIO: Both?

PABLO: The presidency of the Republic and Beatriz González.

(*Blackout.*)

SCENE 5

(*Neruda's voice. Sound of a typewriter.*)

PABLO'S VOICE: Political life came like a thunderclap to take me from my work. I returned once more to the masses. The human multitude has been the lesson of my life. I can approach all those people with the inherent shyness of the poet, with the fear of the timid man, but once in their bosom, I feel transfigured. I am part of the essential majority, I am one leaf more on the great tree of humanity.

SCENE 6

(*Beatriz's room, in darkness.*)

ROSA: Are you asleep?

BEATRIZ: No, Mama.

ROSA: Then what are you doing?

BEATRIZ: I'm thinking.

ROSA: *You* thinking! (*She turns on the light.*)

BEATRIZ: Mama, why did you turn on the light?

ROSA: If you're thinking, I want to see what you look like when you think.

BEATRIZ: Turn off the light, Mama!

ROSA: With the window wide open, in the middle of winter.

BEATRIZ: It's my room, Mama.

ROSA: But I pay the doctor's bills. Let's not beat around the bush, Beatriz. Who is he?

BEATRIZ: Who do you mean?

ROSA: You know very well who I mean. I saw you with him, over there on the rocks.

BEATRIZ: Mama, I'm sixteen years old!

ROSA: And I learned a few things while I was getting these gray hairs. Who is he?

BEATRIZ: His name is Mario.

ROSA: What does he do?

BEATRIZ: He's a mailman.

ROSA: A mailman in Isla Negra? He's lying to you.

BEATRIZ: Didn't you see his mailbag?

ROSA: Oh, I saw his mailbag all right, and I saw what he had in it. He was carrying a bottle of wine.

BEATRIZ: Because he'd already finished his delivery.

ROSA: Who does he carry letters to?

BEATRIZ: To Don Pablo.

ROSA: Neruda?

BEATRIZ: They're friends, you know.

ROSA: He told you that?

BEATRIZ: They go around talking all the time. Haven't you seen them?

ROSA: What do they talk about?

BEATRIZ: About politics.

ROSA: Oh, so he's a Communist to boot?

BEATRIZ: Mama, Don Pablo is going to be president of Chile!

ROSA: Look, dear, if you confuse poetry with politics you'll be pregnant before you can bat an eyelash. And your own mother is here to see that it doesn't happen. What did he tell you?

BEATRIZ: Who?

ROSA: The mailman!

BEATRIZ: He didn't talk much. Most of the time he just looked at me.

ROSA: In the bar. And afterwards, when you went to the rocks?

BEATRIZ: He told me about his work.

ROSA: How interesting.

BEATRIZ: Of course it's interesting. He meets a lot of people.

ROSA: In Isla Negra only one person gets letters. A certain poet. Nobody else can read.

BEATRIZ: Well, the poet keeps him busy. And he gives him good tips.

ROSA: Which he invests in wine.

BEATRIZ: He gives him stamps too. He told me he had an album with stamps from all over the world.

ROSA: Did he invite you to the rocks to look at it?

BEATRIZ: Mama, I want to get some sleep.

ROSA: What did he say to you? I want to know what he said when you went to the rocks.

BEATRIZ: Metaphors. (*Pause.*) What's wrong, Mama? You look so surprised.

ROSA: I am. It's the first time I ever heard you say a word that long. What kind of *metaphors* did he tell you?

BEATRIZ: He said . . . He said my smile unfolds like a butterfly across my face.

ROSA: What else?

BEATRIZ: Well, when he said that, I laughed.

ROSA: And then?

BEATRIZ: Then he said something about the way I laugh. He said that my laugh was like a rose, a spear that shatters, water rushing forth. He said that my laugh was a sudden wave of silver.

ROSA: Then what did you do?

BEATRIZ: I just sat there quietly.

ROSA: What about him?

BEATRIZ: You mean what else he said to me?

ROSA: No, dear. What else did he do to you? Your mailman must have hands as well as a mouth. One thing I've never seen is a one-armed mailman.

BEATRIZ: He never touched me once. He said he was happy just to be near me . . . stretched out beside a girl as pure as a white ocean.

ROSA: What did you say to that?

BEATRIZ: I kept quiet, thinking about it.

ROSA: And him?

BEATRIZ: He said he liked me when I didn't say anything because it was as if I'd gone off by myself . . . He said it seemed like my eyes had taken flight and a kiss had sealed my lips. He also said I resembled the word "melancholy."

ROSA: And?

BEATRIZ: I looked at him.

ROSA: How about him?

BEATRIZ: He looked at me too. Then he stopped looking into my eyes, and for a long time he just gazed at my hair without saying a thing. Then he ran his hand over his own hair and said: "It would take an eternity to praise your hair as I should, counting the strands one by one and singing their glories."

ROSA: I've heard enough. You've got yourself into a real kettle of fish. Men always start with words and then move in with their hands.

BEATRIZ: But Mama, what's so wrong with words?

ROSA: Fancy talk is the worst drug of all. It makes a small town barmaid feel like a princess. Then comes the moment of truth. You return to reality and it dawns on you that words are like a check that bounces. I'd much prefer to have a drunk touching your ass at the bar than for somebody to tell you that your smile reminds him of a butterfly.

BEATRIZ: Unfolds like a butterfly.

ROSA: Unfolds, flits, it's all the same. And do you know why? Because behind those words there's nothing. They're fireworks that vanish in the air.

BEATRIZ: Mario's words haven't vanished in the air. I know them by heart. I like to think about them when I'm working.

ROSA: Okay. Tomorrow morning early you pack your bag, and you're going to your aunt's house in Santiago for a visit.

BEATRIZ: But Mama, I don't want to.

ROSA: What you want doesn't matter. This is serious business.

BEATRIZ: What's so serious about a boy talking to you? It happens to all the girls.

ROSA: First of all, you can see from a mile away that the things he said to you he copied from Don Pablo.

BEATRIZ: He never said they were his own words. He just looked at me and it came out of his mouth like birds.

ROSA: Like birds? You pack your things tonight, and tomorrow it's off to Santiago with you. Do you know what they call it when somebody uses other people's words? Plagiarism! Your Mario can go to jail for going around spouting . . . metaphors. I'm going to call Don Pablo myself and tell him that mailman is stealing his poetry.

BEATRIZ: Mama, what makes you think Don Pablo has time to worry about such things? They've nominated him for President, they may give him the Nobel Prize, and you're going to bother him over a couple of metaphors.

ROSA: A couple of metaphors. Have you seen yourself in the mirror?

BEATRIZ: Why?

ROSA: You're sweating like a plant. You've got a fever, girl, that has only two cures. A trip or a bed. Start packing!

BEATRIZ: I won't. I'm staying here.

ROSA: Dear, a river is strong enough to move rocks, and words can get you pregnant.

BEATRIZ: I know how to take care of myself.

ROSA: What makes you so sure? The way you are now it wouldn't take more than one touch of a fingernail. Just remember that I read Neruda before you did, and I know perfectly well how men turn poetic on you when they've got something else in mind.

BEATRIZ: Neruda's not like that. He's going to be the candidate for the left. He's going to be President.

ROSA: When it comes to getting a girl into bed, there's no difference between a liberal, a priest, or a communist poet. Poets are the worst, and Neruda's charm can do most harm.

BEATRIZ: (*Laughing.*) "Neruda's charm can do most harm." Now *you're* talking in poetry.

ROSA: Go ahead and laugh! Do you know who wrote this? "I love the love of sailors who kiss and go away, leaving a promise never to come again."

BEATRIZ: Neruda.

ROSA: Neruda. And you don't blink an eye.

BEATRIZ: I wouldn't make such a to-do over a kiss.

ROSA: Over a kiss, no, but a kiss is the spark that starts the fire. And here's another of Neruda's verses for you: "I love the love that has its share of kisses, bed, and bread. A love that's free to love and free to love again." In everyday talk that means it even comes as breakfast in bed.

BEATRIZ: Mama!

ROSA: And then your mailman is going to recite to you that immortal Neruda poem I wrote in my notebook when I was exactly your age, young lady. "I do not want this, beloved. So that nothing will bind us, so that nothing holds us firm."

BEATRIZ: I didn't quite understand that.

ROSA: (*Emphasizing each word.*) "I-do-not-want-this-beloved-so-that-nothing-will-bind-us-so-that-nothing-holds-us-firm."

BEATRIZ: Does he mean the wedding ring?

ROSA: Right. The wedding ring. Now pack your suitcase like a good girl. (*Pause.*)

BEATRIZ: Mama, this is ridiculous. Just because a man tells me my smile unfolds like a butterfly I have to go off to Santiago.

ROSA: (*Shouting.*) Don't be a fool! Today your smile's a butterfly, but tomorrow your tits are going to be two doves that want to be cooed over, your nipples two juicy raspberries, your tongue will be the warm carpet of the gods, your ass the sails of a boat, and that thing you have between your legs the dark furnace where the hard metal of the race is forged. Good night! (*The sound of a door closing. Pause. Then Beatriz opens the window and we hear the loud roar of the sea.*)

SCENE 7

(*Beatriz is looking out the window with her back to the audience. Pablo is standing on the opposite side. He walks downstage and speaks directly to the audience.*)

PABLO: Up to this moment, all the parties of the left had their candidates and they all wanted their respective candidate to be the only one to represent the left. When the party proposed me as their candidate, and I accepted, we made our position clear. We would support the candidate who could count on the will of the others. If we didn't join together in a common electoral goal, we'd be overwhelmed in a spectacular defeat. If we didn't achieve such a consensus, I would remain a candidate to the end. It was an heroic measure to oblige the others to come to an agreement, because it was highly unlikely that political unity could be rallied around a Communist.

But my candidacy caught fire. There was no place where I wasn't sought out. I was deeply moved by those hundreds or thousands of ordinary people who pressed against me, kissed me, and wept. I spoke to them all or I read my poems to them in the falling rain, in the mud of the streets, under the Antarctic wind that makes you shiver with cold. I was getting excited. More and more people were coming to hear what I had to say, more and more women were showing up. With fascination and terror I began to think what it would mean if I really was elected president of this headstrong, intractable, debt-ridden country—possibly the most ungrateful republic of them all. Our presidents were acclaimed during the first month and martyred, rightly or wrongly, for the remaining five years and eleven months of their term.

At an opportune moment the news came: Allende was coming to the fore as a possible candidate of Popular Unity. Subject to my party's acceptance, I submitted my resignation. Before an immense and happy throng I renounced my candidacy and Allende accepted the nomination. (*With Pablo's final words there is a blackout and a recording of Sergio Ortega's Piano Variations and Fugue on the theme of "El pueblo unido" [The People United] is heard loudly.*)

SCENE 8

(*The door of Pablo's house. He is painting the doorframe green. Mario comes running up to him.*)

PABLO: You're puffing like a train engine.
MARIO: (*Trying to get his breath.*) Don Pablo.
PABLO: Have a drink of water, man! (*He points to a spigot.*)
MARIO: Don Pablo, I've got a letter for you.
PABLO: Since you're the postman, that doesn't surprise me.
MARIO: Don Pablo, as your friend and neighbor, I'm asking you to open it and read it to me.
PABLO: And why all the hurry?
MARIO: Because it's from Beatriz's mother.
PABLO: Beatriz's mother is writing me? It looks like the cat's out of the bag, as

they say. Which reminds me, I wrote my "Ode to the Cat" today. I've described how he strikes me in three ways: The cat is the miniature tiger of the living room, he's the secret police of bedrooms, and he's the sultan of erotic rooftops. What do you think of it?

MARIO: Please, the letter. (*Pablo tears open the envelope and unfolds the letter.*)

PABLO: (*Reading.*) "Dear Don Pablo, allow me to introduce myself. I am the widow Rosa González, proprietor of the local inn, admirer of your poetry, and a supporter of the Christian Democrats. Although I wouldn't have voted for you in the coming election and I don't intend to vote for Allende, as a mother, a Chilean, and a neighbor of yours in Isla Negra, I am urgently requesting a meeting with you to discuss a certain Mario Jiménez, corrupter of minors. Having stated my purpose, I remain, sincerely yours, Rosa González (widow)." Comrade Mario Jiménez, you've got yourself into a real kettle of fish.

MARIO: (*Shouting.*) Well, what am I going to do?

PABLO: First of all, you can lower your voice. I'm not deaf.

MARIO: I'm sorry, Don Pablo.

PABLO: Second, you're going home and have a good nap. The circles under your eyes are as big as saucers.

MARIO: You expect me to sleep? I haven't slept a wink in a week, and my father's accusing me of being a night owl.

PABLO: If you don't, you'll find yourself stretched out in a wooden box in another week. Mario Jiménez, you have the gift of gab. Now, with your permission, I'll have a look at my other letters.

MARIO: But you can't just leave me stranded like this, Don Pablo. You've got to write that lady and tell her to calm down.

PABLO: My boy, I'm only a poet. I haven't mastered the fine art of defusing prospective mothers-in-law.

MARIO: Poet and future president of Chile: you got me into this mess and you're going to get me out of it. You gave me your books and you taught me how to use my tongue for something more than licking stamps. It's your fault that I fell in love.

PABLO: As the Americans say, there's no point in locking the barn door after the horse is stolen.

MARIO: You've got to help me because this is what you wrote: "I don't like a house without a roof, a window without panes. I don't like a day without work, or a night without sleep. I don't like a man without a woman, or woman without man. I want to see lives joined, giving fire to kisses on lips that were cold. I am a poet who's good at matchmaking." I don't expect you to tell me now that your check will bounce.

PABLO: You probably think they should have put Shakespeare in prison for the murder of Hamlet's father. If Shakespeare hadn't written it, nothing would have happened to the poor man.

MARIO: Don Pablo, don't get me any more confused than I already am. What I'm asking is very simple. Answer that woman's letter and convince her to let me see Beatriz.

PABLO: Are you certain you'll be happy then?

MARIO: Very happy.

PABLO: If she lets you see the girl, will you leave me in peace?

MARIO: At least until tomorrow.

PABLO: That's better than nothing. Come along and we'll give her a call.

MARIO: Right now?

PABLO: (*Pause.*) I can hear your heart beating from here. It's howling like a dog. Muzzle it with your hand!

MARIO: I can't control it.

PABLO: (*Picking up the phone.*) Give me the number at the inn.

MARIO: One.

PABLO: It must have taken some effort to commit that to memory. (*He dials the number. The phone rings a couple of times and someone answers.*) Señora Rosa González?

ROSA'S VOICE: (*From offstage.*) Speaking.

PABLO: This is Pablo Neruda.

ROSA: Aha!

PABLO: I wanted to thank you for your kind letter.

ROSA: It's not your thanks I need, señor. I want to speak with you here and now.

PABLO: Go right ahead, Doña Rosa.

ROSA: Face to face.

PABLO: Where do you suggest?

ROSA: That's for you to say.

PABLO: Then, at my house.

ROSA: I'm on my way.

MARIO: What did she say?

PABLO: She's on her way. At least we'll be playing on our own turf, my boy. (*He goes to the record player and puts on a record.*) I brought you a very special gift from Santiago. The mailman's international anthem. (*"Please Mister Postman" by the Beatles begins. Neruda dances to the music. Mario watches him fascinated. The dance stops when Neruda sees Doña Rosa entering from the audience. Neruda hides Mario behind the door. He stops the record. Doña Rosa walks onstage.*)

PABLO: Won't you sit down, Doña Rosa?

ROSA: What I have to say is too serious for sitting.

PABLO: What's the problem, señora?

ROSA: For the past few days, a certain Mario Jiménez has been abusing my premises. This man has been using improper language with my daughter.

PABLO: What has he been saying to her?

ROSA: Metaphors! (*Pause.*)

PABLO: And?

ROSA: Well, Don Pablo, with these metaphors he's got my daughter as hot as a rock in the midday sun.

PABLO: It's winter, Dona Rosa.

ROSA: My poor Beatriz is totally smitten by this mailman. A person whose only asset is the fungus between his toes. But if his feet are oozing microbes, he's as cool as a cucumber when he starts spouting poetry at an innocent girl. And the most serious part, Don Pablo, is that the metaphors he uses to seduce my daughter have been shamelessly copied from your books.

PABLO: No!

ROSA: Yes! He started by talking innocently about a smile that was a butterfly. But then he told her that her breasts were like a fire with twin flames.

PABLO: And this image, do you think it was visual or tactile?

ROSA: Tactile. He's got my daughter so hot you don't need to light a fire when she's in the house. Just having her around is enough to heat the living-room, the kitchen, the bedrooms, and the cellar.

PABLO: What a savings in fuel!

ROSA: I tried to send her to Santiago, but she refused to go. Then I forbade her to leave the house until senor Jiménez clears out. You probably think I'm cruel to lock her up that way. But just wait until you hear the poem I found stuck between her breasts, ready to go up in flames any moment:
"Naked you're as simple as one of your hands,
smooth, earthly, tiny, round, transparent,
you have moon markings, apple trails.
Naked you are slender as the naked wheat
Naked you are blue as the Cuban night.
You have tangles and stars in your hair,
Naked you are spacious and yellow
like summer in a golden church."
That means, señor Neruda, that the mailman has seen my daughter in the raw. The poem, unfortunately, does not lie. That's exactly the way my daughter looks with her clothes off. For the moment I'm not going to accuse this Mario Jiménez of the seduction of a minor. But you command trust, and I beg you to order this Mario Jiménez, mailman and plagiarist, not to see my daughter again, now or ever. And if he does, you may be sure that I will personally take responsibility for putting out his eyes, like his illustrious predecessor: Michael Strogoff. Goodbye!

PABLO: (*Softly to himself after the Mother has made her exit.*) See you soon. (*He opens the door where Mario is hiding. Without looking at Mario:*) Mario Jiménez, you are pale as a ghost.

MARIO: Don Pablo, you heard what she said!

PABLO: Well, you'd better pull yourself together and start planning your defense. I can see you now delivering letters with a white cane and a black dog, with your eyesockets empty as a beggar's tin cup.

MARIO: If I can't see her, what good are my eyes?

PABLO: You, my friend, are new at this game: you can't separate the music from the dance. This señora González may not carry out her threat after all, but if she does you'll have every right to use all the old clichés about a dark destiny.

MARIO: But she'll go to jail.

PABLO: Only for a couple of hours. Then they'll release her under bond. She'll claim she acted in self-defense. She'll say that you attacked her daughter's virginity with knife in hand: a metaphor as irresistible as a dagger thrust, sharp as a wolf's tooth, tearing through a maidenhead. Poetry, with all its droolings will leave its telltale evidence on your girlfriend's nipples. They strung up Francois Villon from a tree and fastened a rose on his neck for a lot less. What do you intend to do?

MARIO: Try to stop shaking. I don't care if that woman cuts the flesh from my bones. What hurts is not being able to see her, her cherry lips, her sad, dark eyes, and smell the warmth she sheds.

PABLO: From what her mother says, it's a lot more than warmth right now. Maybe a burning radiance would express it better.

MARIO: Why is her mother out to get me? I want to marry Beatriz.

PABLO: From what Doña Rosa says, it's pretty clear that your only negotiable assets are the grime under your fingernails and the fungus between your toes.

MARIO: But I'm young and healthy. And my lungs are strong.

PABLO: It only shows when you're sighing over Beatriz González. Right now you sound as asthmatic as the fog horn on a ghost ship.

MARIO: With the lungs I've got I could blow a sailboat from here to Australia.

PABLO: Mario, if you keep on pining over señorita González, a month from now you won't have enough breath to blow out the candles on your birthday cake. And by the way, when I gave you a couple of my books, I didn't authorize you to sign your own name to them. You gave Beatriz the poem I wrote for Matilde.

MARIO: I thought poetry was the property of the person who used it.

PABLO: That's a very democratic thought, my boy, but let's not carry democracy to the point of taking a vote to see who our father is. (*Mario goes to the telephone, picks it up and holds it in front of Neruda. Resigned, Neruda takes the phone and dials.*) Señora González?

ROSA'S VOICE: (*From offstage.*) Speaking.

PABLO: This is Pablo Neruda again.

ROSA: I don't care if it's Jesus Christ and all twelve of his disciples. That mailman Mario Jiménez will never set foot in this house! (*She hangs up.*)

MARIO: Don Pablo, what's wrong?

PABLO: Nothing, my boy. It's just that I understand now how a boxer feels when they knock him out in the first round. (*He hangs up the phone.*)

(*Blackout.*)

SCENE 9

(*Beatriz is preparing a meal in a cooking pot. Mario enters stealthily.*)

MARIO: (*Slowly.*) Beatriz! (*Beatriz turns around and looks at him. Mario goes toward her. She takes an egg and puts it in her mouth. Mario smiles and reaches out to take the egg. Beatriz, playful and teasing, steps back, leaving him with his arm outstretched. Then she takes the egg in her fingers and begins to rub it slowly over her body. First over her breasts and then down over her stomach toward her vagina. At that point she suddenly lets the egg fall but catches it with her other hand. Then she lifts the egg to her forehead, moves it over her nose to her neck. She holds the egg against her with her chin and gestures to Mario to form a basket with his hands. Mario kneels down and obeys by intertwining his hands. Beatriz goes toward him and lets the egg fall into his hands. He takes it in one hand. Beatriz crouches and Mario begins to move the egg over her body. First over her buttocks and then over her abdomen, moving up to her breasts, and finally replacing the egg against the girl's neck. Beatriz holds it again with her chin. Mario puts his arms around her and takes the egg in his mouth. Then the girl takes the egg from Mario's mouth with her own. Mario takes the egg in his mouth again and walks behind Beatriz to her other side. Beatriz opens the top of her blouse and Mario lets the egg fall into the opening. Beatriz then unfastens the waistband of her skirt and lets the egg fall and shatter on the floor. Mario lifts the girl's blouse and exposes her breasts. Beatriz stoops down and removes Mario's pants. He takes off his shirt and stands nude. Then he removes Beatriz's skirt. She is now nude too. Both turn their backs to the audience and walk upstage. From Mario's side, Neruda enters with a suit for Mario, and Rosa walks on with a very simple wedding dress for Beatriz. Neruda and the Mother dress the couple. Tito Fernández's "Vals para Jazmín" is heard. Beatriz and Mario now turn to the audience again as bride and groom. They walk downstage as in a wedding ceremony. They bow to each other and begin to dance to the waltz music. Neruda invites the Mother to dance. The four dance for a moment. Then Neruda interrupts the dance. He proposes a toast. They all drink. Neruda goes upstage, picks up a suitcase, and waves a silent goodbye to the others. Neruda exits. The others look sad, except Beatriz, who goes on dancing. She teases Mario with her wedding veil. He wraps the veil around her, takes her in his arms and carries her off. The Mother remains onstage alone.*)

SCENE 10

(When the lights come up, Rosa is on Beatriz's bed and is reading a letter from Neruda. There is a package at her feet. Mario and Beatriz listen intently.)

ROSA: *(Reading Pablo's letter.)* "Dear Mario Jiménez, of the winged feet, warmly remembered Beatriz González Jiménez, spark and flame of Isla Negra, most esteemed widow González, dear future heir of Isla Negra, Pablo Neftali Jiménez González, master swimmer in your mother's warm placenta and—when you do come out into the sunlight—lord of the rocks, flyer of kites, and champion seagull-chaser. Four people very dear to me. I haven't written you before as I promised because I didn't want to send you a postcard with Degas ballerinas. I know that this will be the first letter you've received in your whole life, Mario, and if it didn't come in an envelope, it wouldn't count. How did you manage it? Well, you must tell me all about the island and what you've been doing now that all my mail comes to Paris. Hopefully, the Post Office Service hasn't laid you off because the poet left. Or maybe President Allende has put you in charge of some ministry?"

"Well, this business of being ambassador to France is something new and troublesome for me. But it does have its challenge. We've made a revolution in Chile. A revolution Chilean style, that's stirred up a lot of debate. And our enemies on the inside and the outside are sharpening their teeth to destroy it. For the moment we can breathe and sing. That's what I like about my new situation. Chile has become important in the eyes of the world. A warm embrace from your matchmaker and neighbor, Pablo Neruda." *(Pause.)*

MARIO: Is that all?

ROSA: Well, yes. What more were you expecting?

MARIO: There's not one of those things with P.S. they put at the end of letters?

ROSA: No, that's all there was.

MARIO: It's so short. It seemed longer just looking at it.

BEATRIZ: Mama read it very fast.

ROSA: Fast or slow, the words say the same thing. Speed has nothing to do with what things mean. *(Pause.)*

BEATRIZ: Now what's wrong?

MARIO: Something's missing. When they taught me how to write a letter in school, they said you should always put a "P.S." and then say something you forgot to say in the letter. I'm sure Don Pablo forgot something.

BEATRIZ: He probably said all he wanted to in the letter.

MARIO: And if something was missing, I'll bet he wrote it later in a poem.

BEATRIZ: I'll bet he wrote the poem before he wrote the letter.

MARIO: (*Thinking.*) Of course. (*Pause.*) Aren't we going to open the package?

ROSA: I've been waiting an hour. I told you we should have opened the package first.

BEATRIZ: God but you're slow, Mama. We had to open the letter first because we figured it would explain what was in the package.

ROSA: Well, it didn't explain anything, did it? Poets' memories are as flighty as birds. (*To Mario.*) Go ahead and open it. What are you waiting for?

MARIO: "Poets' memories are as flighty as birds." A fine metaphor from a fine mother-in-law!

ROSA: Just open the package before I wet my pants.

MARIO: (*Opening the package. Sound of paper tearing.*) I'm going to tell Don Pablo what you said about poets and birds. He can probably use it. (*Pause.*) What's this?

ROSA: A tape recorder, of course. What do you think it is? What does the card say? Hand it here and I'll read it.

MARIO: Oh no! You read too fast. (*Reading very slowly and deliberately.*) "Dear Mario, comma, push the red button."

ROSA: It took you longer to read the card than for me to read the whole letter.

MARIO: It's because you don't *read* the words, señora; you swallow them whole. You have to take time to enjoy their taste.

BEATRIZ: Please don't start a fight now. Push the red button the way he said. (*Mario presses a button on the recorder. For a moment there is only the hiss of the cassette tape. Then the sound of Pablo clearing his throat, followed immediately by his voice on the cassette.*)

PABLO'S VOICE: "Postscript."

MARIO: (*Excited.*) How do you stop it?

ROSA: Just be quiet.

PABLO'S VOICE: "I wanted to send you something besides words."

MARIO: How do you stop it?

PABLO'S VOICE: "So I put my voice into this singing cage. A cage that's like a bird."

MARIO: Here. Stop. (*The recording is interrupted.*)

ROSA: Why did you turn it off?

MARIO: (*Very excited.*) I was right, señora. "P.S." Postscript. (*He divides "postscript" into two syllables, saying them with emphasis.*) The *post-script* was missing. I told you there couldn't be a letter without a postscript. The poet didn't forget. I knew that the first letter of my life had to come with a postscript! Now it's all clear, mother-in-law. The letter, and the postscript.

ROSA: All right, the letter has a postscript. And you're crying over that?

MARIO: Me?

BEATRIZ: Yes, you.

ROSA: Push the button again or I'm going to bed.

MARIO: From the beginning.

ROSA: Give it to me. (*She presses rewind on the recorder. Sound of tape rewinding. Stop button. Red button. Sound of tape hiss. Poet clearing his throat.*)

PABLO'S VOICE: "Postscript."

ROSA: (*Sharply.*) Shut up.

MARIO: I haven't said anything.

PABLO'S VOICE: "I wanted to send you something besides words. So I put my voice into this singing cage. A cage that's like a bird. It's my gift to you. But I also want to ask a favor, which only you, dear Mario, can do for me. All my other friends either wouldn't know what to do or they'd think I was ridiculous. I want you to take a walk over the island with the tape recorder and record for me all the sounds along the way. I desperately need at least the ghost of my home. Paris is beautiful, but it's a suit that's several sizes too big for me. Send me the sounds of home. Even go into the garden and ring the bells. First record the tingling of the tiny bells when the wind is blowing, and then pull the rope on the large bell, five, six times. My own bell. There's nothing that sounds so much like the word bell, bell, bell, when it hangs in a tower near the ocean. And go out on the rocks and record the sounds of the surf. If you hear the birds, record them, and if you hear the silence of the stars overhead, record that too. (*Pause.*) Here in Paris it's winter, and the wind stirs up the snow like a flour mill. To think that it's summer there, a summer that laughs like a freshly-cut melon. The snow keeps climbing higher and clinging to my skin. It's turned me into a sad king in a white tunic. It's already up to my mouth, it's covering my lips, and I can't get the words out any longer. (*Pause.*) And so that you'll know something about French music, I'm sending you a recording from 1938 that I found tucked away in a second-hand record shop in the Latin Quarter. How many times I sang this song when I was young! I'd always wanted to have the record but I never could. The song is called "J'attendrai" and the words go: "I'll wait, day and night, I'll wait always, until you return." (*The sound of the original version of "J'attendrai," sung by Rina Ketty on the record Les Belles Années des Music Hall, "Voix de son maitre" [HMV] Label: PTX-40331, No. 31*)

(*Blackout.*)

SCENE 11

(*Loud sounds of a Latin "Cumbia" from the radio. Centerstage, Mario is cutting up different types of salad greens to the rhythm of the music. Beatriz accompanies him as she hands him the vegetables. The tape recorder is on the floor.*)

MARIO: (*Into the recorder.*) Dear Don Pablo, many thanks for your letter and the gift. Now I'm trying to invent poems by saying them directly into the recorder without having to write them down. (*Rosa appears upstage, excited, with a tray in her hand.*)

ROSA: Mario!

MARIO: (*Into the recorder.*) But nothing interesting has come out yet! (*He exits carrying a platter of salad.*)

BEATRIZ: (*Into the recorder.*) Mario put off doing what you asked for a long time. It's just that there's a lot to do in Isla Negra in the summer. The labor union at a factory in Santiago got a vacation for the workers, and they signed a contract with my mama to give them room and board at the Inn. Now the restaurant is full of vacationers. (*Mario enters quickly and fills a pitcher with wine.*)

MARIO: (*Into the recorder.*) Now I'm working in the kitchen at the Inn. In the morning I deliver letters and in the afternoon I skin fish and chop onions. But I'm making good money. (*Rosa appears angrily in the doorway.*)

ROSA: Mario! (*Mario follows her offstage.*)

BEATRIZ: As you can see, everything's going well for us all. So, Don Pablo, we don't want to take any more of your valuable time. We just want to tell you how strange life is. You complain of snow up to your ears and we've never seen a snowflake in our lives. Except in the movies. (*Mario enters and lies down beside the recorder.*)

MARIO: How I'd love to be in Paris for a day swimming in snow. I've only seen snow in Yankee movies when it's Christmas. Anyhow, to show my appreciation for your gift, I wrote a poem for you, trying to imitate the snow.

BEATRIZ: "Ode to the Snow on Neruda in Paris." (*Mario climbs up on a chair and begins to recite.*)

MARIO:

"Soft companion of silent footsteps,
milk raining down from the skies,
schoolgirls' dresses starched and white,
a sheet of soundless travelers going
from house to house with wrinkled brow.

Light yet multiple maiden,
wing of a thousand doves,
handkerchief waved in unspoken goodbyes.
Please, my beautiful one,
fall kindly on Pablo Neruda in Paris.
Dress him in your gleaming sailor's suit.
Then change yourself into sheer white sails
to bring him home to this port."

BEATRIZ: . . . where we miss him so much.

MARIO: Well, that's the poem. Now for the sounds you asked me for. One. The wind in the bell tower on Isla Negra. (*He starts the cassette with the sounds on the recorder.*)

BEATRIZ: Two. The bells in your bell tower in Isla Negra.

(*Upstage the lights come up on Neruda's room in Paris. He is listening to the sounds.*)

MARIO: Three. The waves against the rocks that jut out under the terrace.

BEATRIZ: Four. The call of the seagulls.

MARIO: Five. The beehive.

BEATRIZ: Six. The tide going out.

MARIO: Seven. Don Pablo Neftalí Jiménez González. (*Twenty seconds of crying from the son of Mario and Beatriz. The lights of Isla Negra fade slowly. While the child is crying, Neruda is putting on formal clothes. When the child stops crying, Neruda comes down to the stage apron. Mario and Beatriz rest their heads against an enormous radio and listen to Neruda's speech from Stockholm.*)

PABLO: (*Dressed in tails. To the audience.*) Exactly a hundred years ago, a poor but brilliant poet, the most despairing of hopeless men, wrote this prophesy: 'A l'aurore, armés d'une ardente patience, nous entrerons aux splendides Villes.' [At daybreak, armed with a burning patience, we shall enter the splendid cities.] I believe in that prophecy of Rimbaud, the seer. I come from an obscure province of a country cut off from the rest of the world by its geography. I was the most neglected of poets and my poetry was regional, mournful and rainswept. But I always had confidence in mankind. I never lost hope. That's why I've come this far with my poetry and also with my flag. In conclusion, I must say to all men of good will, to the workers, to the poets, that our entire future was expressed in this sentence by Rimbaud. Only with a burning patience will we conquer the splendid city that will give light, justice, and dignity to all men. That way poetry will not have sung in vain. (*As he finishes his speech, Neruda looks toward the radio where Mario and Beatriz are listening. Warm applause over the radio from the audience in Sweden. Deeply moved, Mario and Beatriz hold each other for a long time.*)

ROSA: (*Entering, to Mario.*) Is the soup ready?

MARIO: What, mother-in-law?

ROSA: (*Shouting.*) Is the soup ready? Will you please turn down the radio! (*Mario lowers the volume.*) Instead of working you stand around listening to nonsense.

MARIO: I don't need my ears to cook.

ROSA: The dining room's full and you don't have the soup ready yet.

MARIO: It's coming!

ROSA: Those people are hungry!

MARIO: Doña Rosa . . . with all due respect, if I didn't think so highly of you, I'd tell you to go to hell.

ROSA: How cute! That's the kind of *poetry* that's easiest for you. Why don't you send that to your poet friend?

MARIO: Because I don't have time. (*He uncorks a bottle of wine.*)

ROSA: You don't have time to get the soup ready but you're having yourself a drink.

MARIO: No, Doña Rosa, the wine is for the guests while they're waiting for the soup.

ROSA: You're crazy! The wine doesn't come with the meal. They pay extra for it.

MARIO: No, señora. Today it's on the house. You can take it out of my pay.

ROSA: Fine, but don't think I'm going to forget to deduct it.

MARIO: It won't be necessary, mother-in-law. Here's the money in cash. Now carry the wine to our guests and tell them the soup's coming up.

ROSA: And how do I explain the free wine?

MARIO: Tell them that we're celebrating today.

ROSA: Celebrating what?

MARIO: Don Pablo Neruda's Nobel Prize. (*Euphoric.*) We won, Doña Rosa, we won!

ROSA: *We* won? "We're ploughing, said the fly, as he lit atop the ox." (*Mario turns up the volume again. From the radio, a Chilean "Cueca." Mario and Beatriz take out handkerchiefs and start dancing. The music is interrupted by a newsflash.*)

ANNOUNCER: We interrupt this program to bring you a special announcement. Santiago. A fascist commando has shot and killed Arturo Araya Peters, naval advisor to President Allende. The attack took place at Araya's home in Santiago. At this time President Allende is enroute to the scene accompanied by members of his cabinet. The Central Workers Union calls on all its members throughout the country to remain on alert in their respective posts until further notice. (*Beatriz and Mario separate and walk in opposite directions.*)

SCENE 12

(*While the stage is being set up for the following scene, we hear, in darkness, Mario's cassette with the sounds he recorded for Neruda. When the tape reaches the point of the baby's crying, the sounds of helicopters and gunshots begin to drown it out, increasing in volume until they overwhelm the scene.*)

SCENE 13

(*Neruda is lying in shadow.*)

MARIO: (*Whispering.*) Don Pablo.

PABLO: Mario! How did you get in?

MARIO: Your wife let me in.

PABLO: She let you in here? Into my bedroom?

MARIO: Yes.

PABLO: Then it's all right. Good to see you, boy.

MARIO: I tried to see you yesterday but I couldn't get in. The house was surrounded with soldiers. They only let the doctor in.

PABLO: I don't need a doctor any more. It would be better if they sent me directly to the undertaker.

MARIO: Don't talk like that, Don Pablo.

PABLO: Undertaking is a good profession, Mario. It teaches you philosophy. Remember when Hamlet is caught up in all his speculation, and the gravedigger tells him: "Get thyself a sturdy girl, and leave off all the nonsense."? And if he didn't say it, he should have.

MARIO: How do you feel, Don Pablo?

PABLO: I'm dying. Aside from that, nothing serious.

MARIO: Do you know what's going on?

PABLO: Matilde tries to keep it from me, but I have the tiniest radio ever made in Japan under my pillow. My boy, with this fever, I feel like a fish in a frying pan!

MARIO: It'll go away soon, Don Pablo.

PABLO: Yes, son, it will. And take me with it.

MARIO: Don Pablo, is it true you've got something serious?

PABLO: I'll answer you the way Mercutio did in *Romeo and Juliet*, when he's lying there run through by Tybalt's sword. (*Speaking louder.*) "[the wound] 'tis not so deep as a well, nor so wide as a church door, but 'tis enough, 'twill serve. Ask for me tomorrow and you shall find me a grave man."

MARIO: Please, poet, lie back down.

PABLO: Help me over to the window.

MARIO: I can't.

PABLO: But I'm your male Celestina, your pimp, the godfather of your son. I require in the name of all these titles earned with the sweat of my pen that you help to the window.

MARIO: There's a cold breeze, you have a fever and Doña Matilde said . . . .

PABLO: Listen to this pretty rhyme: A cold breeze can only cause a sneeze! If you could see the icy wind that blows over my bones. It's clean and sharp as the final knife thrust, boy. Take me to the window.

MARIO: But Don Pablo . . . .

PABLO: What is it you don't want me to see? Do you think the ocean won't be there as always when you open the window? Did they take that away? Did they put that in a cage too?

MARIO: The ocean is still there, Don Pablo.

PABLO: Then what's the problem? Take me to the window.

MARIO: The ocean's there, but some other things are too.

PABLO: Then I want to see them. (*Mario carries Pablo to the window. They open it.*) Aha! An ambulance. That was the mystery: an ambulance. Why don't they just send a coffin?

MARIO: They want to take you to a hospital in Santiago. Doña Matilda is packing your things.

PABLO: There's no ocean in Santiago. Only surgeons and stitchers.

MARIO: You've got a fever, Don Pablo.

PABLO: Tell me a good metaphor for dying peacefully in my own bed.

MARIO: Poet, I can't think of any metaphor, but you've got to listen to me. Doña Matilda let me come up here because I have a lot of things to tell you.

PABLO: I hope I last that long. Make it quick.

MARIO: Since yesterday more than twenty telegrams have come for you. I tried to bring them, but I couldn't get past the soldiers. I had to turn around and go back. You'll have to forgive me, Don Pablo, for what I did, but there was no other way.

PABLO: What did you do?

MARIO: I opened the telegrams, and I memorized them so that I could tell you what they said.

PABLO: Where were they from?

MARIO: From all over. Can I begin with the one from Sweden?

PABLO: Go ahead.

MARIO: "Sorrow and indignation assassination President Allende. Government and people offer asylum Pablo Neruda Sweden."

PABLO: Another.

MARIO: Mexico puts airplane disposition poet Pablo Neruda and family. Immediate evacutation."

PABLO: Mario, all my life I've had an owl's face but not his eyesight. What are those people doing over there on the rocks.?

MARIO: Where, Don Pablo?

PABLO: On the rocks, those people on the rocks. What are they doing there, Mario?

MARIO: They're looking for something. They seem to be looking for something.

PABLO: What is that one looking for, and the other one too? Why are they searching beside the water? What are they all searching for on the shore? (*His breathing is more labored. The tone of his voice more feverish; the rhythm becomes gasps.*)
I return to the sea wrapped in sky
the silence between one breaking wave and the next
creates a sense of impending danger.
Life dies, the blood grows still,
until a new movement rises from the deep
and the voice of the infinite sounds once more."

(*Blackout. The sound of an ambulance continues until it fades away in the distance. Silence.*)

SCENE 14

(*Light on the door of Mario's house. Mario and Two Policemen in plainclothes are standing there. The dialogue begins after a few seconds.*)

FIRST POLICEMAN: Are you Mario Jiménez?
MARIO: Yes, sir.
SECOND POLICEMAN: Mario Jiménez, mailman by profession?
MARIO: Mailman, sir.
FIRST POLICEMAN: Born February 7, 1950?
MARIO: Yes, sir.
SECOND POLICEMAN: Son of José Jiménez, fisherman by profession?
MARIO: Fisherman, sir.
FIRST POLICEMAN: Then you'll have to come with us.
MARIO: Why, sir?
SECOND POLICEMAN: Just for a few questions.
FIRST POLICEMAN: A routine check.
SECOND POLICEMAN: There's nothing to be afraid of.
FIRST POLICEMAN: Afterwards you can go home.
SECOND POLICEMAN: There's nothing to be afraid of.
FIRST POLICEMAN: Just a routine check.
SECOND POLICEMAN: You'll have to answer a few questions.
FIRST POLICEMAN: Then you can go home.
SECOND POLICEMAN: Just a check. A routine matter.

(*The three exit. Offstage the sound of a car door slamming. At the same moment, the simultaneous sounds of the car's motor and the Beatles's song "Please Mr. Postman." Final blackout.*)

END

Kathie and the Hippopotamus

a comedy in two acts

Mario Vargas Llosa

to
Norma Aleandro

AUTHOR'S INTRODUCTION

"Life, like man, can only be sustained by lies."
                Simone Weil, *Disordered Thoughts on the Love of God*
"Go, go, go, said the bird: human kind cannot bear very much reality."
                T. S. Eliot, *Four Quartets*

THE THEATRE AS FICTION

In a rough imitation of a Parisian artist's loft, a man and a woman agree, for two hours a day, to lie to each other. For her, it's an amusement, a pastime; for him, it's a job. But lies are seldom gratuitous or insipid; they are fed by our desires and failures and they express us with as much fidelity as the most genuine truths that we utter.

To lie is to invent, adding fiction to life and disguising it as the truth. Morally repugnant when practiced in life, it is an act that seems legitimate, even praiseworthy, under the pretext of art. In a novel, in a painting, in a play, we extol the artist who persuades us, thanks to his skill in manipulating words, images and dialogue, that his creations reflect life, are life. And are they? Fiction becomes the life that didn't happen, that we wish had happened, that couldn't have happened, or which could happen again; the life without which our own always seems lacking. Because, unlike animals which live their lives fully from beginning to end, we only experience a part of ours.

Our appetites and our fantasies always overreach the limits of our mortal being, which has been given the perverse prerogative of imagining a thousand and one adventures and playing the hero in scarcely ten. The inevitable gap between the concrete reality of human existence and the unfulfilled desires that it arouses, yet never placates, is not only the origin of the unhappiness, the dissatisfaction and the rebelliousness of man, it is also the raison d'etre of fiction. It is thanks to the lies that we can skillfully compensate for the insufficiencies of life, expand the suffocating limits of our condition and attain worlds which may be richer, or more sordid or more intense. In each case, we aspire to a world different from the one fate has chosen to give us. Thanks to the deceptions of fiction a life expands, a man becomes many men, the coward becomes brave, the homebody, a wanderer and the prostitute, a virgin. Thanks to fiction, we discover what we are, what we are not and what we would like to be. The lies of fiction enrich our lives, adding to them what they never will have. But later, when the spell is broken, and our lives return to their barrenness, we become brutally conscious of how unreachable is the distance between reality and dreams. For the unresigned, the risktaker, who in spite of everything, still takes the plunge, fiction lies waiting, full of illusions, founded on the seed of our emptiness as if to say, "Enter, come in, play with lies." It is a fame which sooner or later we discover, just as Kathie and Santiago do in their "Paris loft," that one plays with the rather sad truth of what we would like to be or with the harsher reality of what we would do anything not to be.

Theatre is not "life" but it is, in a way, a different kind of life, one of lies and fiction. No other genre besides a play manifests so splendidly the questionable nature of art. Unlike the characters of a novel or a painting, those on stage are flesh and blood and they live the roles they are playing before our eyes. We see them suffer, get angry, laugh and completely enjoy themselves. If the play succeeds, those voices, movements and feelings will completely convince us of their reality. And, in effect, is there anything about them that is not fused with life? Nothing, except that they are pretense, fiction, theatre. Curiously, despite its blatantly deceptive nature and fraudulent talent, there has always been (and there will always be) those who will claim that theatre (i.e., fiction in general) proclaims and propagates religious, historical and moral truth. On the contrary, the mission of the theatre, of fiction generally, is to create illusions, to deceive.

Fiction doesn't reproduce life: it contradicts it, eliminating what is superfluous and adding what is lacking in life, giving order and logic to what in our experiences is chaotic and absurd, or, on the other hand, giving madness, mystery and risk to what is logical, routine and secure. Fiction carries out a systematic rectification of life. As in a photographic negative, it documents human history, its abundantly rich account of deeds, passions, gestures, infamies, manners, excesses and subtleties that men have had to invent because they were incapable of living them.

To dream, to write fiction (like reading it, going to see it or believe it) is an indirect protest against the mediocrity of our lives, a transitory but effective way of mocking it. When we find ourselves bound by fiction's spell, enhanced by its deception, it completes us, changing us briefly into the great villain, the sweet saint, the transparent idiot that our desire, cowardice, curiosity or plain spirit of contradiction incite us to be. We are returned to our normal state, but transformed, more aware of our limits, more contentious, less docile in the face of conformity.

This is the story that the banker's wife and the writer act out in the "Paris loft" of *Kathie and the Hippopotamus*. When I wrote the piece, I didn't realize that its deeper theme was the relationship between life and fiction, an interaction that fascinates me because I understand it less the more I work with it. My intention was to write a comedy, carried to the limits of the fantastic (but no further since total unreality is boring) taking off from a situation which was familiar to me: a lady who hires a writer to help her write an adventure book. She is in the lamentable situation in which culture seems to promise salvation from total failure. He can't get over not having been Victor Hugo in every sense of that exuberant name—romantic, literary, political, and sexual. During their work sessions, beginning with the transformations which the story undergoes between what the lady dictates and what her ghost-writer writes, the lives of both—their two lives, the truthful and the mendacious, what they have been and what they would have liked to be—become real on the stage, conjured up by memory, desire, fantasy, associations and destiny. At some point in the play, as I attempted to animate the characters of Kathie and Santiago, other phantoms intruded, dispersed among the others, finally winning the right to be in the piece. Now I discover them, I recognize them, and once again, I am astonished. The lies of Kathie and Santiago, aside from their truths, reveal my own and, probably, those of all those who by lying boldly reveal the substance with which they shape their lives.

SET DESIGN, COSTUME AND EFFECTS

Kathie Kennety's "Paris loft" is in no way a caricature; it looks realistic and is believable. Kathie, a woman of certain taste, has created a rather convincing image for her study—it is reminiscent of artists' lofts often protrayed in paintings, novels, posters and films, as well as an authentic *chambre de bonne* where students and down at the heels expatriots commonly gather on the Left Bank.

The peaked ceiling has worn rafters and the walls are decorated with the inevitable posters of the Eiffel Tower, the Arc de Triomphe, the Louvre, an impressionistic painting, a Picasso, and, the one essential item—a face or bust of Victor Hugo. There are no elegant or superfluous details, only what is necessary to given an impression of comfort and warmth. This is where Kathie takes refuge from the chaos and the scrutiny of the world, where she feels free to confront her most secret demons face to face. There is a worktable made from thick planks, a wide sofa, covered and worn, large pillows and bolsters on the floor, a tape recorder, a typewriter, a small record player and the obligatory records by Juliette Greco, Leo Ferre, Yves Montand, George Brassens, etc. There are filing cabinets, notebooks, papers and books; however, not too many, as Kathie's idea of culture is not exactly literary.

Kathie and Santiago's wardrobe is not extraordinary or unusual. The story takes place in the sixties and what they wear should reflect the period. Santiago's modest salary and lifestyle as a journalist and professor are evident from his clothing. It wouldn't be a bad idea for Kathie to wear a "Saint-Germain Bohemian" outfit from the fifties: a black turtleneck pullover, tight pants and black high-heeled boots. Juan's and Ana's clothing need not be as specific or detailed. Unlike Kathie and Santiago, who are flesh and blood characters existing contemporaneously to the action, Juan and Ana are characters who are remembered or invented, present only in the memories and fantasies of the two protagonists. Their subjective nature (though not ghostlike in any way) could be suggested in their clothing, without, however, undue exaggeration or extravagance. One possibility is that, since Ana and Juan change psychologically in gesture, voice and name along with Kathie and Santiago's evocations of them, they might also make clothing changes in the smallest details—a hat, a cape, some glasses, a wig, etc.—to underscore their mutable and transformable characters. The same can happen with Kathie and Santiago when, departing from their own identities, they assume those fabricated by each of their fantasies. But none of this should be taken to the unrealistic extremes either of the grotesque or masquerade. *Kathie and the Hippopotamus* is not a farce on a surface level, but in its subtext, the invisible root of what is said and done on the stage.

The action of the play transgresses conventional limits of realism and takes place in the objective and subjective as if they were interchangeable, moving with complete freedom from one direction to another. The distortions of absurdist comedy or excess, be it in word and gesture, would be counterproductive here. The design of the work is not intended to provoke laughter through a crude stylization of human experience but to lead the audience subtly, unknowingly, through the combined techniques of humor, suspense, and melodrama to accept the blending of the separate orders of reality, the visible and the invisible, the real and the dreamed, the present and the past. Objective life is infused with subjectivity and subjective life acquires the physical and temporal concreteness of the objective. In a certain manner, flesh and blood beings become unreal and real phantoms become flesh and blood. The profound issue of *Kathie and the Hippopotamus* is, perhaps, the nature of the theatre in particular and that of fiction in general: fiction that is written and read, but most of all, the fiction that human beings practice every day without even realizing it.

Visual effects may be useful in the presentation, but above all, it is music as an active presence that works to precipitate the different scenes—Paris, Black Africa, the Arab world—that is to say, the cheap exoticism of a good part of the story.

Perhaps it isn't necessary to say that in this comedy, as in my novels, I have tried to give an illusion of totality. Totality, not in a quantitative, but a qualitative sense. The play doesn't attempt to capture the entire human experience, but to show that it is objective and subjective, real and unreal, and that life consists of both. Man speaks, acts, dreams and invents. It is not only history and reason, but also fantasy and desire; not only calculation, but spontenaity as well. Although neither of the two orders is entirely enslaved to the other, neither could do without its counterpart without destroying its very self. Fantasy is an ancient resource we have for escaping from reality when we feel it is intolerable. But, in addition to escapism, it is an indirect way of understanding a reality that, if we were incapable of eluding it, would be confusion, a chaos or a suffocating routine to us. The adventures of the imagination enrich reality and help us to improve our lives. If we didn't dream, it would appear that life could not be improved upon, and if we didn't fantasize, the world would never change.

Mario Vargas Llosa

KATHIE AND THE HIPPOPOTAMUS
Hippodrome State Theatre (Florida)
Directed by Kerry McKenney

CHARACTERS

Kathie Kennety
Santiago Zavala
Ana Zavala
Juan

ACTION

The action takes place sometime in the late 60s in Kathie Kennety's "Parisian loft."

ACT ONE

SCENE 1

(*As the curtain rises, we hear Parisian music from the 40s or 50s. Lights come up on a loft that has been coverted by Kathie Kennety to look as if it belonged to a Parisian artist. Santiago is dictating into a tape recorder while Kathie walks around the room, revising her notes, thinking and remembering aloud. As we begin to hear what they're saying, the background music changes to an Arab melody of flutes, chirimias and tambourines . . .*)

KATHIE: By the time it got dark, I was standing right under the sphinx when, all of the sudden, this bright light came on.

SANTIAGO: (*Thinking of a different way to say the above.*) Let's see . . . As if lost in a dream, I stand there transfixed by the sphinx, totally unaware of the approaching night. Suddenly, . . . a spectral shaft of light illuminates her secret and serene smile. And there we are, face to face, one a woman of flesh and blood, the other of stone, her head held high over magnificent lion claws below.

KATHIE: There were lots of stars. I felt . . . oh, I don't know . . . kind of small and alone in that place, you know, at that time of night and in the middle of all those Egyptian tombs.

SANTIAGO: I wander around the collosal pyramids and by the statues of mighty pharoahs that seem to sleep under the nocturnal firmament, its infinity of stars floating above Cairo in an azure sea of opalescent tones.

KATHIE: It really wasn't very smart to be there by myself. I mean, who would help me if I got in trouble? But I remembered I had my trusty pistol and then I wasn't so afraid anymore.

SANTIAGO: There isn't a living soul in sight. No human, no animal, not even a plant. I'm hardly aware of my solitude as I stand there musing on the ancient beings that erected these monuments, men as immersed in the spiritual as fish in the sea. I begin a silent dialogue with the sphinx. Then, all at once, my reverie shatters and reality reasserts its harsh rule. God! What am I doing there, alone, exposed to a thousand dangers, from ravenous jackals to bloodthirsty criminals. But it steadies me to remember my small pearl-handled pistol, my friend that goes with me through life like a faithful dog.

KATHIE: Then, who knows from where, a man suddenly appeared before me. I couldn't even scream. I was frightened, really terrified. What was he going to do? (*Enter Juan.*)

SANTIAGO: Suddenly, a man in a red robe and white turban looms in front of me. He's like a mirage emerging in the hot desert air from some remote Egyptian past. He's tall, slim, with black eyes and flashing white teeth. I panic. Will he attack me? Rape me? Should I run, scream, cry?

KATHIE: (*To Santiago.*) I don't like that last part.

SANTIAGO: We'll erase it then. Where don't you like it from?

KATHIE: From where the guy appeared. (*Santiago leans over his tape recorder to erase the last part of the dictation. Juan approaches Kathie. The scene shifts to them as they both undergo a transformation: they look like two teenagers chatting on a neighborhood corner.*)

JUAN: Guy? You mean boyfriend.

KATHIE: You, my boyfriend? Ha! Excuse me while I laugh!

JUAN: I'll excuse anything you like except not being my girlfriend.

KATHIE: I am *not* your girlfriend.

JUAN: Maybe not now, but you will be.

KATHIE: Don't you ever get tired of me telling you no, Johnny?

JUAN: I don't quit easy, kitten! I'm going to keep on asking 'til you say yes. You'll be my girlfriend a my fiancé too. We'll end up married. Want to bet?

KATHIE: (*Dying of laughter.*) So, I'm even getting married to you.

JUAN: Well, who do you think you're going to marry if not me?

KATHIE: I've got plenty of guys after me, Johnny.

JUAN: And you'll choose the best.

KATHIE: You are so conceited.

JUAN: Aw, come on. I know exactly who's after you and that you've told them all to get lost. So, how come, huh? 'Cause deep down inside you're just crazy about me.

KATHIE: Boy, you are *really* conceited, Johnny!

JUAN: Only when I've got a reason to be. Want me to prove it?

KATHIE: Go ahead. Prove it.

JUAN: Am I or am I not better than Bepo Torres?

KATHIE: Just how are you better than Bepo Torres?

JUAN: I surf better. He can't even stay up on the board. And, I'm a lot better looking.

KATHIE: So, you think you're the best looking guy around, huh?

JUAN: Better than Bepo Torres. And Kike Ricketts too. Just tell me how Kike is better than me. Is he a better surfer? Is he better looking?

KATHIE: He's a better dancer.

JUAN: Kike? Haha, excuse me while I laugh. Does he do the *mambo* better? (*He does a few steps.*) The *chachacha*? (*More steps.*) The *Huaracha*? (*More steps.*) You've seen them at the parties. They crowd round and cheer me all the time, I swear! Listen, I taught poor Kike all the moves. I taught him how to dance "cheek to cheek."

KATHIE: He dances the *marinera* and the Creole Waltz better than you.

JUAN: The *marinera*? The Creole Waltz? You gotta be kidding! How tacky can you get? Those dances are for old fogeys, kitten.

KATHIE: You're so jealous you can't see straight. You're jealous of Bepo, Kike, Gordo . . .

JUAN: Of Gordo? Me jealous of Gordo? What does Gordo have that I don't? A 50s Chevy convertible. Big deal. So what? I have a '51 Studebaker covertible! Please, kitten, please. I'm not jealous of Bepo, Kike, Gordo, or Sapo Saldivar or Harry Santana or my brother Abel or any of those guys that are after you. None of them even comes close to me and you know it.

KATHIE: (*Reflecting, forgetting Juan and for a minute, leaving her memory or fantasy far behind.*) Kike, Bepo, Harry, Gordo Rivarola . . . God, it seems like ages ago.

JUAN: (*Who hasn't heard her.*) And there's another reason. Shall I be honest?

KATHIE: (*Going back to the imaginary.*) Go on. Be honest.

JUAN: Because I have money, kitten.

KATHIE: You think that matters to me? My daddy has more than your daddy, silly.

JUAN: That's just it, kitten. See, with me you know that I like you and if I want to marry you, it's for you, not your money. How can you be so sure about all those other guys? You know, yesterday, I heard my old man say to your old man, "You better watch out for all those hungry wolves snooping around your daughter. They're looking for the wedding deal of the century. Your money and her looks."

KATHIE: (*Confused.*) Don't be crass, Johnny.

JUAN: (*Also confused.*) That's not crass. Well, if it is, "sorry." But, you can't say anything, can you? It's all true—just ask your old man. See, you can't exactly deny it. You know, I'm already winning you over. I think the next time I ask you to be my girl, kitten, you won't be telling me to get lost. (*His voice has lowered and Kathie moves away. Juan remains in the scene. He acts like a little boy, his hands stuffed in his pockets, wandering around, whistling and looking for something to do. Santiago has finished erasing the last part of the dictation on the tape recorder.*)

SANTIAGO: All done. It's erased. Do you want to take it back to the sphinx or go on, Mrs. Kennety?

KATHIE: You can call me Kathie, you know. Mrs. Kennety makes me feel ancient.

SANTIAGO: Sorry. Do you mind if I ask you something?

KATHIE: No, go ahead.

SANTIAGO: Where did you get a name like Kathie Kennety?

KATHIE: Don't you like it?

SANTIAGO: Sure, it's fine, but where did it come from? How did you choose it?

KATHIE: Well, I thought that if I used my own name, no one would take my book seriously. You know, Peruvian names just don't sound right for writers. On the other hand, Kathie Kennety does. It's foreign, musical, cosmopolitan. (*She looks at him reflecting.*) You know, Santiago Zabala doesn't sound right for a writer either. Why don't we change it? Come on, let me name you all over again. Let me see. I know! Mark! Mark Griffin! What do you think? Can I call you that? Just between the two of us, up here in the loft? Would you mind?

SANTIAGO: (*Laughing.*) No ma'am. I wouldn't mind.

KATHIE: Tell me. Do I really seem so old that you can't call me Kathie?

SANTIAGO: Sorry. Of course not. I just have to get used to it. You have to remember that I'm working for you. I see you as my boss.

KATHIE: Couldn't you see me as your colleague instead? Well, well. Our two hours are running out. Let's begin another episode. (*Going over her notes.*) Let's see . . . My visit to the Cairo museum and the fabulous treasures of the Tutankhamen. (*Once again, we hear Arab music. Enter Ana. Shrinking into a corner, she begins to cry, frightened by Juan's obscene looks and gestures.*)

SANTIAGO: (*Dictating into the tape recorder.*) I spend the next morning marveling at the enameled crowns, turquoise and lapis lazuli necklaces, the coral brooches and the dazzling gold miniatures of King Tutankamen.

KATHIE: In the midst of all those beautiful things . . . there was a pretty young woman, a blonde, sobbing her heart out.

SANTIAGO: Suddenly, through splendid crystal urns and magnificent statuary, sumptuous coffins and sparkling coffers, I spy a blonde beauty, exquisitely alive and delicate. She's shaking with sobs. What could be the matter?

KATHIE: She was a German tourist. The silly thing had gone out alone wandering around Cairo in a mini-skirt. She caused a near-riot in the streets and came in to hide in the museum.

SANTIAGO: Seeking refuge in the museum among the marvels of ancient Egypt, she had excaped from lustful glances, insolent hands, lewd gestures, evil thoughts and the exhibitionist insanities which her long white legs provoked in the Cairo streets. She reminded me of the girl Victor Hugo once called "obscene through sheer innocence." Feeling sorry for her, I offered my help.

ANA: (*Sarcastically.*) And you, don't you feel sorry for yourself, Mark Griffin?

SANTIAGO: (*Without looking at her.*) Go to hell. (*Kathie does not see Ana. She continues to revise her notes and dictate to Santiago as if he were still at the desk with his tape recorder.*)

ANA: I went there a long time ago, Mark Griffin. You sent me there, bound hand and foot. Don't you remember? Think, Mark Griffin, think back.

SANTIAGO: (*Crossing to Ana.*) I can't stand living in this house another minute. Look, marriage certificates are just trash. All that matters is what people feel, nothing else. I'm not in love with you anymore. I can't stay here. It's against everything I believe in. So please, spare me the clinging housewife routine, the crying, the scenes and the threats to kill yourself. You're on your own so why not behave like a real liberated woman.

ANA: Fine. I won't be making a scene and I'm not about to force you to stay. But what should I tell the girls?

SANTIAGO: Ah, so now we get a little emotional blackmail: "The poor abandoned children." What do you want? You want me to lose all respect for you too? This is sounding like some sordid soap opera. Listen, lots of marriages split up and I've yet to see a kid die from it.

ANA: I didn't say they were going to die. I'm simply asking you what to tell them, how to explain that their father won't be living at home anymore. I'm not fighting you or blackmailing you. I'm just asking for advice. They're little and they're going to get hurt. So just tell me what I can say to them so they get hurt a little less.

SANTIAGO: The truth. I mean, what are you? Some bourgeois hypocrite? Don't tell me you believe in telling lies just to be kind?

ANA: The truth? That their father left because he fell in love with one of his students?

SANTIAGO: Exactly. It could've happened to you. It could happen to them later on. If they're at all in touch with their feelings and if they don't turn into a couple of repressed, bourgeois idiots, they'll try to act as I have, like a mature and enlightened human being. (*He returns to his desk and resumes his recording.*)

ANA: So, do you still feel mature and enlightened now, Mark Griffin? Now that you're writing an exotic travel book on the "Yellow Asia and Black Africa" for Kathie Kennety, the so-called writer who has the ideas and pays you to supply the words? You aren't criticizing bourgeois ladies anymore, are you, Mark Griffin? (*Ana crosses over to Juan. A few bars of Arab music are heard.*)

KATHIE: Later on I went to the old part of Cairo and found a Church where the Virgin Mary had taken refuge with Baby Jesus during the flight into Europe. Just beautiful!

SANTIAGO: To my great delight, history and religion blend in the endless and colorful alleyways of old Cairo. I see a chapel emerge from a great cloud of dust, airborne, ancient and graceful. What is it? It's the refuge that provided shelter for Mary and the Child during their Flight into Egypt.

KATHIE: Afterwards, I went to another little church, Jewish, I think it was, where some fellow named Abraham had supposedly been.

SANTIAGO: (*Dictating.*) Why do the walls of this temple out of time exude that special spirituality that penetrates me to the bone? Because Abraham the Patriarch had once walked on these very stones.

KATHIE: Finally, I ended up in a perfume shop.

SANTIAGO: And since in Egypt, material and spiritual worlds are indistinguishable, I soon find myself, that resplendent morning, in a perfume shop.

KATHIE: It was actually afternoon.

SANTIAGO: I soon find myself during that crimson twilight, in a perfume shop.

KATHIE: Some tourists were in the shop. The perfumist explained in really awful English that the shop was very old. He had us try some samples of perfume. The entire time, he never took his eyes off me. It made me nervous.

SANTIAGO: The perfumist is tall, slim, with black eyes and flashing white teeth. His eyes never stray from me while he explains to us in exquisite and seductive French that the shop was as old as the most ancient Egyptian mosques. He told us that his apprentices created marvelous essences whose secrets were transmitted from fathers to sons down through the centuries. He offered us elixirs whose fragrance lasts for years on the skin. And while he speaks, his sensual gaze consumes me with unbridled lust. (*While he speaks, Santiago stands up. He acts like a lithe and sensuous man. He is very close to Kathie.*)

KATHIE: Victor! You? Why are you here? What do you want?

SANTIAGO: To run away with you, for us to escape, just the two of us. Listen, kitten. I've got it all worked out. I have a car. I've talked to a priest from Chincheros and he said he'd marry us. Some friends have even lent us their cottage in the country!

KATHIE: Are you serious, Victor?

SANTIAGO: Isn't it incredibly romantic? To run away and get married in secret to the man you love in spite of your parents? To finally ditch that idiot they want you to marry? Come on, haven't you always claimed to be an incurable romantic?

KATHIE: You've got it all wrong. My parents don't have anything to do with my marrying Johnny. No one tells me what to do. I'm marrying him because I want to. Because I love him.

SANTIAGO: That isn't true! You're marrying Johnny just because your family has forced him on you. They just want to take your mind off me. You can't possibly be in love with that clown.

KATHIE: Don't talk like that about Johnny. He happens to be my fiancé and he's going to be my husband.

SANTIAGO: (*Trying to kiss her.*) You're in love with me, kitten. Haven't you told me so a hundred times? What about all those letters you wrote me? You're making a mistake kitten! If you marry Johnny, you'll regret it for the rest of your life.

KATHIE: I will not regret it. I plan on being very happy with Johnny. So, don't try to see me or call me anymore. Just give up. I am going to marry Johnny.

SANTIAGO: I'll never give up. I'll keep on trying until the last minute. I'll keep trying 'til your priest gives you his final blessing.

KATHIE: Well, you're just going to waste your time.

SANTIAGO: (*Returning to his desk, picking up the tape recorder, becoming himself again. Lights slowly shift back to normal.*) I'll only give up if I'm convinced there's no hope, that there's . . .

KATHIE: (*To an invisible Victor.*) What'll you do? Will you kill me? Will you kill Johnny?

SANTIAGO: Sorry, it just doesn't sound Egyptian, ma'am. Instead of Johnny, how about Ahmed? Or Gamal? Don't you like the sound of Gamal, the sensual and sexy perfumist? Or Ahmed, all lewd and lusty?

KATHIE: Johnny has nothing to do with my book. I was daydreaming, thinking back on when I was young.

SANTIAGO: You still are, ma'am.

KATHIE: If you really believed that, you'd call me Kathie.

SANTIAGO: I'm sorry. I promise that from now on I'll call you Kathie.

KATHIE: I was just thinking about old boyfriends. You know, I had quite a few, Kike, Bepo, Harry, Gordo Rivarola. In those days I was what they considered a great catch.

SANTIAGO: I know. I sort of knew you, though, of course, you had no idea who I was. Actually, everybody knew you. They'd seen you in the society pages, in the magazines.

KATHIE: What were you like back then?

SANTIAGO: (*Dreamily.*) Me? Oh, an idealist, a romantic. I dreamed of being someone like Victor Hugo. I dreamed of having a passionate love like his Adele Foucher, of dedicating my life to poetry, to politics, and art. To something significant, something that would leave my mark on society. I wanted to, you know, fill my life with magnificent gestures.

JUAN: (*Approaching Kathie.*) Can we talk for a minute, Kathie? It's about Victor.

KATHIE: I don't want to talk about Victor. Not now, not ever. Not with you or anyone else, either. I haven't seen him since we got married. Why are you getting jealous now? (*Santiago leaves his desk and stands next to them. He seems transfixed with pain.*)

SANTIAGO: You really married that clown, kitten. You sure aren't the romantic you wanted me to think you were.

JUAN: (*Uncomfortable.*) I know you haven't seen him. And since when have I ever been jealous? I trust you completely. It's just that . . . well, he's come to see me. (*Turning to Santiago in surprise.*) You! But, what a surprise, Victor! Come in, come in. Good to see you, man!

KATHIE: (*Aside, shocked.*) My God! Victor! Victor! How could you do such a thing? And for me, because of me. You did it for me didn't you?

SANTIAGO: (*Extending his hand to Juan.*) How are you Johnny? I know this is a surprise. Yes, at the very least. Look. I don't want to take up too much of your time. I know how busy you must be. I came by to bring you these letters.

KATHIE: I'm sure you did it because of me. I'll never forgive myself. I'll regret it for the rest of my life. Tell me. Do you suffer? Are you happy? Have you at least found peace?

JUAN: (*Leafing through the letters with increasing astonishment.*) What are these, anyway? God! They're love letters. From my wife to you. What's going on, Victor? Why did you bring these to me?

KATHIE: (*Grieving deeply.*) Even though you may be far away across the sea, though you are hidden behind heavy stone walls, even though we may never see each other again, I'm still with you, Victor. Still close by you.

SANTIAGO: As proof of our friendship, Johnny. Kitten is your wife now. I'm sure that neither of you would want our old love letters to get around. You'll see by them that my relationship with Kathie was always honorable. You can keep them, tear them up or do whatever you want with them.

KATHIE: (*Very tenderly.*) I lie with you on the straw mat on the damp stone floor of your barren cell. After a brief sleep I wake with you in the deepest night, the sky still burning with stars.

JUAN: (*Each time more disconcerted.*) Oh, I see . . . look. I don't know what to say. I'm really surprised. I . . . well, the truth is, I just don't know what to say.

KATHIE: With you I pray. I kneel on frigid flagstones and face the mask of death, that skull that stares at us as if to say, "I'm waiting for you." I weep for the evils that have made our world a mire of corruption.

SANTIAGO: Well, you could start by thanking me, I suppose.

KATHIE: With you I do penance for my sins. I scourge my back. I wear a hair shirt. I try til I exhaust my strength to atone for man's infinite capacity to inflict cruelty on himself and on his fellow man.

JUAN: For these letters? Sure. Thank you. (*Looking at him suspiciously.*) You aren't putting me on, are you Victor?

KATHIE: With you I fast. I live in perpetual silence. I go barefoot in the cruelest winter and I don heavy wool in the burning summer. With you I work the land with my hands and I feed the animals.

SANTIAGO: No, Johnny. You have my word.

KATHIE: With you I sing the psalms that will save the world from the brink of destruction. I sing my songs of praise, to a wasp, to a butterfly, to a bird, to a blossom, to pollen, thistle and laurel.

JUAN: Well, I'm sorry. The truth is, you've really floored me, Victor. You're a decent guy, man. Kathie will really appreciate this, too. I'm sure it bothered her that these letters were around especially now that she's a married woman.

KATHIE: With you I have died for the world of the serpent, of sin, of lies, of anguish and pain. I live the slavery that is freedom, the martyrdom that is happiness, the death that is life.

SANTIAGO: That's why I brought them. I was thinking of her.

KATHIE: (*Anxious, tense.*) Do you know why, Victor? Have you guessed? Do you know?

JUAN: (*Getting friendlier.*) Well, this is a relief, Victor. I thought that you might have a grudge, even hate me.

KATHIE: Because I love you. Yes, Yes, Yes, Victor. I love you! I love you! I've always loved you! Always, always, always.

SANTIAGO: Because Kathie married you? Not really, Johnny. I mean at first, it hurt, but I got used to it soon enough. And now I really think it was best for everyone that she married you.

KATHIE: (*Exalted, transported.*) Yes, it's true. Your Adele loves you, has loved you, will love you. My Lord, my love, my master, my king. Oh, Victor, Victor, Victor.

JUAN: Right, right. I always thought so, too. Kathie and you are very different. You wouldn't have gotten along at all.

KATHIE: (*Sad again.*) When you're gone, I have no air to breathe, no light for my eyes, no voice in my throat, no blood in my veins.

SANTIAGO: (*Turning to an invisible Kathie.*) You didn't marry me because you thought I was just after your money.

KATHIE: (*Still talking to the same phantom.*) I didn't marry you because I was stupid . . .

JUAN: (*To Santiago.*) Kathie and I, on the other hand, get along just great.

KATHIE: . . . because I was ignorant, blind, a coward, a fool.

SANTIAGO: (*To the same invisible Kathie.*) I thought you were more of a dreamer, an idealist, an innocent, less calculating. What a disappointment, kitten. You're not like Adele Foucher at all, Adele!

KATHIE: (*Upset, desperate.*) Forgive me! Forgive me!

JUAN: (*To Santiago.*) Look, Victor. Now that you've cleared things up, we ought to see more of each other. You should come over and have dinner with us one of these days.

KATHIE: Come back. Turn back. There's still time. Listen to me! Answer me! Come back, Victor!

SANTIAGO: (*To Juan.*) That won't be possible, Johnny. I'm going on a trip. Far away. I don't think I'll ever come back to Peru.

KATHIE: I want to be your slave, your servant, your dog.

JUAN: (*To Santiago.*) That sounds pretty mysterious.

KATHIE: I want to be your whore, Victor.

SANTIAGO: You could say that. Listen, what's happening is that I'm on my way to Spain. To Burgos. I'm going to join the Trappists.

KATHIE: I'll go down to the docks and strip in front of the filthiest sailors. I'll go down on my knees and lick their tattoos if you want me to. Whatever whim, whatever fantasy, Victor. Any madness you can imagine. Whatever you want.

JUAN: What are you going to do?

KATHIE: You can spit on me, humiliate me, beat me, lend me to your friends. Just come back, come back.

SANTIAGO: Of course. You don't even know what it is. It's a cloistered religious order. It's very old and very strict. I'm going to become a monk.

KATHIE: Come back even if it's just to kill me, Victor.

JUAN: (*Breaks out laughing.*) Why don't you try being a bullfighter instead? I knew sooner or later you'd be pulling my leg. You just can't help yourself, can you, Victor?

KATHIE: (*Desolate, resigned.*) But I know that you don't hear me now and that you never will. I know that your Adele has lost forever her reason to live, to die, to go on.

SANTIAGO: I'm not pulling your leg. I am going to enter the monastery. What's more, I'm even asking for your help. I don't have a dime and the trip to Spain is expensive. I'm asking my friends to help me get up the money for a third class ticket on the Queen of the Sea. Could you give me a hand, Johnny?

KATHIE: (*To Juan.*) Why are you telling me all this? Why should I care?

JUAN: Because you're my wife. Who else should I tell? Do you think it's true about the Trapper, Trappet, Trappen convent?

SANTIAGO: (*To Kathie.*) What did I need your money for? I've told you so many times. I don't need to be rich. I just want to be happy. Tell me, is your father happy? Is Johnny happy? Well, maybe Johnny is, but not because he's rich, . . . because he's stupid. You would've been happy with me. You would've had the most unforgettable wedding night in history, Adele.

JUAN: (*To Kathie.*) Of course, I didn't believe him at first. I thought he'd come to give me some sad story, to hit me for money. But I don't know now. If you'd only heard him . . . He was talking just like a priest, you know, sort of soft and delicate. Said he'd heard the call. What do you want to do with all these letters, kitten?

SANTIAGO: (*To Kathie.*)So, now we'll never get a chance to live in Chincheros, to breathe the pure air of our beautiful mountain village. Now we'll never share the life we planned, simple, free and together. But I'm not blaming you, kitten. Actually, I'm really grateful to you. You see, you've been the key to my salvation. Through you I opened my eyes to a greater being than you or me. Now I can see what He wants from me. So thank you for leaving me and thank you for marrying Johnny. You know I'll always remember you and pray for your happiness. (*He returns to his desk.*)

JUAN: (*To Kathie.*) Of course I haven't read them! (*He instantly regrets his lie.*) Okay, I did. God, what romantic letters, Kathie! You were really in love with Victor, weren't you? I had no idea. I also had no idea you were such a romantic. You wrote him some pretty amazing things, kitten. (*Smiling, he seems to forget Kathie. He crouches, gets his balance and gives the impression that, suddenly, he has begun to surf.*)

KATHIE: (*Kathie lost in her thoughts.*) Johnny darling, Johnny darling. What a clown you turned out to be!

SANTIAGO: (*Without looking at Kathie, absorbed in his own thoughts.*) Well, at least as far as his name goes. "Johnny darling" doesn't give the impression of someone to take very seriously.

KATHIE: (*Casting a glance at Santiago who is still immersed in his own fantasies.*) What a relief it would be to confide in you about my disastrous marriage, Mark Griffin.

SANTIAGO: Go ahead, Kathie. Tell me. That's really why I'm here in this Parisian loft. It's part of my job. What were your problems? Did Johnny darling treat you badly?

KATHIE: I guess I didn't realize it then, but I do now. I felt terribly let down. Two, three years after we got married, life became so incredibly boring. Was marriage that routine? Did I get married for this?

SANTIAGO: What did your husband do?

KATHIE: He went to the Waikiki.

SANTIAGO: You mean that surfing club on the beach at Miraflores?

KATHIE: Every day of the year, winter or summer. It was the main thing in his life.

JUAN: (*Youthful, athletic, carefree, gazing at the horizon.*) I like it. I have a right to. I'm still young and I want to enjoy life.

KATHIE: (*Absorbed in her thoughts.*) But Johnny darling, Hawaiian surfing isn't the only way to enjoy life. Don't you ever get tired of spending all day in the ocean? You know, you're going to grow fins.

JUAN: (*Looking straight ahead.*) Every day I like it even better. I plan on doing it more and more every day until I die. Or 'til I'm so old I can't catch a wave.

SANTIAGO: (*Finally looking at Juan as if he were conjuring him up before his very eyes.*) Did he really spend his whole life surfing? Wasn't he a little ashamed?

JUAN: Ashamed? Just the opposite. I feel proud. I like it. It makes me happy. Why should I be ashamed? What's wrong with surfing anyway? Here in Miraflores, in Hawaii, in Australia, in Indonesia or in South Africa? It's the greatest thing in the world! You see, I slip into the water real slow and I slide right into the waves playing them this way and that. I cut them, I cross them, I glide through them. I go on and on and the current pulls me just past the big breakers. Then I sit up on the board and wait like a jockey for the starting pistol to fire. I start to size up and figure out which one of those little waves will swell and grow. Which one will be the best? This one! This is it! God, the tension! Your muscles tingle! Your heart goes crazy! Pum, pum, pum, pum! Not a second to lose, Johnny! I get in position, I wait, now a quick stroke to the water, and then there it is, it catches me, it takes me, I got it just before it breaks. I spring to my feet, I'm up, then down the board, crouching, then standing tall. Now it's all in your waist, your balance, your resistance, your intelligence, your experience. You're not going to throw me, you little wave! I've ridden waves that could snap a skyscraper in two. I've caught the tube of waves as big as waterfalls, mountains, caverns, waves that could have shredded me to pieces if I'd lost my balance. I've surfed through coral reefs, through seas full of sharks. I've nearly been drowned, deafened or crippled hundreds of times. I've won surfing championships on four continents and, if I haven't won in Europe, it's because European waves aren't worth shit for surfing. So you tell me, why should I be ashamed?

KATHIE: (*Still immersed in the dream.*) What do you think about out there beyond the surf, sitting on your board for hours on end?

JUAN: (*Scrutinizing the horizon, the ocean surface.*) How big will the next wave be? Will I catch it? Or miss it? Will it wipe me out or take me into shore?

SANTIAGO: Doesn't he ever think about anything besides waves?

JUAN: Sometimes, when the sea is dead calm, I start thinking about that sweet little thing I met this morning, yesterday, or the day before yesterday. The chick that really turned me on. Will she be easy or . . . hard to get. Will I get my nooky on the first date . . . or the second? Am I going to have to work at it a little? Be a little sneaky, maybe? How . . . when . . . where will we make it? (*Becoming embarrassed, like a child caught in a prank.*) Sometimes my little dicky bird wakes up and I have to put it back to sleep, so I think about the bank . . . you know, interest rates, balances, contracts . . .

KATHIE: I'm sure you've even fooled around on that board! It wouldn't surprise me a bit. But tell me when you're riding high on the crest of a wave, flapping your arms around like some ridiculous puppet, what do you think about?

JUAN: I wonder . . . are they watching me from the terrace of the Club Waikiki? How about the people in the pool or on the beach? Or the ones driving on Shore Drive? Do they see me? Are they saying great things about me? Are they jealous?

SANTIAGO: And what do you feel?

JUAN: I feel bigger than life! I feel handsome. I feel real macho . . . I feel like a god. What's wrong with that?

KATHIE: Do you care if I watch you? Do you care if I think you're great?

JUAN: Before we got married . . . yes. Afterwards, no. Come on. What's the big deal? You're my wife. You're supposed to think I'm great. Now I do it for all the other sexy little girls . . . the new ones, the ones I barely know, the ones I don't know at all.

SANTIAGO: (*In his own thoughts.*) You mean, it never occurred to you that it was a crime to waste time that way, especially when there are so many creative, productive things to do in life?

JUAN: (*Contending with the waves.*) Of course not. I would never think such a dumb thing. Do I hurt anybody? If I stop surfing, do I solve anyone else's problems? (*Derisively.*) Is working in a bank any more "creative" or "productive" than good surfing or fooling around with a pretty girl?

KATHIE: (*Tormented by the memories.*) Was this what my married life was going to be like? Watching Johnny Darling surf and screw around on me?

SANTIAGO: (*Pensively.*) The real bourgeois were even more bourgeois than we ever imagined. Even more than the ones in the pamphlets, the ones we hated in principle, because of our ideology. At least I didn't mislead you about them, Anita. (*Ana approaches Santiago who appears not to see her.*)

KATHIE: (*Still remembering.*) Go to bed late . . . Get up late. You going to the bank today, Johnny?

JUAN: For a little while. Got to keep up appearances, right? But let's meet at the Waikiki around one, okay?

KATHIE: The damned waves . . . the damned surfboards . . . the damned championships . . . the damned trips to Hawaii. The incredible boredom in Hawaii, in hotels with plastic palms and plastic lawns. And all just to watch them, entertain them, flatter them. And to gossip . . . who's screwing around on whom and with whom. Who broke up, who got together again. Get ready for "cocktails," "dinner," the "shower," the "luau," the "party," the "surprise." Think about your hairdresser, your dress, your manicure. Yesterday the same . . . and tomorrow the same. Is this how the rest of your life is going to be, Kathie?

SANTIAGO: (*Brusquely aggressive and sarcastic.*) That's ridiculous! I know what the real truth is and so do you, but you're too ashamed to admit it.

KATHIE: (*Not seeing or hearing him.*) Things will be different with children, Kathie. Taking care of them, teaching them, watching them grow up . . . All that will give some meaning to your marriage. Ridiculous, of course! Instead of going by yourself, now you go to the Waikiki with Alejandra, and then with Alejandra and little Johnny junior. Instead of getting bored alone, now you get bored with a family. Is this marriage? Is this motherhood? The children didn't change a thing, they didn't fill the emptiness. Is this what you sighed for, what you dreamed about all those years in school? To spend your life watching an idiot doing pirouettes through the waves on a flimsy piece of wood?

SANTIAGO: Ridiculous! Want me to let you in on the real story? Kathie Kennety got bored because her beautiful surfer ignored her. He left her alone every night, awake and waiting with no loving at all. The surfing idol was no Victor Hugo, Adele. After all that surfing, his dicky bird just couldn't take off.

ANA: (*To Santiago.*) You speaking from your own experience? When you left with your little Lolita, it'd been months since you'd even touched me. And you didn't even have to surf for your little bird to be totally grounded.

SANTIAGO: (*Acknowledging Ana.*) That's not true. You just didn't attract me anymore. I was making love every day with Adele . . . several times a day. One day, nine times. Just like Victor Hugo on his wedding night. Isn't that right, Adele?

KATHIE: (*Transformed into a vivacious, flirtatious young woman.*) No, it's not,

Professor. But I'll keep your secret. You never could make love to me more than twice in one day and even then you needed a real long time in between . . . hahahaha.

SANTIAGO: (*To Ana furiously.*) I'll tell you something else. The thought of night coming revolted me because I'd have to go to bed with you. That's why I left.

KATHIE: (*Returns to being herself, still immersed in her memories.*) Going to bed . . . even that became boring, like going to the Waikiki and to the "parties."

ANA: (*To Santiago.*) Or was it that you were becoming what you hated most . . . the perfect bourgeois bore? Wasn't it you who always said there was nothing more despicable in the world? Don't you remember all your lectures on how I should become a truly liberated, aware and enlightened woman?

SANTIAGO: (*Lectures very seriously to Ana who listens spellbound. Kathie, transformed to Adele, paints her nails and looks at him mockingly from time to time.*) Not passion-love, but solidarity-love, that's what ours will be Anita. Passion-love is just a bourgeois fraud, an illusion, a trap. You see, love that's based on sex alone, that tries to justify everything in the name of pleasure, of instinct, is mendacious and ephemeral. Desire can't and shouldn't be everything, much less the primary bond. No couple can last if the only thing holding them together is a dicky bird. (*Kathie, as Adele, tosses off a laugh, but Ana, wanting to believe, agrees.*)

KATHIE: (*Smiling, becoming herself again.*) And yet in the beginning it was beautiful. At night, when we held each other close and you told me all those wonderful dirty little things, Johnny darling. My face would be on fire. I felt dizzy, embarrassed, thrilled. It seemed like a dream come true, that it would give my life meaning, that I'd be happy and fulfilled.

SANTIAGO: (*Continuing Ana's education.*) In solidarity love, sex is just one factor among the many and is certainly not the most important one. Solidarity love is based on understanding, the sharing of ideals, sacrifice, struggle on working for a mutual spiritual, intellectual and moral identity.

ANA: (*To Santiago.*) I pleased you. I did what you wanted me to so that we could share your so called solidarity-love. Did I or didn't I? Didn't I quit my job at the boutique? Didn't I start studying sociology like you told me to, instead of interior design which was what I wanted?

JUAN: (*From the heights of his surfboard.*) So, am I or am I not as good in bed as I am on the surfboard, Kathie? Am I or am I not better than Victor Hugo, Adele?

KATHIE: You are, Johnny darling. That's why so many girls throw themselves at you. Blondes, brunettes, redheads. That's why you could cheat on me in so many languages and on so many continents, Johnny darling.

ANA: (*To Santiago.*) I pleased you by dressing the way you wanted me to, didn't I? I quit using lipstick, painting my nails and fixing myself up because according to you all that was bourgeois friviolity. And what did I get out of pleasing you? Not pleasing you is what I got.

SANTIAGO: (*To Kathie, all sweetness.*) You know, you have very pretty hair, Adele.

KATHIE: (*Becoming Adele, coy and cooing.*) I give it a secret treatment twice a week to get it like this. It makes it super-soft, shiny and real full. Want me to tell you about it, Dr. Griffin? But you have to promise not to breathe a word to any of the other girls, OK? You use one egg yolk, one avocado and three teaspoons of oil. Beat well in a blender for thirty seconds than rub the paste into your hair and let it dry for three quarters of an hour. Then you wash your hair with a good shampoo and rinse. It's beautiful, isn't it?

SANTIAGO: (*Fascinated.*) Unbelievably beautiful. So soft, so shiny and full. And your hands are just as pretty as your hair, Adele.

KATHIE: (*Looking at them, showing them off.*) I have another secret for them you know. It's so they don't get rough and hard, so they feel like silk, like satin, like two little Angora kittens. Actually, I have two secrets. I rub them with lemon juice for ten minutes every morning and with coconut milk for ten minutes every night. They are pretty, aren't they?

SANTIAGO: (*Bewitched.*) Yes. They're just like silk, like satin, like two little Angora kittens. When I see them in class, they look like two white doves fluttering above your books.

KATHIE: What a poetic compliment! You really like them, Dr. Griffin?

SANTIAGO: And your hair, your lips, your eyes. I like everything about you. Except, you keep calling me Dr. Griffin. Are you trying to make fun of me?

KATHIE: Well, you are my professor, aren't you? It's a matter of respect. I mean, what would all the others at school think if they heard me call Dr. Griffin, Professor of Golden Age Spanish Literature, Mark, or Mark Griffin?

SANTIAGO: Is that why you're being so formal with me?

KATHIE: You're supposed to be polite to your elders.

SANTIAGO: So, I seem that ancient to you?

KATHIE: Not ancient, no. But an older man, married with two children, yes. By the way, do you happen to have a wallet photo of your two daughters to show me?

SANTIAGO: You know, you really are wicked, Adele.

KATHIE: Wicked or not, a lot of people seem to like me just fine.

SANTIAGO: Yeah, me for instance. I like you a lot. But you know that already, don't you?

KATHIE: Hmmm . . . news to me. What do you like about me?

SANTIAGO: That you're such an outrageous flirt.

KATHIE: You think I'm a flirt?

SANTIAGO: You're the devil herself.

KATHIE: And what don't you like about me?

SANTIAGO: That you won't go out with me.

KATHIE: What a sly dog you are, Dr. Griffin.

SANTIAGO: No, seriously, Adele. Why won't you? Because of some stuffy bourgeois hangup? I mean, what's wrong with going to the movies? Or to hear a little music?

KATHIE: O.K. I'll go. But on one condition.

SANTIAGO: Whatever you say.

KATHIE: That we go with your wife and your little girls. And now, if you'll excuse me, I'm going to go study just to make sure you don't flunk me in your class. If you're real good, next time I'll tell you even more beauty secrets. I'll tell you how to keep your teeth white and your eyes bright, how not to get a double chin, broken nails or freckles. Ciao, Dr. Griffin.

SANTIAGO: Ciao, Adele. (*To himself.*) She's so gorgeous, . . . so delicious . . . exciting.

ANA: I stopped being gorgeous, delicious and exciting because you kept preaching it was nothing but bourgeois frivolity.

SANTIAGO: (*Pensively.*) It was. (*Seeing Ana.*) And it is, Anita. Can I help it if all that silliness gets the dicky bird going? Is it my fault if liberated women are so serious and sober that they put it to sleep? Kill it? You can't control your own nature, Anita. You just can't fight human nature or natural instinct with moral or political convictions.

ANA: What? Didn't you teach me that there was no such thing as human nature?

SANTIAGO: (*Pontificating.*) It doesn't exist! Human nature doesn't exist, Anita! It's just another bourgeois fraud they use to justify exploitation!

ANA: Liar. Cheat! Bastard!

SANTIAGO: (*Professorial.*) Man is malleable material, Anita! Everyone can be whatever he wants to be! That's why you can really believe in human progress, Anita!

ANA: What a fool you made out of me, Mark Griffin!

SANTIAGO: What a fool Jean-Paul Sartre made out of me, Anita!

KATHIE: (*Becoming herself, again.*) You could never fool me Johnny darling. I could always spot your lies in a minute.

JUAN: (*Without diverting his attention from the waves.*) That time you caught me with Maritza, you really tore into me! The scratch marks on my face lasted at least a couple of weeks.

KATHIE: In the beginning, your cheating just destroyed me. I couldn't sleep. I cried all the time. I fell apart. The world had ended. I ground my teeth with the humiliation. I lost weight. I always had dark circles under my eyes. I cried and cried and couldn't stop.

JUAN: They sure got a good laugh at the Waikiki when they saw those scratch marks!

ANA: Instead of listening to your anti-bourgeois sermons, I should have paid attention to my mother. You never would've left me for Adele if I had.

SANTIAGO: And what advice did she give? That petit bourgeois from Santa Beatriz aspiring to be a high style bourgeois by moving to Orrantia.

KATHIE: (*Sermonizing to Ana as if she were a little girl.*) You just have to treat men bad, Anita. Use your smarts, honey. Your husband may be an intellectual or whatever, but what's really important is the dicky bird. And listen baby, I may not know anything about professor types, but I know everything about dickies. I'm warning you, if you don't want him to leave you or cheat on you, you've got to keep him dancing on his toes.

ANA: And what do I do to keep Santiago on his toes, Mom?

KATHIE: You go hot and cold. By day, you act like a perfect lady and by night, the all time whore. Use perfume, music, mirrors. Be wild! Extravagant! Fantasize! Make him feel like he's died and gone to heaven. But not every day. Only when you want to and when it'll do you some good. Hot and cold. Some days the whore turns to ice, sometimes the lady of pleasure acts like a sweet little nun. And top it off with the best trick there is—jealousy. Quick exits, mysterious phone calls, whispers to his friends, contradictions and white lies. Make him suspicious. Shake him up. Now it may get you a beating now and then, but that doesn't really matter. There's no love without a good fight, right? Just keep him on his toes and his dicky bird will sing for life!

ANA: But you always had complete faith in me and that really did me in. On the other hand, Adele made you work a little and you panting after her like a dog, Mark Griffin.

JUAN: Jealousy is fantastic, kitten. Like when we make up after a good fight. You look so sexy when you're angry. And you know our very best lovemaking is when we go from insults to kisses. Remember Hawaii when you caught me with that Eurasian girl on the beach? God, you really took after her with that shoe! And it was terrific afterwards, remember? Just terrific! We did it in the sand, in the ocean, on the astroturf and then in the ocean again. It was really fantastic, wasn't it, "darling?"

KATHIE: It wasn't all that great.

JUAN: Well, the sad fact is Kathie, you're no champ in bed, yourself. You're sort of drab. You get tired, you get embarrassed, you giggle. You just don't take the dicky bird seriously, darling and it's the most serious thing in the world. It's like surfing, Kathie!

KATHIE: There are some who have better things to say about their time in bed with me, Johnny darling. (*Juan and Ana disappear.*)

SANTIAGO: (*Sarcastic and aggressive.*) Yeah, like the horny perfumist in Cairo for example?

KATHIE: What are you trying to insinuate, Mr. Mark Griffin?

SANTIAGO: You know damn well what. You're just one more rich society woman, hysterical, menopausal. You leach off of the more progressive minds and talents of others. You're a pretentious hack. You know damn well, Kathie Kennety.

KATHIE: (*Without flinching in the slightest.*) Is that so?

SANTIAGO: (*With ferocious aggressiveness, as if purging old wounds and resentments.*) Come on, you don't take those exotic trips just to satiate your great thirst for spirit and beauty. You travel so you can play the grand whore without the fear of gossip, so you can indulge in a lot of extravagant and baroque fornications a long way from your Lima friends. Orientals, Blacks, Arabs, Eskimos, Afghans, Hindus! All the dicky birds of the world. Do they charge by the hour like I do? By the way, how much did you have to pay your Cairo perfumist to act excited for you?

KATHIE: (*Who has listened to him amiably, vaguely entertained.*) Aren't you exceeding the minimum limits of respect between an employee and his employer, Mr. Griffin? You're asking me questions that I can't answer without risking my modesty or breeding.

SANTIAGO: (*Demoralized, his rage begins to dissolve.*) No, I haven't forgotten you're the boss-lady or that as a writer, you're just a cheap fake. If it weren't for the money, I'd only disdain you, maybe pity you. Because it must be pathetic, isn't it? I mean, to travel around the world spending fortunes, writing books that you don't write and no one reads just so you can screw around. It must be very sad, right Kathie? (*He returns to his tape recorder and begins to dictate again, moving his lips silently. Kathie looks at him sadly, but with growing admiration. The Parisian music from the beginning is heard again in the distance.*)

KATHIE: What's really sad is being shut up here in this loft, day in and day out, missing out on all the wonderful things in Paris, just beyond my reach, through that door and down the stairs of the hotel. On the other hand, you really know how to live in this "City of Light," Mark. If you didn't have to work on the book about Black Africa and Yellow Asia, would you let me go with you? I wouldn't bother you. I wouldn't say a word. I'd learn so much just following you around to galleries, libraries, theatres, concerts, lectures and bistros. I'd feel so small and ignorant listening to you talk with all your brilliant friends. I know they've read all the books and know simply everything. (*Santiago is not focusing on Kathie, but there is no doubt that he is listening to her with great satisfaction.*) Because that's the life you have when you're not here, right, Mark Griffin? You stroll the banks of the Seine, you explore the old book stalls, you go to concerts, operas, ballets. You go to the symposium at the College of France, you catch all the art films, you never miss a gallery preview. God, how wonderful to spend an evening discussing philosophy with Sartre, feminism with Simone de Beauvoir, anthropology with Levi-Strauss, theatre with Jean-Louis Barrault, fashion with Pierre Cardin! I'd be hanging on their every word, just dazzled by their sheer brilliance. You have an amazing life, Mark Griffin. My life is so empty in comparison. But . . . our time is slipping by . . . we'd better get back to work. Let's get back to Cairo . . . the old city . . . to that little street with the perfume shop. (*The Arab music revives in the distance.*)

SANTIAGO: (*Dictating.*) Soon enough I would understand what the perfumist was insinuating. In honeyed tones he begged me to wait until he'd taken care of the other tourists. He brought me a cup of tea and I in utter naivete, accepted his offer and stayed.

KATHIE: Doesn't that "in utter naivete" sound a bit tacky?

SANTIAGO: (*Correcting.*) You're right . . . And I foolishly accepted the offer.

KATHIE: And doesn't "foolishly" sound a little . . . severe?

SANTIAGO: Uhhh, okay. And I accepted the offer.

KATHIE: Then, all of a sudden all the other employees seemed to vanish and the perfumist began to offer me vials of perfumes and sparkling jewels!

SANTIAGO: (*He stands up and starts acting out what according to Kathie, the perfumist from Cairo did. The Arab music of flutes, chirimias, little drums and castanets floats in the air.*) Take whatever your heart desires, beautiful stranger. Perfumes, essences, elixirs, resins, for the hair, for the ears, for the throat, for the breasts, for the belly, for the pubis, for the thighs, for the wrists, for the fingers, and the soles of the feet. Take whatever you want, beautiful stranger. Necklaces, rings, earrings, bracelets, anklets, lockets, tiaras, pins, diadems. Of amber, of tortoise-shell, of turquoise and butterfly wings.

KATHIE: (*Pleased and a little frightened.*) Thank you very much, Monsieur. Your perfumes are intoxicating and your jewels are so tempting. But I don't wish to buy anything. However, I appreciate your courtesy, Monsieur.

SANTIAGO: (*Sensuous, serpentine, he revolves around Kathie, his hands and eyes in constant motion.*) But who spoke of buying anything, beautiful stranger? Who's thinking of money, exotic lady from the exotic kingdom of Peru? Everything in this shop is yours. Take whatever you want. It is a homage to your beauty.

KATHIE: Your generosity overwhelms me, Monsieur, but I cannot accept gifts from strangers. I'm a decent, respectable woman, from Lima, Catholic, the mother of children. I'm not one of those loose American tourists that I'm sure you're more accustomed to, Monsieur.

SANTIAGO: I'm a prurient perfumist, Madame. Let me squire you through the Cairo night. We'll luxuriate in secret temples of pleasure, in sybaritic salons of sensuality. Madame, Cairo is the most corrupt city in the world!

KATHIE: Stop. Control yourself, Monsieur. Please, have some respect, be a gentleman. Don't get so close. Take your dirty hands off me!

SANTIAGO: We'll see the pyramids bathed in moonlight and walk barefoot in the desert. We'll go to a cabaret where voluptuous belly dancers writhe in wild frenzies. By dawn, we'll be lulled into dreams by aphrodisiac music that makes snakes hiss and camels climax!

KATHIE: Help! Help! Don't touch me you filthy half-breed! Savage! Let me go or I'll kill you. Kathie Kennety doesn't scare this easy. Hands up or I'll shoot. (*She threatens him with her small woman's pistol. Santiago returns to his desk. He continues dictating. An alarm clock goes off.*)

SANTIAGO: On seeing this pistol, the perfumist lets me go. I run from the perfume shop and lose myself in the dusty alleyways of the old city . . .

KATHIE: As I returned to the hotel, I was shaking all over, remembering that dirty, disgusting man.

SANTIAGO: Lost and wandering, asking my way through the Cairo labyrinth, I finally found the path to my hotel. I shudder with revulsion remembering that snake's slippery hands all over my body and my nostrils still sense the pungent poison of his perfumes. (*The sound of the alarm stops.*)

KATHIE: Well, those two hours went fast.

SANTIAGO: Yes, they really flew by. But we work pretty well together, don't we Kathie? (*They smile.*)

ACT TWO

(*The set decorations are the same. As the lights go down, Parisian music can be heard,* Les feuilles mortes, J'attendrai toujours *or something equally well-known and dated. All four characters are on stage, but the lights single out Santiago seated at his desk, dictating into the tape recorder and Kathie, papers and maps in hand as she wanders about, remembering and narrating. African music begins to replace the Parisian melody. We hear tribal tom-toms, the roar of wild beasts, the song of birds, the thundering of a waterfall. In an imaginary caricature of the scene, Ana and Juan can mime the narration.*)

KATHIE: My first night in Murchison Falls, a really terrifying noise woke me up.

SANTIAGO: It was a windy and moonlit night on the banks of Lake Victoria, not far from Murchison Falls. Suddenly, strange indecipherable sounds rip through the African night, waking me up with a start.

KATHIE: I couldn't tell what it was. It was something besides the waterfalls. I was camped out in a tent in the garden. They'd put me there because the hotel was full. The canvas danced in the wind. It seemed like the whole thing was ready to fly away.

SANTIAGO: As shelter they'd given me one of the fragile Bedouin tents in the camp. It seemed as thin as rice paper and shook wildly in the wind.

KATHIE: I raced to get dressed and to see what all the noise was.

SANTIAGO: Frightened and confused, I sit up in my woven reed hammock. I part the mosquito netting with a sweep of my hand and reach for the pearl handled pistol I have under my pillow.

KATHIE: What was going on? What was happening?

SANTIAGO: What's going on? What's happening? Could it be the waterfalls overflowing? The lake flooding? Is it an earthquake? A herd of elephants attacking our camp? A tribe of cannibals?

KATHIE: No, not quite. It turned out to be two hippos fighting over a "hippa."

SANTIAGO: (*Switching off the tape recorder for a moment.*) Hippos? Oh, hippopotamuses. That was the noise that woke you up? Two hippopotamuses fighting over a hippopotama?

KATHIE: Shouldn't you say female hippopotamus?

SANTIAGO: Nah, you should say whatever sounds good. Hippopotama is sort of resonant, strong, original. (*Dictating again.*) Could it be the waterfalls overflowing? The lakes flooding? Is it an earthquake? A herd of elephants stampeding? A tribe of cannibals attacking out camp? No, once again it's the eternal love triangle. The same old saga of desire, duel and abduction. In the deep quagmire of the banks of Murchison Falls two hippopotamuses were bellowing and thundering, trying to kill each other over a hippopotama.

KATHIE: The night was jet black. I couldn't see a thing, but I could tell by the sounds that the fight was ferocious.

SANTIAGO: (*Each time more enthusiastic.*) I saw them in the coal black shadows, prehistoric, ungainly, with huge heads, massive round bodies and ridiculous short legs, furiously chomping at each other's flanks.

KATHIE: The female was all aflutter, a little dizzy and excited just waiting on the side to see which of the macho hippos would win her.

SANTIAGO: Meanwhile, the coveted prize who had unleashed this titanic lust and fury, waddles about swinging her monstrous hips, all impassioned by the spectacle before her. She waits for the one who will claim the right to possess her, to ravish her, to impregnate her?

KATHIE: To ravish her probably. A German, a Dutchman or something like that, who was staying at Murchison Falls ... very smart, a scientist or something said that the hippopotamus was a very peculiar beast.

SANTIAGO: (*Talking with a heavy German accent.*) This primitive, wrinkled and thick-skinned specimen which you see before you, Frau Katherina, the hippopotamus, has a throat so delicate that he can only manage to eat little birds, butterflies and those unfortunate and confused little creatures who land on him thinking he is a tree trunk. But he is a beast of insatiable sexual voracity, a libidinous brute of cataclysmic potency. It is not unusual that after the first experience hippopotamas are forever disenchanted with sex, just like Adele Foucher, since the least inclined hippopotamus easily surpasses the record established for the human species set by Victor Hugo on his wedding night. (*Resuming his natural voice.*) What the Prussian zoologist said was true. Throughout the entire night, we heard the thrusting victor and the submissive hippopotama copulating with a thunderous roar. Soon they overpowered the sound of the waterfalls.

KATHIE: (*Laughing.*) What will my children say about "copulating with a thunderous roar?" (*Juan and Ana appear as Kathie's children. They approach her.*)

JUAN: So what are you writing, Mother? A travel book about "Yellow Asia and Black Africa" or a pornographic paperback?

ANA: You want everyone to laugh at us?

SANTIAGO: (*Stopping the dictation.*) Are your kids a bit critical?

KATHIE: Yeah, I suppose they are. At least in front of me. I wonder what they're like when they're alone? With their friends, lovers or whoever. Do my children have lovers?

JUAN: We have a surprise for you that you're not going to believe, Mother.

SANTIAGO: Actually, you don't talk much about your family.

ANA: Can't you guess? It's the tickets! For your trip to Black Africa and Yellow Asia!

KATHIE: I don't have much reason to talk about them. This is a travel book, not an autobiography.

JUAN: You'll be going to forty-two countries and more than eighty cities!

ANA: You'll explore every country, race, language and religion! It'll set your head spinning, Mother.

SANTIAGO: Did it take much persuading to get them to let you go on such a long trip?

KATHIE: Hardly. It didn't take much of anything in fact. (*She turns on her children.*) I don't need my head spinning, young lady. Why did you go ahead and buy the tickets? I haven't decided if I'm going to go yet.

JUAN: Because you're dying to do it. All you needed was a little push. So, there you go, we just gave it to you.

ANA: You'll learn so much. Those other worlds are so different, so exotic. Just think of the exciting adventures you'll have. And all to put in your book!

JUAN: Naturally, we got you first class hotel reservations all the way and every excursion has a personal guide and private car.

ANA: Who deserves it more, Mother?

KATHIE: (*Mockingly.*) Aren't you going to miss me?

JUAN: A lot. But this is for you, so that you can really enjoy yourself and write that book you've always wanted to.

ANA: Haven't you always said that you're fed up with your Lima life with all the cocktail parties, the boring dinners, the endless weddings at the Gomez's, the Lopez's, the Sanchez's? That Lima's frivolous social life doesn't leave any time for culture? Well, you've finally got the chance. Eight months to dedicate yourself to your cultural pursuits.

JUAN: You'll travel with a diplomatic passport so you won't have any trouble with customs.

KATHIE: My, what marvelous, splendid children I have! (*Changing her tone.*) You know, you're a couple of real hypocrites. You must be just dying to get rid of me for a while.

JUAN: How could you say that, Mother? God, it's impossible to make you happy. And we thought that we were going to give you the time of your life with this trip.

ANA: You have to twist everything around. Why should we want to get rid of you?

KATHIE: (*Rubbing her thumb and fingers together.*) For my money, my sweet, for the little *soles*. Because when I go, you'll have the legal power to do whatever you want with it. Isn't that so?

JUAN: Of course it isn't. Boy, it's always the same old story. Your suspicion, your distrust. It had to come up.

KATHIE: It's because you're sick of me sticking my nose into everything, of me questioning everything you do. Don't you think I sense your irritation every time you have to get me to sign every little thing?

ANA: It was just a bad idea when Johnny suggested the bank transfer . . .

KATHIE: The infamous transfer of powers that so cleverly divies up between you two everything that belongs to me before I'm even dead.

JUAN: No, no, no! It was so you wouldn't have to worry over the senseless little details, so you wouldn't have to spend all your time in board meetings, law offices, banks and all.

ANA: You've got an insufferable persecution complex!

KATHIE: Maybe I do, but I'm still not going to give you that transfer because I don't like feeling dead before my time. So, now that the transfer didn't work out for you, you want to send me on a trip around the world.

ANA: Don't be unfair, Mother!

JUAN: It was your idea to take the trip. It never would've occurred to us otherwise.

ANA: (To Juan.) She can't appreciate anything. Take the tickets back and don't bother going to any more trouble for her.

KATHIE: Only the trouble of buying them young lady. Don't you forget that I paid for them.

JUAN: All right. Enough said. It's done. Let's not fight. I'll return the tickets, period.

KATHIE: No, don't. I'll go on the trip and I'll write my book. But don't kid yourselves. I don't intend to be eaten by a tiger or run over by an elephant. I'll be coming back in one piece and then you'll answer for what you've done with my money while I've been gone. My money, don't forget. (Juan approaches Kathie and it looks as if he were trying to begin a mute conversation with her. She rejects it, taking refuge in deep thought. Ana approaches Santiago.)

ANA: A hippopotamus, huh? How ironic. Doesn't it remind you just a little of yourself, Mark Griffin? Oh, come on, don't pretend you don't hear me.

SANTIAGO: How do you mean?

ANA: Oh, on the outside you seem so strong, so sure, anyone would think you could eat a tiger up, claws, fangs and all. But all you can eat are little birds, beetles and butterflies. You're pure bluff.

SANTIAGO: (Fantasizing.) I know what way I'm like a hippopotamus.

KATHIE: (Kathie becopmes Adele.) Listen, my love, my dear sweet Teach, don't pay any attention to that spiteful bitch. Forget her. Don't let her spoil our life.

SANTIAGO: (Lustily.) Wouldn't think of it, kitten. Now come here so I can smell you, tickle you, lick you. Come here. You can't get away from me!

KATHIE: (Lifting her up and taking her into his arms.) Where should they end up?

And what of it? Aren't you glad you drive your husband wild, Adele?

KATHIE: Drive my lover wild, you mean. I'm not your wife, that mean old witch is.

SANTIAGO: Not anymore she isn't. I've left her for you, silly. Now you're my wife and my student, my lover, my pet.

KATHIE: Hey, take it easy, sweetie. We don't have time now. Don't you have your Spanish mystics class now?

SANTIAGO: The Spanish mystics can go to hell. The only class I want to give is to you alone and in the bedroom. Come on, let's go.

KATHIE: (*Mesmerized.*) Again? Have you gone crazy? We made love last night and again this morning.

SANTIAGO: (*Wildly.*) And we'll do it again before and after lunch, at teatime and at dinner. We'll do it nine times! Nine times!

KATHIE: Who would've ever thought Professor Mark Griffin was such an animal?

SANTIAGO: It's your fault. You unleash a volcanic fury in me! When I see your lovely body, feel it, hear it, smell it, you set my blood on fire!

KATHIE: (*Pouting.*) I'm not the only one to set your blood on fire, Victor. Don't you think I know what's going on with you and Juliet Drouet? Do you think I don't know about your fooling around? I see all those little sluts that hang all over you.

SANTIAGO: (*Arrogant, chastizing.*) They're just insignificant little flings, Adele. They don't even begin to touch my true feelings or to inspire my poetry like you do. They only prove that no lover comes close to my *Adèle chérie*.

KATHIE: (*Whimpering.*) It makes me sick to think of you fooling around with them. I suffer. I really suffer.

SANTIAGO: Jealousy is the spice of love. It colors it, perfumes it, excites it!

KATHIE: Yeah, sure, but nothing in a skirt gets by you. Look at my poor nails. They used to be so long and now look! And all because of you and your fooling around. Every time you go out I go crazy. I start to think which little slut is he with now? What's he saying to her? What's he doing to her? And where? And how many times? Nine times?

SANTIAGO: Listen Adele, dear. For some reason God, Nature or the Devil has endowed me with greater urges than your ordinary man. For me the gift of poetry has come hand in hand with the fury of love.

KATHIE: But don't we make love every day, Victor?

SANTIAGO: It's just not enough, Adele. Somehow I have to satisfy this yearning, to cool this fire.

KATHIE: You're a marvel of nature!

SANTIAGO: I am.

KATHIE: You're insatiable, inexhaustible, indomitable!

SANTIAGO: I am.

KATHIE: You're Victor Hugo, Mark Griffin!

SANTIAGO: As air is to others, so is woman to me. I must have her constantly. Without her, I cannot breathe. I'm addicted. Like absinthe for alcoholics or opium for drug fiends, so is woman to me.

KATHIE: You know more secrets than the Kama Sutra, than the Ananga Ranga, than Casanova, than the divine Marquis.

SANTIAGO: I do. What do women feel like when I make love to them, *Adèle chérie?*

KATHIE: Like butterflies pinned in a golden clasp, like nightingales caught in a honeyed web, like little chickens on the spit. (*Ana laughs mockingly, breaking the spell. All turn to Kathie and Juan.*)

JUAN: (*Again as Johnny darling.*) What about our son?

KATHIE: (*Becoming herself again.*) My son! My poor son! He didn't turn out at all like his father. (*To Juan.*) You were a charming rogue, an entertaining devil, Johnny darling. Your only interest in money was spending it. Little Johnny on the other hand, works like a mule. He's the stiffest, dullest, most disagreeable man I've ever known. The only thing about money that interests him is making more of it.

JUAN: That's not so Kathie. You're slandering him.

KATHIE: I'm not. The only things he cares about are the Bank, board meetings, and the hacienda. His major preoccupation in life is whether or not the Agrarian Reform will happen some day.

SANTIAGO: (*Thinking aloud.*) Do you even know what the Agrarian Reform is, Kathie?

KATHIE: It means taking away the haciendas from the decent people and giving them all away to the Indians. Sometimes I wish it would happen just to see Little Johnny's face.

JUAN: Do you think as badly of our daughter, too?

KATHIE: She's an empty-headed flit. Just like you, Johnny darling. A revised and improved edition. All she thinks about are the beaches, parties, clothes and men. And in that order.

JUAN: Looks like you detest your children as much as you detested me, Kathie Kennety.

KATHIE: No, I don't. Besides, they're the ones that hate me. It's because I don't let them do whatever they feel like with my money.

JUAN: That's what you'd like to believe, but you know you're lying, Kathie.

KATHIE: Yes, you're right. Actually, they hate me because of you.

JUAN: They detest you because they hold you responsible for the death of their father. And they're justified.

KATHIE: They are not justified. They never knew and they never will know what happened.

JUAN: They may not know the details, but they suspect it, they sense it, they smell it. And that's why you hate each other.

SANTIAGO: (*Cautiously.*) Did you and your husband ever separate, Kathie?

KATHIE: Johnny and I were never separated. I . . . was widowed.

SANTIAGO: Oh, I thought that . . . but what about the gentleman I kept passing in the hallway, in the stairwell, the one in all the newspapers, he's not your husband? I'm sorry, I didn't know.

KATHIE: There's no reason that you should know. And you don't have to be sorry either. Hundreds and thousands of women are widowed in the world. What's so unusual about it?

SANTIAGO: Nothing, of course. I guess it's as frequent and natural as a divorce. (*Santiago looks at Ana.*) Hundreds and thousands of women in the world split up with their husbands. Do they all turn it into a Greek tragedy?

KATHIE: I don't like Greek tragedies. But in this case, it was because Johnny darling didn't die a natural death. Actually . . . he killed himself. (*Santiago appears not to hear her as he is now concentrating on Ana who has returned to the scene with a bitter laugh.*)

SANTIAGO: So, are you laughing out of spite? Jealousy? Envy? Or just plain stupidity?

ANA: Curiosity, Professor.

SANTIAGO: Why don't you go cook, clean house, take care of your children. Get busy with the things you were born for.

ANA: Just answer one little question for me. I'm dying to know why Adele left you, hahaha . . . (*The music of African tom-toms suddenly breaks in as if conjured up by Santiago to avoid an unpleasant scene. Confused, he quickly grabs the tape recorder.*)

SANTIAGO: I don't have time for you. I'm extremely busy, the two hours are almost up. Get lost! (*Dictating.*) We traveled for countless hours through an exuberant tropical forest of bamboo, ebony and breadfruit trees, sweating and suffocating in our rickety bus. Finally we stopped in a small village between Moshe and Mombasa.

KATHIE: When we got there we saw something unbelievable in this small hut.

SANTIAGO: (*Dictating.*) There, before our very eyes, we see a horrifying, blood-curdling scene.

KATHIE: Some little naked kids, their bellies all blown up, were eating dirt just like candy.

SANTIAGO: We see some naked children with bellies swollen by parasites, hungrily consuming morsels of suspiciously white meat. What am I seeing? Paralyzed with horror, I realize that these voracious little creatures are devouring, a little hand, a foot and a shoulder of another child's body.

KATHIE: (*Disconcerted.*) You mean cannibals?

SANTIAGO: (*Stopping the dictation, demoralized by Ana's mocking glances.*) Well, so it'll sound more dramatic, more original, more exotic. I mean children eating dirt happens here in Peru all the time. It wouldn't surprise anyone.

KATHIE: (*Astonished.*) Here in Peru? Are you sure?

SANTIAGO: Kathie, Peru isn't Lima. And Lima isn't your San Isidro neighborhood. I realize that you'd never know it, living here, but in certain barrios and other places up in the sierra things like you saw in that African village happen all the time. You know, you've made two or three trips around the world, but you hardly seem to know your own country.

KATHIE: Once I took a tour with Johnny to those Inca ruins in Cuzco. The altitude made me queasy. You know you're right. In Peru, we're more interested in other countries than our own. I suppose we're actually terrible snobs.

ANA: (*Dying of laughter.*) Yeah, what snobs we are, we . . . we, the multimillionaire Peruvians!

SANTIAGO: (*Resigned, he puts down the tape recorder and looks at Ana.*) Look, you got what you wanted, didn't you.

ANA: What a ridiculous picture, Mark Griffin! You abandon your wife and daughters, run away with a Lolita, make yourself the laughing stock of the University. And for what? After a while the little vamp sends you packing and you come home begging my forgiveness like a mangy dog. (*Very ironic.*) Come on, won't you tell us why Adele kicked you out, Victor Hugo?

KATHIE: (*Kathie becoming a furious Adele, to Santiago.*) Because I'm young, because I'm just beginning my life, because I want to have fun, because I've got no reason to live like a nun. If I'd wanted to be a nun, I would've gone into a convent. Understand?

SANTIAGO: (*Remorseful, intimidated.*) Of course, I understand, kitten. But don't exaggerate. It's not all that bad.

KATHIE: You know damn well I'm not exaggerating. You spend all day telling me you love me, that you'd die for me, but at the moment of moments, at the moment of truth, when we're fooling around . . . psst . . . gone, like a punctured balloon.

SANTIAGO: (*Trying to get her to speak softer, to calm her so that no one will hear.*) Be a little more understanding, kitten.

KATHIE: (*More and more angry.*) You're pure bluff, Mark, you're a joke. A hippopotamus. A real terror at first, but all you catch are tiny little birds.

SANTIAGO: (*Terribly uncomfortable.*) I've got a lot on my mind, kitten. Ana is harassing me to the point of a nervous breakdown and my Spanish mystics classes, you know, they're a little heavy on sermons and theories in asceticism, well, you see, they seem to have a certain dulling effect on the psyche, on the libido. Want me to explain what the libido is? It's very interesting, you'll see. There was this man named Freud . . .

KATHIE: I don't give a damn about the psyche or the libido. They're all just stories, excuses, lies. The fact is you're a wimp, a dud, you're . . . you're . . .

ANA: Impotent, maybe?

KATHIE: That's it! You're impotent. That's your real problem. You can't get it up!

SANTIAGO: (*Not knowing where to hide.*) Don't say that, Adele. Don't shout so, please. The neighbors'll hear. (*To himself.*) How embarrassing. (*To her.*) When things get calmer during vacation, you'll see . . . (*Ana listens to them dying of laughter.*)

KATHIE: Do you really think I'm going to wait until summer to make love?

SANTIAGO: But we were fooling around just the other night after that movie. . .

KATHIE: Three weeks ago! You think I want some old man who can only do it once a month and then only after seeing a porno film? Is that what you think?

SANTIAGO: (*Wishing the earth would swallow him.*) Passion-love based on crude animal coupling is not everything in life, kitten. It's not even the best thing there is. On the contrary, it's ephemeral, a mere sandcastle in the wind. Solidarity-love, on the other hand, based on understanding, a sharing of ideas, sacrifice, struggle . . .

KATHIE: Well, find another idiot to make solidarity-love with. What I like is the other kind. What's it called? Love of passion, passion-love? The dirty kind, the animal kind. That's the one I like. Adios, teach. Let's hope I never see you again. Ciao, you phony. Some Victor Hugo, hah! (*She goes over to cheer on Johnny who is performing his surfing feats on a rough sea.*)

SANTIAGO: (*Santiago, crestfallen, overwhelmed, to Ana who looks at him compassionately.*) You made a mountain out of a molehill. It never was that big a deal. What do you want from me? Blood? You're just overreacting.

ANA: Undoubtedly another one of my bourgeois defects.

SANTIAGO: Every marriage gets in trouble once in awhile. Couples split up and get back together again all the time. No hassles. No big deal. But you had to turn this into a Greek tragedy.

ANA: Blame it on all the education you gave me. Weren't you the one who radicalized me? Well, from your social, moral and revolutionary perspective, you were a real bastard with me. (*She approaches him affectionately.*) Anyway, those are your problems, not mine. I let you leave and I let you come back. I put up with your nonsense about the psyche, the libido and solidarity love and we fool around, oh, about every time a bishop croaks. It's not my fault you like Greek tragedies, Mark Griffin. (*Santiago rests his head on her and she caresses him like a child.*)

SANTIAGO: You're right. I'm a hopeless romantic. But wouldn't it be great to star in a Greek tragedy just once in your life? (*Both turn to look at Juan who proud and cocky, after surfing, receives the congratulations of an invisible crowd. He holds up the cup he has just won in a surfing championship. He seems happy and a little drunk.*)

JUAN: (*To Kathie.*) Why didn't you come to the victory party they gave me "darling?" You never seem to be around when I need you. Everyone asked about you and I didn't know what to tell them. Why weren't you there? They gave the party to honor the champion, Kathie, and the champ is your husband! Doesn't that mean anything to you?

KATHIE: Not a thing, Johnny darling. Nothing. I'm fed up with your championships, your surfing, and your "parties." That's why I didn't go and that's why I'm through with your surfing—forever. I've never seen anything as idiotic nor as many idiots as surfers.

JUAN: I know what your problem is. You're envious.

KATHIE: Of you?

JUAN: Yes, of me. Because I'm a winner. All over the world, in Peru, in Hawaii, in Sidney and in South Africa. Because they cheer me, they idolize me, they photograph me and throw "parties" for me. You envy me. People only know about you because you're my wife. A famous nobody. Admit it. That's why you hate surfing. Pure envy!

KATHIE: (*Laughing.*) You honestly believe that, don't you, Johnny darling?

JUAN: And jealousy. I dare you to deny it! You're jealous of all the girls that play up to me. And believe me, I've got girls by the hundreds everywhere I go.

KATHIE: You're right. They all go crazy for a jerk who knows how to balance on a board.

JUAN: You're jealous as hell. You didn't come to the "party" because you didn't want to see all the pretty girls coming on to me. Because they're young and pretty and you're getting old and ugly. Because you're just dying of jealousy.

KATHIE: I used to be at the beginning. Those first months. Those first years. But not anymore.

JUAN: And you still are. Everytime a girl flirts with me it tears you up. You think I don't notice?

KATHIE: (*Not hearing him, lost in the past.*) I couldn't believe it. Every time I caught you I died. With Adelita? Yes, with Adelita. With Julie? Yes, with Julie. With Jessy? Yes, with her, too. All my best friends and enemies. I felt humiliated, hurt, destroyed. You're right. I was dying of jealousy. Life was over for me. I felt like the most abandoned person on earth. How could you fool around on me right and left like that and still tell me you loved me?

JUAN: (*A little confused, trying to make peace.*) What's that got to do with anything. Love is one thing, fooling around is another. Of course I loved you and I still love you even if you didn't come to my "party." You just annoyed me, silly. I've already told you about fooling around. It doesn't count. It just doesn't count. I take those girls to bed, then psst . . . they're out of my mind. They're just little flings, a little ordinary refreshment, like having a "drink" or changing my shirt, just some harmless recreation for the ol' dicky bird. My feelings don't enter into it. My dicky bird is for the world, but my heart's just for you. It's like when we were going together, don't you remember? When I used to tell you, "We can't go out tonight 'cause tonight's my night, my night to fool around." A girl doesn't get jealous because her boyfriend fools around a little with a few little sluts. It's the same thing, don't you understand?

KATHIE: Sure, I understand. That's why I'm not jealous. That's not why I didn't go to your party.

JUAN: (*Conciliatory*.) Well, I only said that 'cause I was really mad at you. I'm over it now. I'll let it go this time, but just this once. Just don't pull another stunt like that again. (*Smiling*.) So, now, come on, just whisper in my ear. Do you or don't you just die of jealousy.

KATHIE: Never, Johnny darling.

JUAN: (*Teasing, cajoling her*.) Aw, come on. Tell me it kills you. I love it. Don't you just die of jealousy over your little hubby?

KATHIE: You're only jealous when you're in love. I quit loving you a long time ago, Johnny darling!

JUAN: Are you serious?

KATHIE: When I began realizing what a complete fool you were . . .

JUAN: Do you realize what you're saying?

KATHIE: . . . how empty your life was, the mess you made of my life. That's when I stopped being jealous.

JUAN: Oh, so you really want to pick a fight? I mean first you stand me up and then on top of that you insult me.

KATHIE: When I really began to despise you, my jealousy just disappeared. There isn't a trace of it left. As far as I'm concerned you can give your dicky bird and your heart to any girl you want, Johnny darling.

JUAN: Oh, so that bit about the ol' dicky bird and the heart really got to you. You know, I was ready to make up, you silly woman. Look, let's change the subject. I'm tired of hearing your same old complaints. You're worse than a broken record.

KATHIE: No, let's go on with the subject. You picked it. How many girls did you cheat on me with?

JUAN: (*Once again furious*.) With more than you can possibly imagine.

KATHIE: Twenty? Fifty? A hundred? It couldn't be much more, could it? (*Calculating*.) Let's see . . . in ten years of marriage, a hundred would make around ten a year, almost one a month. You're right. It could be more. A hundred and fifty? Two hundred?

JUAN: As many as I wanted.

KATHIE: You don't even know how many. On the other hand, I do know how many I cheated on you with, Johnny darling.

JUAN: Careful, Kathie. This isn't something to joke about.

KATHIE: Eight to be exact. Some surfers too, by the way. Even champions, I think.

JUAN: Cut it out, Kathie. This isn't funny.

KATHIE: With Bepo Torres in the summer of '57 on the beach of the Kon Tiki Club. You know, in Bepo's little cottage close to the lighthouse? His wife had taken her mother to the United States for a facelift, remember?

JUAN: (*Only now beginning to believe her*.) You can't be serious. Are you serious?

KATHIE: With Ken, the Australian guy, the first time we went to Sydney. In

1958, wasn't it? Remember the one that really impressed you, the guy that always surfed right in the tube of the wave. You were fooling around with his girlfriend, Sheila, weren't you? Well, I was with him, Johnny darling.

JUAN: (*He goes from disbelief to horror and rage.*) I'll smash your face in. I'll kill you. Is that what you're looking for?

KATHIE: With Kike Ricketts, the race car driver. In 1960 in Hawaii with your good friend, Rivarola, the skindiver. The next year in South Africa with the German safari guide who took us to the ostrich hatchery. Hans what's his name? And the next year with Sapito Saldivar.

JUAN: (*He clamps his hand over her mouth. It appears as if he were about to strangle her.*) Are you telling the truth, you bitch?

KATHIE: (*Without resisting.*) Don't you want to know who the other two were?

JUAN: (*Undecided, he lets her go. He's sweating, watching, overwhelmed.*) Yes.

KATHIE: Harry Santana and . . . Abel.

JUAN: (*Enraged.*) Abel?

KATHIE: Yeah, your brother Abel. Is he the one that hurts the most? So, that makes him exactly eight. (*She looks at him.*) Who's jealous now?

JUAN: (*Shattered, he looks at Kathy dumbfounded.*) This isn't the end of this. You're going to be really sorry. And those bastards are going to be even sorrier than you. That's for sure. That's for real sure. (*A sob chokes him. He hides his face in his hands while he gasps and cries under the indifferent gaze of Kathie.*) Why did you do this to me?

KATHIE: (*Profoundly depressed.*) God, I don't know. To get back at you for all the pretty girls you slept with right under my nose. Out of boredom. To fill the emptiness somehow. To find someone worthwhile, someone I could fall in love with, someone to make my life better.

JUAN: I'll kill you for this. I swear I'll put a bullet in your brain.

KATHIE: Go ahead, Johnny darling. Just shoot straight. I probably told you all this so you would kill me. I'm sick of myself, of my life.

JUAN: And your children?

KATHIE: Them too. They didn't change a thing. I just don't seem to care anymore about seeing them grow up or seeing how they'll do in life. I already know what's going to happen to them. They'll be a couple of idiots, just like you and me.

JUAN: God, you have no feelings. You're a monster!

KATHIE: I wasn't when I married you, Johnny darling. I guess I was a little spoiled, but I was alive and curious. I wasn't just rich and pretty. I wanted to learn, to improve myself, to do things. And there was still time to change. But you killed that. Living with you made me just like you. (*She turns towards Santiago.*) I should have met you when we were young, Mark. (*As the following scene unfolds, Juan is getting drunk.*)

SANTIAGO: Do you know what I was like when I was young, Kathie?

KATHIE: I can see it right before my eyes.

SANTIAGO: (*Anxious, hopeful.*) So . . . what was I like, Kathie. Tell me.

KATHIE: Let's see . . . You were born in the slums, in a sordid and savage world. Although an orphan, you still managed to go to school. You scratched out a living shining shoes, guarding cars, selling lottery tickets and newspapers.

ANA: (*Caressing his head, compassionately.*) What really happened was you went to the private Salesian Fathers Academy. Your family wasn't poor, just lower middle class. And you didn't even begin to work 'til you were twenty.

KATHIE: You didn't go to the exclusive Catholic University. You were poor and an atheist too, so you went to the national University of San Marcos instead. You were a brilliant student from the start. Always the first to arrive at the department and the last to leave. How many hours did you spend in the library, Mark?

SANTIAGO: Hundreds.

ANA: And how many in the Azangaro street pool halls? Did you ever make it to metaphysics class? Or how about Ancient History? You were terribly lazy, Mark.

KATHIE: How many books a week did Victor Hugo read? Two, three? Sometimes one a day!

ANA: Actually, you really didn't study all that much. You didn't have the patience or the perseverance. Did you ever understand Heidegger? Did you translate even one verse of Latin? Or learn a foreign language?

KATHIE: You were too poor to keep up with the rich kids from Miraflores and San Isidro. You didn't have a car. You couldn't buy clothes, or join the Waikiki Club, or surf, or have a beer with your friends on Saturday.

ANA: How about those wild drunks at the Palermo bar? Didn't they count on having a beer with your friends? And what about the trips to Señora Nanette's whorehouse on the Avenida Grau, which always left you with such socialist remorse.

KATHIE: What did Victor Hugo care about Miraflores socialites and San Isidro snobs? His days and nights were dedicated to profound and elevated things, to absorbing the ideas of great men so he could go on to do great things himself.

ANA: So why did you drop out then? Why did you cheat on your exams? why didn't you write the term papers? How come you cut your classes?

KATHIE: What importance could surfing ever have had for you? Only the spiritual, the artistic, the revolutionary mattered to you. Because you believed in fighting social injustice. Right, Karl Marx?

SANTIAGO: (*Transported.*) It's true. The secret Marxist study groups . . .

ANA: . . . bored you to tears. Did you understand *Das Kapital*? Did you even read *Das Kapital*? Did you ever finish the *Dialectic of Nature*? What was the name of that book? You know, the real tongue-twister. *Materialism and Empiricism* something? Empirioclassicism? Empiriocriticism? Empiriocretinism? God, what a laugh!

SANTIAGO: (*With a melancholy smile.*) Those were the days. What a spirit there was! Maybe there weren't too many of us in the Party, but we were militant!

KATHIE: Yes, yes, the militance, the spirit. Teaching the poor to read, giving out food and clothing, organizing strikes and revolutions. Planting bombs!

ANA: It was more like plotting and scheming ad nauseum at the universities and downtown coffee shops against Tom, Dick and Harry. Or accusing the Maoists of being Trotskyites, the Leninists of being Stalinists, the socialists of being revisionists and everyone else of being fascists, nazis and spies.

KATHIE: That was the life, Victor Hugo! That's what being young and alive is all about, Karl Marx! Art, literature, politics . . . prisons, revolutions, executions. You didn't feel empty for a single minute of your life did you?

SANTIAGO: I didn't have time for that, Kathie.

KATHIE: (*Taking his hand.*) And the women who became your girlfriends?

SANTIAGO: "Girlfriends" is an alienating and petit bourgeois expression. Those of us in the struggle, in the Party, called them "comrades."

KATHIE: (*Eager, hopeful.*) Yes, and your comrades, just by following you around, by typing your manifestoes, bringing food to you in jail, supporting you and collaborating with you. They got to share in the glory. Isn't that so?

ANA: (*Still affectionate and compassionate.*) No, it isn't. Isn't it true that it's not true, Mark Griffin?

KATHIE: When you're young, you do great things greatly. (*A doubt shakes her. She looks at Santiago, suddenly disconcerted.*) But . . .

ANA: But, Mr. Mark Griffin, Mr. Victor Hugo, Mr. Karl Marx, you still haven't done any of those great things. Why?

SANTIAGO: (*Anguished.*) Why? In spite of being so ready to do great things . . .

ANA: . . . you've only done little tiny things, just fooled around.

SANTIAGO: What happened to those books you never wrote?

ANA: What happened to those political parties you never joined?

SANTIAGO: What happened to those strikes you never organized? To those revolutions you never carried out.

ANA: What happened to all those women you dreamed about? To those pleasures you never had? To all the love you never made?

SANTIAGO: What happened to all those intellectual, social and sexual conquests?

KATHIE: What happened, Victor Hugo?

ANA: What happened, Karl Marx?

KATHIE: What happened, Mark Griffin?

SANTIAGO: (*Looking from right to left, searching desperately to find an answer.*) I married the wrong woman. She never understood me. She never helped me. She weighed me down with her ignorance, her pettiness, her stupidity. That's what happened! I married a miserable bitch that fought me, that frustrated me, that castrated me.

KATHIE: (*Glowing, Kathie moves to Santiago and embraces him.*) I knew it. I knew it. It happened to you too. We're so much alike. We just didn't know how to choose. Our lives would have been so different with other people. Oh, isn't it wonderful that we met? That we're so alike, Mark?

SANTIAGO: (*Embracing her too.*) You're the one that I've needed all along. The one who would've understood me, inspired me, excited me. You would have believed in me, given me strength and courage . . . (*Ana's giggling forces Santiago to look at her.*) And I didn't just make one mistake, I made two! Adele didn't help me either. She demanded what I didn't have and what I couldn't give. She brought my fantasies to life then turned my life into a nightmare. She twisted everything I believed in. She humiliated me.

ANA: (*Making a face.*) Dicky, dicky, dicky bird . . .

SANTIAGO: That's exactly what happened to me. My wife killed me and my lover finished the job.

KATHIE: And Bepo, Ken, Kike, Gordo, Hans, Sapito, Harry and Abel did the same to me. We chose the wrong lovers too. Nobody understood, inspired or excited us. They fought us, smothered us, castrated us.

SANTIAGO: (*Looking in her eyes, filled with hope.*) Oh, it's so wonderful that we met, that we're so alike, Kathie.

KATHIE: You'll take me away from the country clubs, from the barbecues, the "showers," the "parties," you'll save me from the hell of surfing.

SANTIAGO: With me, you'll read all the best books, you'll see all the exhibitions and go to all the concerts.

KATHIE: And I'll take you your meals in prison. I'll type your manifestos. You'll teach me to make bombs, to kill.

SANTIAGO: We'll discuss novels, poems, and plays together. You'll be my inspiration, my strength, my faith to go on. I'll read you what I write and you'll give me ideas, concepts, words.

ANA: Who'll do the dishes, mop the floors, change the diapers, cook the meals?

KATHIE: We'll learn Chinese, Greek, German . . .

SANTIAGO: . . . Russian, Japanese.

ANA: And the dicky bird will sing every quarter, every semester, once an academic year.

KATHIE: The arts, love . . .

SANTIAGO: The revolution, pleasure . . .

KATHIE: Oh, oh!

SANTIAGO: And when I have you naked in my arms, we'll be "two sublime creatures, the emperors of paradise."

ANA: Isn't that a phrase from Victor Hugo?

KATHIE: I love you, I love you. Love me too, Mark.

SANTIAGO: I love you and tonight the dicky bird will sing nine times! (*He kisses her passionately while Ana laughs. But her laughter is drowned out by Juan returning home, roaring drunk, with a pistol in his hands.*)

JUAN: I'll kill all nine. The eight samurais and you. And then me. Goddamn,

goddamn! This isn't the end of it. (*He sees his reflection.*) What are you look-
ing at, you sorry bastard. Look at you. What's the word? Cuckold! That's it.
You're a cuckold. Cuckold, cuckold, cuckold! That's just what you are,
Johnny darling. She really put a pair of horns on you, didn't she? You're a
goat, a big goat with horns . . . huge horns. (*A sob breaks his voice.*) How can
I face the world now? What did I do to make you act like that, you whore?
Did you cheat on me because of the surfing? Did it get you that mad? And
you call me stupid . . . Who did I hurt by surfing? What's wrong with enjoying a sport? Is it better to drink, or snort or shoot up? Don't you understand
that I'm the wholesome type? Am I a drunk, by any chance? I only drink
enough to enjoy myself some! Am I a dope fiend? I'm not. I smoke a joint
now and then just to get a little high. Hell, you'd rather have me be a drunk,
snort coke or shoot smack or even be a fag than a surfer, wouldn't you, you
whore. You were just jealous. You couldn't stand me being a winner. In
Lima, in Hawaii, in South Africa and in Australia. Yeah, oh yeah, you
bitch. I've ridden waves three, four, eight meters high. Huge waves. The size
of the horns you put on me. So you did it with Abel too. You thought that
was really going to get me, didn't you. Well, you're wrong. He doesn't matter
at all. At least you kept it in the family. I could have done it with his wife
years ago if I'd wanted to. I didn't do it because she had hair under her arms
and women who don't shave, puaff, they make me sick. No, this isn't going
to be the end of it. Oh, God! God! (*Another sob cuts him off as his drunkeness
sends him reeling.*) You can never look anyone in the eye again, Johnny darling. How can you walk around with these horns crashing against walls,
knocking down innocent people in the streets. The next time you try to surf
these horns will take you right to the bottom. You can win every surfing
championship, you can ride the most dangerous waves. What good will it do
you? These horns will be here till you die, as solid as rocks. And after you
die, you'll still have them, Johnny. Johnny? What Johnny are you talking
about? Oh, that one! The goat, the sorry bastard! It's worse than original
sin, worse than a cancer. I'd rather go blind. I'd rather get leprosy or syphilis.
I'd rather go to hell. You're a cuckold eight times over, Johnny. What a slut!
What a slut! (*Sobs.*) And what if she lied to you? Just to hurt you? She hates
you, Johnny, she hates you. Because she's a bitch and you're "nice." You're
"Johnny darling." Everyone likes you and all the girls go wild for you. Why
do you hate me so much? You whore! Because I don't spend my life in the
bank like my old man and Abel? For what? To get more money? What do I
need more money for? I want more out of life. Anybody who wants to work,
let 'em. Let 'em get all the money they want. Screw them. When the old man
dies, I'll blow the inheritance . . . psst . . . just like that. Do you want me to
throw my life away . . . busting my ass so I can die rich? So I can leave more
money to my children who aren't even my children? (*He sobs.*) Are your
children my children? You're gonna tell me that! You whore! How could

you? How dumb, how stupid to turn into a whore just because you were jealous. None of those girls meant a thing to me. Anybody but you would've understood that. It was just to pass the time. Sometimes it was just to be polite, not to look bad. You should feel proud, not jealous, you bitch. (*He finally reaches Kathie, staggering.*) I want to know right now if my children are mine or the eight samurais'.

KATHIE: (*She looks at him indifferently, paying no attention to the pistol.*) Alejandra is yours without a doubt. About little Johnny, I'm not so sure. He might be Ken's, the Australian. I always had a few doubts about him. Now we can share them.

JUAN: (*Staggering, overwhelmed.*) You're lying to me. Now you really are lying to me. All this has just been a joke, a bad joke. All that about little Johnny and the samurais. Isn't it true that it's not true? That you invented it to drive me crazy? (*His voice breaks. He falls to his knees, imploring.*) "Darling," Kitten, in the name of all that you love, I'm begging you. Tell me it's not true. Tell me you haven't cheated on me. Tell me little Johnny is my son. I'm begging you on my knees, kissing your feet. (*He drags himself to her, whimpering.*) Even if he's not, tell me he is so I can keep on living, Kathie.

KATHIE: (*Looking at him carefully.*) Everything I told you is the pure truth. You'll just have to accept it for now and for always. What's really too bad is that even seeing you like this, I don't feel sorry. I resent you too much. I must be a monster. You don't evoke any pity or regret in me.

JUAN: (*Standing with the pistol in his hand.*) Then you're going to pay, you whore.

KATHIE: Go on, shoot. Right here at my heart. You're trembling. Get close so you don't miss. You see, I'm not running away. I'm not afraid. You finished off my life a long time ago. You think I couldn't care less if I die now? Go on, finish the job. (*But Juan isn't able to shoot. His hands tremble. His body shakes, he collapses at Kathie's feet. He holds the pistol to his temple and closes his eyes. Sweating, trembling like a leaf. He can't shoot. Kathie finally seems sympathetic.*) If you can't kill me as much as you hate me now, you could hardly kill yourself. It's a lot harder to commit suicide. You need a little more courage than you do for riding eight meter waves. You need a sense of the grand gesture, of tragedy. You need a romantic soul. You haven't got any of those things, Johnny darling.

JUAN: (*Sobbing with the pistol at his temple.*) But you do. Help me, kitten. Help me. I can't go on living knowing what I know, what you've done. What you've told me. Help me. Help me. (*With his free hand, he places Kathie's hand over the hand he has on the trigger.*) Go ahead. Pull it. Get back at me for all those things you say I've done to you. For the surfing, the Waikiki, the emptiness. Make yourself free. (*With a sudden movement, Kathie presses Juan's finger on the trigger. The shot explodes powerfully and Juan slumps to the ground. The scene remains frozen for a few seconds.*)

SANTIAGO: What do you do here in Paris, Kathie? That is, when you're not working on your book on Yellow Asia and Black Africa.

KATHIE: (*Discouraged and tired.*) Well, I go to the Louvre, to the Jeu de Paume, to l'Orangerie, to the Museum of Modern Art, the galleries on the Rue de Seine. I walk for miles. I'm on my feet for hours. I get very tired. My feel swell. I try to make up for lost time, I guess.

SANTIAGO: (*To Ana.*) Why don't you try to make up for lost time? You're just the same as when I met you.

ANA: Sorry, I haven't had time to improve myself or to be different. Your tiny salary at *The Chronicle* was never enough to hire a maid and by the time you started teaching classes at the University, it was "Ana, I'm sorry, but my principles don't allow me to have servants." But your principles didn't stop you from turning your wife into a servant. You're right. I'm about the same. How about you? Have you changed much? Yes, I think you have . . . but are you sure it's for the better? (*She helps Juan up and the two leave arm in arm like ghosts disappearing.*)

KATHIE: I'm not sure that it's never too late to learn. Sometimes it is too late for certain things. You have to learn to see them and enjoy them at the right time.

SANTIAGO: What do you mean? Are you talking about all the modern painting and avant-garde music and literature you've been around?

KATHIE: Yes, and about the old masters, primitive music, and rearguard literature for that matter. I get bored. And I don't understand it. I don't know how to judge when a painting is good or bad. And the same for music, or theatre or poetry. That's the truth, Mark. I wouldn't ever tell anyone else, but it's true.

SANTIAGO: Modern art is very confusing. Believe me, we all get lost in that jungle.

KATHIE: I'm going to confess something else to you . . . when my life was simply frivolous and stupid, I had a great longing for the world I was missing out on, a world of depth, intelligence, art and literature. But now that I try to read and go to all the exhibitions, concerts and lectures, I get so bored. It makes me wonder if a life of culture is essentially just as stupid and as much a lie as the other one.

SANTIAGO: By the looks of it, we both go against the grain. We want what we don't have and we don't want what we have.

KATHIE: And the worst of it is now I don't even know what to want. I realize that I've lost my illusions, my dreams. Is this what it is to grow old?

SANTIAGO: What a pessimist you are today! I don't believe a thing you've told me. If you were totally disillusioned, you wouldn't be writing the book on Black Africa and Yellow Asia.

KATHIE: Am I really writing it? Or are you writing it?

SANTIAGO: I'm just the one who puts in the periods and commas and chooses one adjective over another. The book is yours from beginning to end. (*The alarm clock rings indicating that two hours have passed.*)

KATHIE: My god, the two hours are over and we've hardly written anything. Can you stay another half hour?

SANTIAGO: Sure, and don't worry. There's no overtime.

KATHIE: Don't be silly. Overtime's the last thing I'm worried about. A few *soles* more or less aren't going to break my husband. Let Johnny spend a little on "culture."

SANTIAGO: All right. In that case I'll charge you a half an hour extra and take Anita to the movies. She spends her life complaining that I never take her out.

KATHIE: Your wife's name is Ana? You'll have to introduce us. By the way, there's something I've wanted to tell you for awhile now. Do you think it's a little strange that I've never invited you to my home outside of work hours?

SANTIAGO: No, not at all. I know how busy your life is. I see your picture in the paper attending some cocktail party or reception almost every day it seems.

KATHIE: Those are all Johnny's banking functions. It wouldn't look good if I didn't go with him. Actually, it's the least I can do for him because he's so good to me. No, it's not that. It's because you'd be bored with him. You're so different. Johnny's the sweetest soul in the world, but he's a bit culturally retarded.

SANTIAGO: No, he can't be that bad. Not after getting as far as he has.

KATHIE: No really, he is. He even says so himself. According to Johnny, culture and business don't mix. "I'll leave art to you, kitten, and you can leave the practical things to me." Eventually you'll meet him and then you'll see.

SANTIAGO: Actually, I sort of know him already. I've run into him coming and going out of the house. You know, he looks at me as if I were some sort of strange bird. Have you ever told him what kind of work I do for you?

KATHIE: Yes, but I'm sure it's gone in one ear and out the other.

SANTIAGO: (*Taking up the microphone.*) Shall we go on then?

KATHIE: Yes . . . (*Meditatively, doubtfully.*) You know, I don't think I'm going to do it.

SANTIAGO: What?

KATHIE: Invite you and your wife over for dinner.

SANTIAGO: Well, whatever, but now I'm curious. Why?

KATHIE: Don't get me wrong. (*She looks affectionately at her Paris loft.*) It would be like mixing oil and water. I don't mean you and Johnny. I'm thinking more about myself. I don't know. See, when I come up here, I seem to be able to leave San Isidro, Lima, Peru, behind and I swear I'm really in a Paris loft where there is only culture and fantasy. I can actually forget being a banker's wife. Here I get to be Kathie Kennety. I can be anything I want, single, married, a widow, a saint, a little wild. I can be a woman who has experienced everything in the world, who lives to keep her spirit alive. You make my dreams real and my reality a dream. I don't want to mix the two. I want our friendship to remain in this little room of lies. That's why it's better for you not to meet my husband and why I don't want to meet your wife. Let them stay out there. You understand, don't you?

SANTIAGO: Perfectly. And I think you're right. And you know, after listening to you, I think I know why I never really wanted to bring Anita here.

KATHIE: Have you told your wife about my Parisian loft?

SANTIAGO: I told her that you had made a playroom in your loft. And, you know how curious women are. She drives me crazy trying to get me to introduce you. I always give her excuses with the pretext that you wouldn't want to, but I think there's another reason.

KATHIE: And what's the real reason?

SANTIAGO: The same as yours. It seems that without realizing it, I've begun to play this game too. And to think I made so much fun of you and now it's got a hold on me too.

KATHIE: Well, I did think you got a good laugh out of the Parisian loft and Kathie Kennety.

SANTIAGO: Of course, I did. I thought of you as an eccentric rich lady playing a very expensive game. I had a good laugh and came out here a couple of hours every day for the money. But I don't think so anymore. The truth is that for a while now I've been enjoying this game too. I enjoy these two hours of lies that become truth and truths that become lies, and it helps me to get through the rest of the day too.

KATHIE: That's good to hear. You've taken a weight off my shoulders. I'm really glad I trusted you from the beginning. My intuition didn't betray me. Thank you, Mark.

SANTIAGO: I'm the one who should thank you. When I come here I get to play out a secret life too. I guess I can be just a little more than *The Chronicle* reporter writing mediocre articles for an even more mediocre salary. The mediocre professor of mediocre students stays behind somehow. I mean, here Mark Griffin is born, writer, dreamer, inventor, creator, a judge of intelligence, of good taste. Here while we work, I have the lovers I never had. I live through Greek tragedies I hope never to have. Here, thanks to you, I not only travel to Yellow Asia and Black Africa, but to many other places no one would ever suspect.

KATHIE: You said something about mediocre, mediocrity. Isn't this game a little too mediocre as well?

SANTIAGO: Maybe it is, Kathie. But at least we haven't lost our imagination, our dreams. We can't let them take away our little game because we haven't got another one.

KATHIE: (*A laugh.*) How well we understand each other. And what good friends we've become.

SANTIAGO: Friends and accomplices.

KATHIE: Yes, accomplices. And, by the way, shall we begin again?

SANTIAGO: Sure, let's go. Where were we? Black Africa. (*He picks up his tape recorder. Exotic music, somewhere between African and Arab begins, sensual, caressing and mysterious.*)

KATHIE: (*Sorting her papers.*) Let's see. Let's see. On the island of Zanzibar. Our little airplane landed at dusk.

SANTIAGO: (*Dictating.*) The shadows are descending rapidly as I climb down from the small airplane among whispering bushes and coconut palms of Zanzibar, land of a thousand adventures, crossroad of every race, religion and language.

KATHIE: The small hotel where I had my reservations was an old house. It was filled with flies and Arabs.

SANTIAGO: Enraptured by the palaces, the minarets and the gleaming white fortresses, the mystery of the island begins to take hold of me. A coolie trots through the semi-deserted streets, pulling my rickshaw to the inn, a spectacular Muslim tower guarding the city.

KATHIE: I asked for a cup of tea which I drank on the run. Then I dressed in a flash and ignoring the innkeeper's warning, I hurried out to explore the exotic city made famous by the film.

SANTIAGO: Dark servants, who speak Swahili and perform magic, offer me a brew of herbs. It dissolves my fatigue. A steambath and a massage by black girls with skillful hands and erect breasts restore my energy, my sense of adventure. Even though they told me of the dangers a woman risks in the Zanzibar night—robbery, assault, rape, I venture out to explore the city.

KATHIE: The streets were very narrow. They smelled of animal and plants. Some men passed by me dressed in native clothing and then after a long walk, I reached a building that looked like a palace.

SANTIAGO: Soon I find myself lost in a labyrinth of narrow paths surrounded by a maze of indecipherable landscapes of staircases, terraces, balconies and stone arcades. I hear the neighing of wild horses in the forest and I become hopelessly intoxicated by oil of clove lingering in the air. I come to a beautiful building with filagreed jalousies, bronze studded doors and swirling columns. I realize it's the palace of the Sultan! I keep going. I pass turbaned Muslims, insistent beggars, shrill prostitutes and boys of ebony skin and flashing white teeth who strip me naked with their eyes. I arrive in a courtyard. A shiver of excitement tells me that this used to be the slave market.

END

Orchids in the Moonlight

Carlos Fuentes

ORCHIDS IN THE MOONLIGHT
American Repertory Theatre (Cambridge)
Directed by Joann Green

CHARACTERS

Maria
Dolores
The Fan
The Nubian slave girls
The Mariachi band

SCENE

Venice, the day Orson Welles died.

STAGE NOTES

1) Both women shall be of an indefinite age, somewhere between thirty and six-
ty years old. At certain moments, they will be nearer the first age; at others,
nearer the latter. Throughout the performance, Dolores shall be dressed as a
very stylized Mexican peasant woman: Braids heaped on top of her head, rose-
colored ribbons and bows, bougainvillea flowers covering her ears, a provincial,

calico dress with high boots and a *rebozo* around her shoulders. Maria, on the other hand, will change wardrobe many times. The physical type of the two women shall not be predetermined. Ideally, the roles would have been interpreted by the Mexican actresses Maria Felix and Dolores del Rio. Even more ideally, one and the other would have alternated in the parts. In their absence, the roles can be interpreted by actresses who resemble their two models: tall, svelte, dark, with a notable facial bone structure: high, brilliant cheekbones, sensual lips, quick laughters and angers, challenging chins, eyebrows at odds with each other. This should not be an obstacle for the perversion, if necessary, of having the roles played by two rosy-hued, blonde and plump women. Finally, and in absence of all the former possibilities, the two roles can be played by men.

2) The stage should be conceived as a territory shared although in permanent dispute between the two women. Maria is identified with the style of certain objects and decors: White bear rugs, a white satin divan, a wall of mirrors. Dolores shall put emphasis on her taste for rustic Mexican furniture, paper flowers and piggy banks. Each one of them shall possess, on opposite parts of the stage, a sort of small votive altar in homage to her own person: Photographs, posters of old films, statuettes and other prizes. The common territory shall be the vast clothes closet upstage center, formed by mobile clothes hangers such as those found in hotels and receptions. There hang all the imaginable clothes, from the crinoline to the sarong and from the Mexican folk dress of the *china poblana* to the latest cry from Emmanuel Ungaro. They are all the dresses the two actresses have used on the screen during their very long careers. Left stage down there is a door of metallic, almost penitentiary aspect. Center stage, in front of the wardrobes, a white toilet with a white phone on the toilet seat.

FIRST AND ONLY ACT

(*The illuminated area is down center. Dolores is seated next to a colonial table of light walnut covered with a tablecloth of colored paper and a service of Tlaquepaque earthenware dishes, paper flowers and jug of fruit water. Dolores gazes intensely at the audience during thirty full seconds, first with a certain challenge, arching her eyebrows; but little by little she loses her self-possession, lowers her gaze and looks to left and right as if she awaited someone's arrival. Finally, with trembling hands, she serves herself from a kettle, again looks at the public,.first with challenge, then, again with terror. She lets the cup fall noisily and smothers a shrill scream, in which theatricality is suffocated by authentic tears. She repeats her moan several times, throwing her head back against the chair, lifting her hand to her brow, hiding her mouth behind the other, trembling. From between the clothes hangars upstage appears slowly, but with enormous contained tension, moving like a panther, Maria. Her dark hair falls on the fur collar of a gown of thick brocades, which seems to be copied from the czar's ceremonial gown in Boris Godunov. Maria advances towards Dolores with a growing air of pragmatism; she arranges her coiffure, fixes her gown over her breasts and embraces Dolores from behind. Dolores responds to Maria's embrace caressing her hands and trying to move her face close to that of the other woman.*)

MARIA: It's very early. What's wrong with you?

DOLORES: They didn't recognize me.

MARIA: Again?

DOLORES: I was sitting here, having my breakfast, for more than half an hour, and they did not recognize me. (*Maria sighs and kneels to pick up the cup. The trembling loneliness in Dolores's voice slowly gives way to a very insinuating tone of supremacy. Maria's presence has sufficed.*) Before, yes, before they recognized me.

MARIA: Before? (*Dolores looks scornfully at Maria on her knees.*)

DOLORES: They asked me for my autograph.

MARIA: Before.

DOLORES: I couldn't leave a restaurant without a crowd of people coming together to stare at me, to undress me with their looks, to ask for my autograph, yes . . .

MARIA: We haven't gone out. (*Dolores looks at Maris with a mute interrogation.*) I mean, we are alone.

DOLORES: Where?

MARIA: Here. In our apartment. Our apartment in Venice. (*She pronounces the name of the city with an atrocious English mimesis: Vi-Nais.*)

DOLORES: (*Correcting her patiently.*) Ve-Nice, Ve-Niss. How do you say Nice in French?

MARIA: Nice.

DOLORES: Well then add a vee. Ve-Nice.

MARIA: The fact is that we are here alone and that we have not gone out. Don't go off the track. (*Dolores looks astonished. She stoops to come nearer Maria's face.*)

DOLORES: Don't you see them there in front of us, sitting there, looking at us?

MARIA: Who? (*Dolores dramatically points towards the audience. But her hurt, secret voice does not coincide with her words.*)

DOLORES: They. The public. Our public. Our loyal public who has paid good greenbacks to see us and applaud us. Don't you see them sitting there in front of us? (*Maria laughs, stops herself so as not to offend Dolores and starts removing the Indian sandals from Dolores's feet, shaking her head.*)

MARIA: We should get dressed.

DOLORES: I'm ready.

MARIA: No. I don't want you to go out barefoot again. (*She puts her cheek near Dolores's naked foot.*) You hurt yourself the last time.

DOLORES: A thorn. It was nothing. You took it out. I like it so much when you take care of me. (Maria kisses Dolores's naked foot. Dolores caresses Maria's head.) Where are you going to take me today?

MARIA: First promise me that you won't go out barefoot again. You are not an Indian girl from the Floating Gardens of Xochimilco. You are a respectable lady who might hurt her feet if she goes out barefoot in the street. You promise?

DOLORES: (*Nodding.*) Where are you going to take me today?

MARIA: The beach?

DOLORES: Not on your life! We only sun ourselves by the moonlight.

MARIA: O.K., what's your pleasure? (*She starts putting a pair of antiquated button-up boots on Dolores's feet.*)

DOLORES: I don't want to go to the studios anymore.

MARIA: To the film museum then?

DOLORES: No, no. It's the same thing. They don't recognize us. They say we are not we.

MARIA: It doesn't matter. There's no reason why we should announce ourselves.

DOLORES: The thing is that we don't receive the treatment we used to get. They don't reserve the best seats for us, nothing of the sort . . .

MARIA: I tell you it's of no importance. We sit in the dark and we see ourselves on the screen. *That* is important.

DOLORES: But they don't see us now.

MARIA: Better still. That way we see each other as the others see us. Before we couldn't do that, you remember? Before we were divided, looking at ourselves on the screen as ourselves while the public divided itself, asking itself: Shall we look at them on the screen or shall we look at them looking at themselves on the screen?

DOLORES: I think the more intelligent preferred to look at us while we looked at ourselves.

MARIA: Is that so? Tell me why.

DOLORES: Well, because they could see the film again, many times, and many years after the opening. Whereas they could only see us that night, the night of the premiere, you remember? Wilshire Boulevard . . .

MARIA: The Champs Elysées . . .

DOLORES: The spotlights, the photographs, the autograph-hunters. . .

MARIA: Our cleavages, our pearls, our white foxes.

DOLORES: Our fans.

MARIA: (*Interrupted in her dream.*) Our elephants?

DOLORES: (*With a superior tone.*) No, our admirers, our fanatics, f-a-n-s.

MARIA: Pardon me but I don't speak Tex-Mex.

DOLORES: Ah, you envy me Hollywood, it was always thus.

MARIA: Listen, I never had to disguise myself like you did as a Comanche Indian and talk English. God forbid! Besides, how am I going to envy you something that does not even exist? My success was in Paris, señorita, that really exists, it has existed for two thousand years. You look out the window and just tell me where Hollywood is. We've been living here twenty years now from . . .

DOLORES: (*In a hurry.*) Shhh, shhh. Forget Hollywood, forget Paris, remember where we live now, we have Venice . . .

MARIA: (*Coming to a halt, closing her eyes.*) We'll always have Venice.

DOLORES: If you look out the window you'll see the Grand Canal, yes, the gondolas going by, and the *motoscafi*, here from our apartment in the Palazzo Mocenigo which was Lord Byron's palace in Venice, look out the window, tell me if I am right.

MARIA: (*Without opening her eyes.*) Yes, you are right. We are in Venice. We shall always have Venice.

DOLORES: (*Happily.*) What more do you want? Do you want more?

MARIA: (*Without opening her eyes.*) No. This is a good place to die. There are no prints left on the water. The whole city is a ghost. It does not demand proofs of our existence. Here we shall never know if we have died or not. Venice.

DOLORES: Well, then that's cleared up. Then no one can see us, right? I am right.

MARIA: (*Opening her eyes.*) I'm telling you that today we see ourselves as the others see us, on the screen, you and I very quietly seated amongst all the rest, very decent and well-behaved, right? (*Maria stops putting the shoes on Dolores and stands up, visibly irritated, takes a small black cigar and lights it up. Dolores observes her with curiosity.*)

DOLORES: How irritated you get by your own dreams.

MARIA: They are nightmares when I have them with you.

DOLORES: You'd do better never to close your eyes again. You look so defenseless, you poor thing.

MARIA: (*Laughing.*) I tell you, señora, you must start behaving yourself. We can't go around playing the wanton vamp anymore. We ain't what we used to be. Now we are elderly, decent people. Don't you ever forget it. (*Dolores withdraws into herself, finishes buttoning up her boots with rapidity and precision, while Maria lets her lighted cigar fall into Dolores's breakfast kettle without the latter noticing it.*)

MARIA: (*Striking a pose.*) The orgy is over, Borgy. (*She quickly goes upstage and chooses a get-up of emerald green pants and jacket. While she dresses, Dolores finishes with her shoes. Then she takes a rococco style mirror from her dressing table and puts it in front of her feet, trying to look at the reflection of her shoes as other women look for the reflection of their facial makeup.*)

DOLORES: There's no need for you to throw the book at me. I was always a decent woman.

MARIA: Well I wasn't and I'm not sorry.

DOLORES: It's not a question of being sorry. No one chooses her cradle.

MARIA: Nor her bed either.

DOLORES: Do you really think so?

MARIA: (*Laughing.*) If in my life I have slept in one hundred beds, I assure you I've only chosen ten of them.

DOLORES: And the other ninety?

MARIA: (*Directly.*) They were called hunger, ambition or violence. (*She appears fully dressed and swirls around like a professional model.*) What do you think?

DOLORES: Divine. You look like a deluxe asparagus.

MARIA: (*Laughs and goes toward her wall of mirrors.*) I dress in the color of your envy, darling, to save you the mental effort. Don't go withering on me, bouganinvillea. (*In front of the mirror, she puts on her jewelry. The serpent theme is predominant: bracelets, rings, a necklace in the form of a cobra entwined around Maria's neck.*)

DOLORES: Who gave you all those jewels? Your lover or your husband?

MARIA: Both of them.

DOLORES: You haven't told me where you are going to take me.

MARIA: Guess.

DOLORES: (*Suddenly fearful, she ceases to observe her own feet in the mirror.*) No . . . again . . . again? . . . No . . . you can't . . .

MARIA: You're right. When you see me dressed in black, it means we're not going to a funeral.

DOLORES: (*Violently.*) Give me the paper. (*She holds out her hand. She lets the mirror fall. The glass breaks. Maria reacts slowly: hers is a smothered anger, a caricatural resignation.*)

MARIA: Seven years' bad luck. It's nice to know we won't live them out. Although perhaps that would be the bad luck: to continue here together for another seven years.

DOLORES: Don't change the subject. Give me the newspaper.

MARIA: What for? You know his life by heart.

DOLORES: It isn't that, it's because of Mummy.

MARIA: Mummy?

DOLORES: You're very careless. You leave the newspaper forgotten anywhere, on top of the toilet, Mother comes in to . . . Mother comes in and reads it.

MARIA: So what?

DOLORES: You know she can't stand reading about somebody else's death. I have told you many times . . .

MARIA: Other people's? Listen, honey, I doubt whether she can read the newspaper to find out about her own death. Mummy's a tough one, but not that much.

DOLORES: I have told you to shred the newspaper and flush it down the toilet. Mummy . . .

MARIA: I doubt she will survive herself.

DOLORES: No, something even more painful, she can survive you and me. Us.

MARIA: (*Goes on.*) Although who knows, the old buzzard can even beat us at that game: not to survive us, but to survive herself. Some mothers are like that, you know.

DOLORES: Shhh, don't let her hear you, please, what if she . . . ?

MARIA: I tell you not to worry. This time around, the dead person is younger than Mummy.

DOLORES: (*With a sigh of relief.*) Ah, then she'll be happy.

MARIA: Sure. Let her find out. It isn't she who should be unhappy, but you.

DOLORES: (*Naively.*) Did I know him?

MARIA: You're quite sure it was a man, aren't you?

DOLORES: Did I know *her*, then?

MARIA: Right the first time, failed the second.

DOLORES: I did know him. (*She looks uneasy.*) Don't tell me. I don't want to know. I want to imagine. (*She stands up.*) I'm depressed when I know a former lover dies before I do. They are going to think he was older than I. And I have never had a lover older than myself. I shall be no one's widow. I told all my men: Our life began the moment we met. (*She walks towards the white sofa.*) Now I'm going to rest. Bring me some cotton for my eyes, please. (*She reclines on the white sofa. Maria offers her the cotton pads. Dolores covers her closed eyelids with them.*) Don't you want to rest before we go out?

MARIA: I don't need to.

DOLORES: Excuse me. I was forgetting. How many months did you spend in that sleeping cure in Switzerland?

MARIA: (*With a cold anger.*) I've already told you, it was not a dream, it was a nightmare. I had the nightmare that I had been spending God knows how many years taking care of you, seeing to it that on Mondays, Wednesdays and Fridays you pass the whole day in the dark, with drawn blinds, on your back and with cotton covering your peepers . . .

DOLORES: What a curious way of speaking. You are badly educated.

MARIA: Shut up. Seeing to it that on Tuesdays and Thursdays you spend the whole day in a bathtub full of ice cubes, taking care of you, you taking care of yourself and I wasting away my life in order that on Saturdays and Sundays I can unleash you and you can run like a gazelle through the woods, so that everyone can say, how *does* she do it?, her debut was in 1925!, she danced with don Porfirio Diaz!, she learned Spanish along with la Malinche!, Sir Walter Raleigh was her godfather!

DOLORES: (*Coldly.*) I tire easily. Now I only go out on Sundays, to picnics. Never again at night. You know it, my beautiful Mariquita. (*Pause.*) You aren't recognized either. (*Maria remains as immobile and cold as a statue, facing her mirrors.*)

MARIA: Insult me. (*Dolores remains silent.*) Go on. You have my permission. Take your vengeance on me. (*Dolores clings to an obstinate silence.*) Say whatever you please. Use those sticky names I hate so much, call me beautiful Mariquita, Marucha, Marujita, butterfly, beautiful Maria, call me . . .

DOLORES: Maria Felix. (*Maria more immobile than ever. Then a shudder of gratitude. She turns around. She stops looking at herself in the mirror. She looks at Dolores, who is lying down with her eyes covered. She comes near her.*)

MARIA: Really? You do believe it? (*Dolores nods.*) You're not deceiving me? You're not flattering me? (*Dolores shakes her head.*) For you, I am . . . she? (*Dolores gets up with her eyes blinded, looking like a female Oedipus. She offers her hands in a gesture of beatitude. Maria rushes into her arms. The cotton pads continue to blind Dolores's eyes.*) The most beautiful Maria Felix?

DOLORES: (*Caresses Maria's head.*) The youngest, most beautiful dead woman in the world, a dead woman on horseback, in the arms of her lover the brave *charro*, trotting towards the peak of dead souls . . .

MARIA: (*Leaving Dolores's blind embrace.*) I, the devourer, I, the bandit woman, I, the warrior nun, I, the *cucaracha*.

DOLORES: The woman without a soul. You were a few pounds overweight then.

MARIA: (*Goes up to Dolores and rips the cotton pads from her eyes.*) Look. Look at me well. A goddess does not grow old. When I'm ninety years old, I'll go out in the streets dressed exactly as you see me now, very well made up, very dignified and impeccably groomed, and when the children see me they'll say: "It is she, it is she!" and I will disperse them thus, thrashing them with my cane, you stinking brats, you Peeping Toms, what are you staring at? (*She stops, adopting a haughty pose. Dolores profits from the pause to say precipitately*)

DOLORES: Now you tell me all I was in Hollywood, Bird of Paradise, Carmen . . . (*Now it is Maria who clings to her silence.*) Madame DuBarry . . . (*Maria goes back to her mirror.*) Ramona.

MARIA: Oh yes, I saw that film when I was a child in Guadalajara. (*She gazes at herself in the mirror.*)

DOLORES: You saw me?

MARIA: I saw *her*. (*Long pause. She stops looking at herself in the mirror with a sigh.*) I think that after all I will change to go to the funeral of your former lover, if he can be so called.

DOLORES: Who? Who was it?

MARIA: (*Disappears into the closet.*) How should I know? All this happened before I was born. Mummy told me. Ask her.

DOLORES: Shhh! Don't let her hear you. You know that she . . .

MARIA: Ha! She told me that piece of gossip with great pride, the big idiot.

DOLORES: María! She's our mother.

MARIA: She made an example of you. Why has Lolita managed to maintain herself always so young, so luscious?

DOLORES: Mummy dearest . . .

MARIA: Because no one has ever touched her.

DOLORES: Nine months in her womb . . .

MARIA: That is, not that she is a virgin, no . . . (*Dolores embraces herself with anguish and proceeds to imitate the acts Maria describes as Maria dresses again outside the gaze of the audience.*) . . . but no one has ever touched her breast. That is why she has these beautiful, bouncy tits of a fifteen-year-old with happy rose-colored nipples that no one has ever messed around with, like this. No one has ever laid flat upon her, she's never felt eighty kilos of a macho on top of her, no, everything with her has always been so delicate, always sideways, like this . . . (*Maria appears totally dressed in black, exaggeratedly black, old-fashioned, funereal clothes: a long, black skirt, a high black blouse buttoned up to her ears, veils. She is adjusting a pearl necklace. When she sees her, Dolores remains immobile.*) La señora has no child, she has never given birth, her tummy is not like custard cream, her ass doesn't wobble like a flan. La señora, I say, is perfect: A dark silky Venus, la señora . . . la señora has left all of us with our peepers creepers.

DOLORES: What do you know about these things? You have no idea what it meant to live in Hollywood, to be a Latin in Hollywood, fighting against prejudice first, against advancing age immediately, why do you scoff at age?, it is the climbing vine, the invisible leprosy of an actress and those who had children had to hide them or negate their existence and hate them, beat them, a star with a growing son, giving her away, thirty years, forty years, an actress must be like a goddess, you've said it, yes, a goddess, not someone humiliated, forced to go to the supermarket and then come back burdened with cans and steaks and oranges and cauliflowers . . . I wanted to be weightless, winged, a dark flame.

MARIA: Nothing hurt Dolores.

DOLORES: I think of her from time to time. Her light was brighter than anyone else's. When it goes out, it shall be night in the world.

MARIA: (*Observes her with a sardonic smile.*) You stole that from one of my pictures.

DOLORES: (*With resignation.*) It's probable. God wrote our destinies but not, unfortunately, our scenarios.

MARIA: And the directors we had!

DOLORES: Apart from Buñuel and Welles.

MARIA: Who used us as furniture.

DOLORES: No, he used me as an animal. I was the leopard woman in *Journey into Fear*. (*She growls, amused.*)

MARIA: Darling, at least a panther has history . . .

DOLORES: Leopard.

MARIA: Panther, leopard, cats in any case: at least you know what to imitate. But what about those directors who only told me, "You know, Maria, give me a lot of Ummmm, eh?, you know, lots of Ummmmm," "What is that, señor?" "What I'm saying, Ummmm."

DOLORES: Ummmm.

MARIA: Ummmm. (*The two women start a parodical game of UMMMS, inventing scenes and dramatic situations until, without ceasing to UMMM, in crescendo, they embrace, they kiss and from love they instantly pass to hate, they make believe they are clawing at each other, they fall, they roll on the stage floor and the UMMMS are no longer able to designate fury or laughter, but a sort of constant commerce between both. Maria is the first to separate herself and stand up, shaking off the dust from her black clothes, replacing the veils over her face, arranging herself in front of the mirror.*)

MARIA: When I'm ninety years old, I'll go out into the street dressed exactly the way you see me now, very well groomed, and I shall disperse the curious with my cane, what are you looking at, what are you looking at?

DOLORES: You repeat yourself, darling.

MARIA: (*Starts to lose her bearings with fury and tears.*) What are you looking at? Am I no longer the woman you desire, the most beautiful woman in the world, the sexpot who excited your fathers, your grandfathers? Am I no longer the most dazzling hunk of flesh your sad eyes ever had the good luck to see? Is there no one anymore to write boleros for me, to send orchids and pâté de foie by hydroplane to me every afternoon to the location at Lake Pátzcuaro? Is there no longer a single bullfighter who will dedicate a bull to me? (*From the floor, Dolores has been watching her with growing skepticism, shaking her head.*)

DOLORES: No, no no no. she would *never* say such things.

MARIA: Do you really think so?

DOLORES: Of course not. It's as if I said I am no longer the little girl who went to the Convent of the Sacred Heart and learnt to write with a spider's scrawl, I am no longer the teenager who married a Mexican aristocrat at seventeen and who scandalized all the well-to-do families by abandoning him at nineteen in order to become a shining star of the cinema.

MARIA: But it's true.

DOLORES: Ah, so it's true. Then you admit *I am* Dolores del Río?

MARIA: Don't invent things I haven't said. I said that was true for her life, not for yours, Lolita, because you are not she.

DOLORES: I don't like to insist, my darling, but I would like to have you understand that both of them only live—we only live—on the screen, in the image of Doña Bárbara and Maria Candelaria, not in anyone's private biography.

MARIA: You said I was Maria. You admitted it.

DOLORES: And you did not answer in kind. Please forgive my lie. I praise your sincerity. (*The two women observe each other for a moment.*)

MARIA: Have you read today's paper?

DOLORES: No. You beat me to it. That's how you found out about his death before I did, do you remember?

MARIA: That appeared in yesterday's paper.

DOLORES: But his funeral . . .

MARIA: Already took place. Yesterday.

DOLORES: Then you fooled me.

MARIA: I don't see why, precious.

DOLORES: You are all dressed up in black.

MARIA: Excuse me. We are going to the cemetery today, of course we are, to present our respects to the deceased, who was buried yesterday, yes. Do you want me to go dressed as if for a carnival, like you? (*Dolores now comes out of her sleepy vacillation on the floor, stands up and occupies the place in front of the mirror as if the news of the death awakens in her something more than the flirtatious instinct.*)

DOLORES: I carry my pains in my heart, not in my clothes.

MARIA: Ah, the pains of Dolores are not the pains of her rags.

DOLORES: Simplicity is the sign of a wealthy cradle.

MARIA: No, madame. If you're a swell, you have a right to dress as a swell and show the riffraff that you are the swell. You will do me the immense favor of dressing up like a Christmas tree. And if you don't, why the hell all the sweat if you're to end your years, with all your millions, dressed as a humble little peasant?

DOLORES: You're not capable of understanding.

MARIA: Why?

DOLORES: Because it cost you to make it to the top. Because you have a desperate need to stand out from them.

MARIA: From whom do you mean?

DOLORES: You just said it, the riffraff, the ugly little people. Because, in one word, my darling, you do not have aristocratic qualities.

MARIA: And that's why I should go around dressed like a ranch hand, like you?

DOLORES: You would never understand it. These are things one suckles from birth.

MARIA: I won't compete with you in that department. I understand your wanting to disguise yourself as the humblest little Indian girl in order to have them forgive you. That I understand.

DOLORES: Nobody's menacing me.

MARIA: They're menacing us. And even if you dress up like a piñata, they're going to discover you. Or do you think that the Reds are going to hang the bankers and are going to spare us who have made more money than any banker?

DOLORES: We are national glories.

MARIA: Tell that to your pal Madame DuBarry.

DOLORES: Besides, besides we are far from Mexico, there's not going to be any revolution here . . .

MARIA: Here. In Venice? Did I pronounce it well this time?

DOLORES: Here. In Venice.

MARIA: Where we have retired with our bags full of the gold we won in the national cinema of Mexico.

DOLORES: We brought hard foreign currency into the country. That makes us quits. Besides Madama DuBarry resembled you, honey, not me.

MARIA: Whoa there! Do we live in life or on the screen? You are Madame DuBarry because your idol interpreted her on the screen. Biographies don't count, what counts is Madame DuBarry who is she who is she who is you, ça va?

DOLORES: With the qualification that I am Dolores del Rio.

MARIA: Read today's paper.

DOLORES: (Alarmed.) What does it say?

MARIA: Listen to this. It says here that Maria Felix flew to France yesterday to be present at the Grand Prix at Deauville where one of her fillies is going to run.

DOLORES: Doesn't surprise me. That woman's fondness for the sport of kings is well known.

MARIA: Wait a minute. It then goes on to say that Dolores Del Rio has accepted to play the part of an ancient woman of the Seminole tribe who is Marlon

Brando's grandmother in a production by Metro . . .

DOLORES: I, the grandmother of Marlon Brando? But that's a lie. I would never accept such a deal. Why, Marlon Brando could be my father, I . . . But these two ladies are a pair of imposters! They are making the world believe they are us!

MARIA: When I tell you that we are being menaced . . .

DOLORES: Well, I mean, of course, we should unite forces, forget old feuds, our dissimilar origins . . .

MARIA: Shhh! But don't let Mummy find out.

DOLORES: You're right, shhh. She doesn't understand that we are already grown up and can make our own decisions.

MARIA: No, what she would not understand is your crack about our dissimilar origins.

DOLORES: Bah, the fathers can be different.

MARIA: Yes, little sister.

DOLORES: Shhh, don't let her hear us . . .

MARIA: Mummy?

DOLORES: No, silly, the Fourth Power, the gossip columnists, what would they say?

MARIA: That it is time to take tea.

DOLORES: It is a good English custom.

MARIA: They also drink tea in France, you know.

DOLORES: Are we going to start that all over again?

MARIA: To each his spiritual home.

DOLORES: Well, I only speak English at teatime.

MARIA: And I only speak French. (*Maria sits down next to the table. Dolores, standing up, prepares the two cups and picks up the kettle.*)

DOLORES: (*With an English accent.*) How do you prefer your tea, with lemon or with milk?

MARIA: (*With a French accent.*) I preferz eet sans lemon et sans meelk.

DOLORES: (*With an English accent.*) I'm so sorry, we do not have it without lemon or without milk.

MARIA: (*French accent.*) Alors sans ze zugar, please. (*Dolores serves tea in Maria's cup.*)

DOLORES: (*English accent.*) Without white sugar or without brown sugar?

MARIA: (*French accent.*) Non, I priferz eet hot. (*Dolores serves herself a cup of tea. She drinks it. Maria observes her with her own cup of tea on her knees. Dolores violently spits out the tea. Maria covers her mouth like a little girl who has been caught at her prank. Dolores furiously rubs her mouth.*)

DOLORES: Ashes, ashes . . . (*Dolores plunges her hand into the kettle and brings out Maria's wet cigar. Maria has advanced downstage. She stops at the end of the stage. She moves her hand and arm as if she were throwing apart a curtain and looks far away out of the window.*)

MARIA: Venice . . .

DOLORES: (*With hysterical fury.*) I'm speaking to you! You threw your cigar into my kettle!

MARIA: What am I looking at? The campanile of San Marco or an oil derrick?

DOLORES: You have put your wet, stinking, old fag in my beverage!

MARIA: (*Looking impertinently towards her imaginary Venice.*) On what cupolas is the sun shining? Santa Maria Maggiore or Howard Johnson's motel?

DOLORES: I hate you! Ashes in my breakfast! That's what you are! Ashes disguised as flame!

MARIA: Don't you understand me, Lolita? Where are we, in Venezia or in Venice, are we overlooking the Grand Canal or Centinela Boulevard? (*Each one of these options scares Dolores more than the other. She ends up serving herself a new cup of tea and drinking it with an expression of bitter nausea.*)

DOLORES: (*With disgust.*) All right. We are in Venice, overlooking the Grand Canal. Can't you hear the gondoliers singing? "Bandera rossa, color' del vin' . . ."

MARIA: (*With cold obstinacy.*) Finish your breakfast. You must build up your strength. (*Dolores drinks, closing her eyes as if she were drinking castor oil. Then she wipes her lips with her hand.*) Very good, Lolita. I thought I heard another song through the open window. (*She hums the tango "Orchids in the Moonlight."*)

DOLORES: (*With an abrupt gesture, abrupt yet soft, recognizing herself for the moment in Maria's power.*) All right! That's enough . . .

MARIA: (*Stepping back from the window.*) Good. We have now restored ourselves. So tell me, what should we do with those two imposters?

DOLORES: Denounce them.

MARIA: On what grounds?

DOLORES: That . . . that . . . you know what . . . that they are . . .

MARIA: Say it: That they are us?

DOLORES: You say it, you say it.

MARIA: (*Seriously, yet with an edge of mockery.*) Shhh . . . but don't let Mummy find out. (*Dolores trembles. Maria arranges her black veils in front of the mirror. Dolores looks around the apartment. She goes towards the paper flowers and caresses them. She then takes a piggy bank and sits downstage with the piggy in her arms, on the floor, like a woman vendor in a popular Mexican marketplace.*)

DOLORES: (*To the piggy.*) Shhhhhh . . . Don't let Mummy find out.

MARIA: I tell you not to worry. I make the papers disappear every day.

DOLORES: What do you do with them? It's not true. You leave them lying around. I've told you to flush them down the toilet.

MARIA: Don't worry. I don't collect them. She doesn't see them. She doesn't know who dies.

DOLORES: You do well. She'd be very sad if she read the obituaries of her contemporaries, of her friends, of the people she lived with.

MARIA: No, I don't do it for that reason. I simply don't want her to read the obituaries of people younger than she. I want to make her suffer through ignorance that there are people younger than she who die all the time.

DOLORES: But you would make her suffer if you also let her know that there are people her own age who die, wouldn't you?

MARIA: I think she's really going to suffer more by ignoring that people die and finding out one of these days that there is no one left in the world, no one but she, alone: Mummy.

DOLORES: (*Visibly frightened.*) No one? Not even we?

MARIA: (*Starts playing with her black veils, dancing like a funereal Salome.*) No one. Our vengeance shall be to die before she does.

DOLORES: But . . . but don't you think she already gives us up for dead?

MARIA: (*Notoriously arching her eyebrow.*) She's not the only one who thinks so, honey. Or what have we been really talking about all this time, you tell me? (*Maria is now a real whirlpool of black veils.*) No one remembers us, no one remembers us, no one remembers us . . .

DOLORES: You cried, Maria. You said it: We are no longer the desired women, nobody dedicates their bulls or their boleros to us . . . (*She hums.*) "Remember Acapulco, remember those nights, beautiful Maria, Maria of my soul . . ." (*Maria advances with all her black veils towards Dolores. She dances around her sister, wreathing her in veils.*)

MARIA: Shut up! I'm not talking about that, I'm talking about Mummy. For her, we died the day the first hair appeared in our armpits.

DOLORES: Such vulgarity. I don't know how I can live with you. (*She wraps herself up in the Mexican rebozo, without letting go of the piggy.*)

MARIA: Yes! As soon as our first menstruation came around, she ceased to speak to us, you know it well. She hated us because we grew up, because we grew old, because we were not her little precious babies, her little darling daughters, forever. (*She lifts the veils for a moment in order to mimic.*) Do you remember the way she used to imitate us, the way she used to tell her friends about the funny things we did? (*Mimics.*) "Lolita doesn't like it if we call her thenolita, she cries and she screams saying I ain't no thenolita, I'm a fat juicy baby!"

DOLORES: (*Continues the mimicry, but talking to the little pig.*) "This little pig went to market, this little pig stayed at home . . . "

MARIA: "I was a fat juicy baby."

DOLORES: "This little pig . . . " (*She abruptly changes her song and her tone and continues humming the melody of the tango "Orchids in the Moonlight." Maria looks like a buzzard who flies down on poor Dolores, waving her black veils.*)

MARIA: Shut up! Don't sing that song! I'm telling you that she hates us because we're no longer her little girls with pink ribbons and ruffled bloomers! Ruffled, oh yes, but above all without blood stains!

DOLORES: (*Takes her hand to her head and touches the ribbons.*) I am! I am!

MARIA: You fool! Haven't you realized that she doesn't want to see us again . . . as long as we live?

DOLORES: But . . . but then it's never going to matter to her if we die.

MARIA: Yes, oh yes, it *is* going to matter.

DOLORES: Why? Haven't you just said that . . . ?

MARIA: You trust me. You just trust me and keep your eyes wide open, 'cause this one (*she points at herself with a finger*) is going out of sight.

DOLORES: I don't understand you. (*Dolores sighs and arises.*) But I do agree that you have a much keener intuition than I do, even if you *are* ignorant and badly educated . . . (*She puts the piggy down on the table.*) Life, you know, is very different when one has read books . . . (*She hugs herself in a smug fashion*) . . . when one has cultivated the, how should one call it?, the garden of the soul . . . (*Maria has disappeared anew into the clothes closet.*)

MARIA: Don't be pretentious. You've never read a book in your life. (*A long silence. Dolores silently goes towards the white telephone which is on top of the toilet.*)

DOLORES: It's true. It makes me sad to think of it. That's why I count so much on you. Because even if you know nothing you do have a good memory. (*She moves her hand toward the phone. She is frightened and draws her hand back.*)

MARIA: (*Laughing from the closet.*) What would you do without me, bougainvillea? Frankly, how would you prove your own existence? (*Dolores hears this and dares to put her hand on the telephone.*) Let's see, who directed *Flying Down to Rio* (*Dolores hangs her head but leaves her hand on the phone.*)

DOLORES: Archie Mayo, of course, who doesn't know that . . . ?

MARIA: (*With an incredulous voice.*) You don't know who directed that picture where you dance . . . what, what is the name of the dance you dance, Lolita, what you dance in *Flying Down to Rio* . . . ?

DOLORES: (*Insecure.*) No, I don't remember . . . a bolero, Maria Bonita, remember Acapulco, Archie Mayo, Busby Berkeley . . . (*She lifts the receiver as if she clung to a floating timber, keeps the receiver in the air, without daring to put it close to her ear.*)

MARIA: (*Laughs.*) You say you are Dolores del Rio and you don't remember that, you don't . . . ?

DOLORES: (*Presses the receiver against her mouth.*) It's because it was so hot on the sets, the klieg lamps, the confinement, you see these were the first talkies and they were afraid of noises on the set, they isolated us, they suffocated us, the lights, the playback, the tango, the passion, we were suffocating orchids, orchids burnt out by the spotlights . . . Orson Welles and Ginger Rogers dancing the tango . . . Such memories! Such confusion!

(*Music: "Orchids in the Moonlight." Maria comes out from the closet dressed in white, clinging satin — that is, dressed as Dolores del Rio in* Flying Down to Rio. *Dolores lets go of the telephone, without being able to put the receiver in its place before Maria can see her. The receiver hangs inertly and one should distinguish a very distinct buzz behind the tango music. The buzz will grow and grow until it becomes unbearable and drowns out the tango. Now Maria approaches Dolores with stylized tango steps, she takes her by the waist and both of them dance, Maria with fervor and joy, Dolores with her initial fright surmounted at last by the happiness of dancing in Maria's arms. The dance ends with an elegant turn by Dolores with her arm on high, detained that way by Maria for an instant. The buzz from the telephone becomes unbearable. Maria lets go of Dolores. Dolores doesn't change her position, she remains like a statue with her arm up high. Maria goes to the toilet seat and, in a routine fashion, rehooks the telephone.)*

MARIA: *(Cuttingly.)* What were you doing with the phone in your hand? *(Dolores continues in her fixed position.)* You know we do not touch the telephone. *(She glowers at Dolores and goes towards her.)* You know that the telephone is there like the apple in Paradise as a temptation. The first one of us who makes a call shall be damned, do you understand! Damned, do you remember, do you understand?

DOLORES: A temptation . . .

MARIA: You'll go to hell, *capiche?*, the illusion shall break, we shall no longer be where we are, but in . . .

DOLORES: *(With an attempt at coyness to interrupt Maria's thoughts.)* To hell did you say, with the devil? He has prettier names, you know. Beelzebub, Mephistopheles, Lucifer, Asmodeus.

MARIA: Everything has more than one name. But you, when shall you call a spade a spade?

DOLORES: *(With the same tone of frivolous excuse.)* A spade is a kike is a dago is a spick is a frog is a Polack is a . . .

MARIA: *(Interrupting violently.)* A greaser, madame, a dirty Chicano greaser!

DOLORES: *(With fright.)* Yes . . .

MARIA: "Orchids in the Moonlight." That's what the tango was called. But you don't remember it. You're not she.

DOLORES: No, you remember for me, Mariquita, you do me that favor, I'm dependent on your good memory, it's not that I am not I, it's not that I don't exist, no, it's that . . . I forget things.

MARIA: At least say thanks.

DOLORES: Thanks.

MARIA: That's the way I like it, my wild Mexican flower.

DOLORES: *(Aggressively.)* Who directed *French Can Can?* Quick!

MARIA: *(With her back towards the public and Dolores, amused.)* Jean Renoir. My white little teddy bear.

DOLORES: *(Even more aggressively.)* What's your son's name? Quick! *(A silence. Maria remains with her back to the public. She hangs her head slightly.)* How many times did you see him as a child? Tell me! What did you play with him? Did you ever go on all fours with your baby? Tell me! Mary had a little lamb, here comes the A, here comes the B, did you teach him the games, the riddles? A cold mother, unhinged by success, egoistic, perverse, how many times did your bald, fat juicy baby find you in the arms of a man who was not his father, eh? (*Maria continues with her back to the public, motionless. Dolores, flushed by her audacity, runs toward the phone posed on top of the toilet, picks up the receiver, quickly dials a number and waits for the answer, twirling the tassels of her shawl and with her tongue firmly stuck in her cheek—a grotesque image of some of the roles she played, a caricature of her Madame X.*) Hello? With whom do I have the pleasure? . . . Oh, I see . . . Could I speak to . . . ? (*Maria comes out of her paralysis, violently goes towards Dolores and takes the receiver away from hand, even menacing her with it. Dolores covers her head as she shrieks with laughter. Maria hesitates between putting the receiver to her ear or putting it back in its place.*) Go on, don't be afraid, listen . . . listen to yourself . . . it is she. (*Maria quickly hangs up.*)

MARIA: You have no reason to hurt me this way. I had a son because I had the courage to have a son. I have atoned for my omission. I have purged my guilt.

DOLORES: (*Wildly gestures, imitating a movie director.*) Cut! Print it! Wrap it up!

MARIA: You poor thing. You have nothing for which to be forgiven.

DOLORES: Again, F for failure. I shall tell you my story. So that my son could go to school, I took to the streets, I was a taxi dancer, a fly-by-night, a street-walker, you remember? To pay for my little boy's university career, I became spent, old, used-up, but my son grew in honor and promise, as tall and strong as an oak, as dignified as a king, as beautiful as the sun and he was going to marry señorita O'Higgins, can you beat that, he was going to marry a girl from Puebla descended from emigré Irishmen, Baby O'Higgins, related to generals and presidents, heiress to millions and millions in rubber, bottled waters and sport sheets: my boy born from the fog was going to enter Mexican high society thanks to my sacrifice, Maria. I did see the wedding from the street, in the Lomas de Chapultepec, under the drizzle, I the old whore, poor, dark, fucked-up, toothless, bathless, I without Social Security, I without an American Express credit card, I the last of the abandoned women, looking at my son marry a Puebla girl with Irish origins . . . (*Maria advances, trying to interrupt her.*) Let me finish! I let you tell and retell your sinister soap operas, your Aztec versions of Sappho and Camille.

MARIA: But my melodramas end differently each time, Sappho is safe and Camille marries her father-in-law, which is what both wanted from the very beginning. And they lived happily ever after. You do nothing but repeat the same soap opera all the time . . .

DOLORES: The policeman came up to me, pushed me, said this is not your place, old hag, scram, out of here.

MARIA: This is not your place.

DOLORES: What?

MARIA: It's the same thing they told us when we crossed the border.

DOLORES: What are you talking about?

MARIA: When we left Mexico.

DOLORES: Oh yes, when we retired to live our autumn days in Venice.

MARIA: Venice.

DOLORES: Very good. That's the way to pronounce it.

MARIA: Venice, California. (*Dolores stops in sheer terror. Nervously she takes one of the dresses from the closet and starts ironing it, disguising her anguish with this activity. Maria smiles as she sees her do this.*) Aren't we far from the place where we were born.

DOLORES: We shouldn't complain, Mariquita . . . Venice is . . .

MARIA: (*Brutally.*) A suburb of Los Angeles.

DOLORES: Maria! I called you Maria . . . (*Imploringly.*) I did not prick the balloons of your illusion, I called you Maria, I didn't say you were a . . .

MARIA: The same as I, a retired Chicana living in a stinking suburb of L.A. . . . . (*She walks downstage and repeats the gesture of drawing open a curtain.*)

DOLORES: No . . . (*She lets the iron fall, she knocks over the ironing board, she stops without daring to touch Maria.*)

MARIA: Here's your Venice. A fake Venice, invented by a crazy gringo so as to make other crazy gringos believe that they lived in a second Renaissance: look at the flaking columns, look, look at the canals buried under the garbage, look at the gondolas next to the Ferris wheel and the carousel, look at your fucking Venice, go on living on illusions, Dolores . . .

DOLORES: Dolores yes, not Venice, no, but Dolores yes, please?

MARIA: Look at your Venice. It's up for auction.

DOLORES: We came looking for Hollywood, you remember?

MARIA: Yes, like two elephants in search of their cemetery. When nobody offered us any films in Mexico, we decided to come to die in Hollywood, to bury ourselves in the fresh cement of the Chinese Theater. (*Pause.*) They didn't want us, not even here. Old Chicanas, old movie stars? To the trash can. Everything here is a trash can. Nothing should be useful for more than ten days.

DOLORES: (*Dizzily.*) Orchids in the moonlight . . .

MARIA: Everything becomes old as soon as it's used for the first time. The automobile, the mixer, the T.V. set, and the rags we use. The heart we bear.

DOLORES: The stars.

MARIA: Look outside, Dolores. Venice, California, the same as Moscow, Texas; Paris, Kentucky; Rome, Wisconsin and Mexico, Missouri: The dress has been borrowed, the names have been auctioned, the illusions are going to the highest bidder. Yes, you *are* Dolores del Rio . . .

DOLORES: Maria! (*She makes a gesture as if to approach Maria. Then she stops.*)

MARIA: Dolores del Rio Mississippi. Maria de los Angeles Felix Florida. Something else, no longer they, no longer we. A mirage. A nostalgia. Two crazy Chicanas . . . (*Dolores embraces Maria. Both remain standing up.*)

DOLORES: . . . who love each other, who nourish each other in the desert, yes, who came looking for what had never existed . . .

MARIA: Your Hollywood . . .

DOLORES: The dream factory . . . that dreamed us . . .

MARIA: The place of illusion . . . that turned out to be one more illusion . . .

DOLORES: Our mirror . . .

MARIA: Our mirage . . . (*Embracing, they sing "Orchids in the Moonlight" in a duo.*)

MARIA & DOLORES: "When orchids bloom in the moonlight
And lovers vow to be true;
I still can dream in the moonlight,
Of one dear night that we knew.

There's a dream in the moonbeams,
Up on the sea of blue;
But the moonbeams that fall,
Only seem to recall,
Love is all, love is you."

(*The song is brutally interrupted by a noise: a mixture of heartbeat and knocking.*)

DOLORES: Creepers! (*The two women embrace even more.*) Madre mia de Guadalupe . . . (*Dolores separates herself from Maria and repeatedly strikes her breast.*) Santo, santo, santo. (*The strikes on Dolores's breast amplify themselves and become solid: someone is knocking at the door. The two women embrace again.*)

MARIA: (*Overcoming the situation as she gulps.*) Who can it be?

DOLORES: Mummy . . .

MARIA: I tell you she has forgotten us.

DOLORES: And if suddenly she remembered?

MARIA: What are you more afraid of, that she remembers us or that she forgets us?

DOLORES: I don't know, I don't know . . . (*The knuckles insist on the door.*)

MARIA: Did you warn someone?

MARIA: (*With a cold anger.*) When you phoned a while ago, stupid. Didn't I tell you that . . . ?

DOLORES: No, I swear it, I was faking, it was another number, it was not her number.

MARIA: Another number? Listen, who are you calling behind my back?

DOLORES: Not her, believe me.

MARIA: I believe you. Are you calling a man?

DOLORES: How can you think that?

MARIA: I can think it.

DOLORES: Don't even think it.

MARIA: Okay. I don't think it. I intuit it, I smell it, I smell it and it smells like a dead rat, like an all-too-living skunk. Who are you two-timing me with, you little Xochimilco sailor girl? (*The knocking becomes more insistent. Dolores nervously glances towards the door.*)

DOLORES: Any number, I dialed the first number that came into my head, I swear it on this . . . (*She makes the sign of the cross with her fingers and kisses it. Maria moves away from Dolores.*)

MARIA: Then . . . *anyone* may be knocking at our door, the first slob that came into your head, you fucked-up imbecile . . .

DOLORES: But how was I to know? I didn't give him the address . . . He couldn't find out . . .

MARIA: I'll inform you. One can call the police and have a number traced, a number that has just called us, and then an address can be put on that number and even a name: our names!

DOLORES: But why was this gentleman going to go to all that trouble to find out the whereabouts of two women he doesn't even know?

MARIA: Two old Chicanas languishing in the Venetian suburb of a Hollywood that no longer exists.

DOLORES: Ay, that never existed.

MARIA: Two retired old mad women, right?, two stars that are burning out, two floozies, from the old Klondike days, right?

DOLORES: Oh, we're not that, don't say that, our pictures live, they do not burn out, Enamorada, The Bird of Paradise, you yourself have sai . . . (*Maria decisively leaves Dolores with the words in her mouth and walks with a martial step towards the door. Courage seems to fail her for an instant. She takes a deep breath, stretches out her hand and opens the door. With his fist in the air, about to knock again, is a thin young man, wearing horn-rimmed spectacles and carrying a bouquet of flowers in the same fist with which he knocked. He is dressed like a nice young man of the forties: striped shirt, bow tie, a double-breasted suit with a Prince of Wales pattern and black shoes. A felt hat with the front brim raised in the style of the news reporters of the times. It is the only revealing detail. In fact, the newcomer looks like a disquieting mixture of Harold Lloyd and James Cagney. Under his arm, he carries a can of film and in his hand a film projector.*

Maria and Dolores look with amazement at the young man. They look at each other, Maria asking with a movement of her head if this might be the taxi driver who is in love with Dolores, Dolores denying with her head, trying to make Maria understand that she has never seen him before, inquiring if, rather, he might not be Maria's secret lover. The young man hasn't got enough arms to sustain his flowers without damage. He is carrying a bouquet of forget-me-nots, the canned film under one arm, the movie projector and now the newspaper, which he picks up, before coming in or even being invited to come in, with the same hand as he holds the bou-

quet and then puts under his chin.)

FAN: *Pardon me ... I'm not an octopus ...* (*He offers the flowers to Dolores but the newspaper slips from his chin and falls on the floor. The young man is attentive above all to his canned film, saving it from any accident. He places the film projector on the floor and at last he is able to take off his hat. Dolores nervously stoops to pick up the paper, the young man does so at the same time. They bump their heads. Maria sees to it that Dolores does not pick up the newspaper by stepping on her hand. Dolores represses a cry of pain. The young man tries to help her and his hat falls on the floor. But he never lets go of the can.*)

MARIA: (*To Dolores.*) Don't be so curious. (*The young man picks up his hat and shakes the dust off it.*)

DOLORES: (*Nursing her hurt hand.*) I wanted to know. I wanted to read the news of his death. (*She looks towards the young visitor.*) Besides, this is not he.

FAN: Beg your pardon?

MARIA: It's not he? But he's offering the flowers to you. Go on, take them. (*But even before Dolores can touch them, even when she has timidily put forward her hand, Maria interrupts her. Dolores stands up.*)

DOLORES: I have a right, I have a right to a beau of my own! (*Maria observes this with irony.*) I won't spend all my life going to the supermarket on the corner of Rialto and Pacific or hiking all the way to Olvera Street only to find your preferred Mexican dishes, you devourer but not of men, you devourer of tacos and tamales!

MARIA: (*Takes no notice of Dolores. She addresses herself to the Fan.*) Come on, señor, give her the dried-up day of the dead flowers before they really wither.

FAN: They are forget-me-nots. (*He gives the bouquet to Dolores and blushes.*) Ever since I saw you in *The Jungle of Fire* I can't forget you, señorita.

DOLORES: (*In ecstasy.*) A fan!

MARIA: (*Solicitous.*) Do you need air?

DOLORES: A fanatic, you ignoramus, an enthusiast, a groupie . . . (*She modestly sniffs at the flowers.*) A fastidious follower of my artistic endeavors.

FAN: So it is, señorita, at your feet. I have seen everything you have filmed, with one exception.

DOLORES: (*Flirtatiously.*) Then you have seen more than I. But come in, come in, make yourself at home . . . (*The Fan enters the set.*)

FAN: I did not expect more from your proverbial politeness. When in the film called *The Little House* you invite Roberto Cañedo to visit you in . . .

DOLORES: (*To Maria, in an authoritarian voice.*) Girl, will you please close the door?

FAN: Exquisite! That is the way, in the film called *Bougainvillea*, you treat your Indian maid servant. (*Maria, without batting an eyelash, closes the door. The noise on closing is that of a prison door, a metallic sound. We hear the clang and even an insinuation of chains and inviolable locks. Maria rests herself, with her hands joined behind her back, against the door. But nothing can separate Dolores and her Fan from their pavan of courtesies and reminiscences.)*

DOLORES: And what might that gap in your culture be?

FAN: I beg your pardon?

DOLORES: I mean that picture of mine you have not been capable, as yet, of . . . admiring.

FAN: Oh! Well it's nothing less than your film version of *Carmen*, directed by Raoul Walsh in 1926, based on the homonymous novel by Mérimée and on the celebrated opera by Bizet. (*He breathes.*) The only extant copy is in the archives of the Cinematheque at Prague, the capital of Czechoslvakia.

DOLORES: (*Smiling.*) Aaaaah! (*Dolores takes a flower from the bouquet and puts it between her teeth. Music: The "Seguidilla" from the Bizet opera. The actress imitates the vibrating ferocity of Dolores del Rio playing the role of Carmen: her hair is undone, thrown forward in order to cover her face, then thrown back to show it: her movements are those of a savage little tiger until, exhausted, she plants herself torero-fashion in the center of the stage as the music mounts to the martial crescendo of the "Toreador March" and the fan screams.*)

FAN: Olé, olé! (*Maria, still leaning against the door, makes the Roman Imperial gesture of condemning to death: the thumb signalling down. But nothing can repress the enthusiasm Dolores and her Fan have mutually given themselves.*)

FAN: *Ramona, 1927. (Dolores drapes herself in an Andalusian shawl she takes from the closet and walks around with little steps, evoking the virgin girl of a catholic town. Music: the song "Ramona.")*

FAN: *The Bird of Paradise, 1932. (Dolores puts a Hawaiian lei around her neck and dances hula-hula to Hawaiian music.)*

FAN: *Flying Down to Rio, 1933. (Music: the tango "Orchids in the Moonlight." Dolores starts to dance it alone. Then she sees Maria. She stops. She rushes towards her. She embraces her. She tries to draw her away from the door, almost sobbing.*

DOLORES: Pardon me . . . pardon me . . . (*The two women take each other in their arms and adopt a stylized but immobile posture of tango dancers. The Fan observes them open-mouthed, without ever letting go of his can. Repeating.*) Pardon me, pardon me . . . (*Maria firmly holds Dolores. The music ends.*)

MARIA: What should I pardon you for?

DOLORES: You know.

MARIA: You flatter me, I don't understand anything.

DOLORES: (*Looking flirtatiously towards the Fan.*) I am still remembered. I have still got one fan in this world. He . . . he searched for me? (*She observes Maria with compassion.*) While you, my beautiful little Maria . . . (*Maria, with slow deliberation, steps away from Dolores, picks up the paper from the floor and starts browsing through it. The Fan feels he is responsible for the tension and tries to find a way of relieving it.*)

FAN: *Caramba . . . por Dios . . .* please forgive me . . . but I had no idea that you . . . two . . . of all people . . . lived here together . . .

MARIA: (*Sighs as she picks up the paper.*) The original version of the odd couple.

FAN: (*Laughs.*) The odd couple? In an L.A. suburb . . .

MARIA: The Venuses of Venice, yes, sir.

FAN: (*To Maria.*) If I'd only known, I would not have missed bringing you your flowers as well, señorita . . .

MARIA: (*Stops reading with mock wonder.*) You flatter me, señor. (*To Dolores.*) You see. You won an admirer. But the two of us regained a public.

FAN: (*To Maria.*) Believe me, there also exists a most exclusive club of your admirers, your true fans.

MARIA: How exclusive? More than two members?

FAN: Few, it's true, but select.

MARIA: Recalcitrants, eh? (*With these words she dismisses the Fan and addresses herself to Dolores with the open newspaper in her hands.*) I think you should know, honey, that necrological news is prepared with great anticipation. As soon as you show promise in any activity—politician, artist, banker, gangster, *fille au pair*, child prodigy, medium or matricide—the paper opens a file with all the facts of your life, in case you should suddenly kick the bucket. If you are not fortunate enough to die young, the facts just go on accumulating, the dates, the prizes, the film titles, the years at Alcatraz, the gossip, the photographic proofs that you are no longer the same and can only blame . . . yourself. (*Dolores, listening to Maria, has again taken the elaborate hand mirror with rococo framing, identical to the one she uses in the film Madame DuBarry, and observes herself fixedly in it. The Fan cannot but exclaim.*)

FAN: *Madame DuBarry*, 1934!

DOLORES: (*Looking at herself in the mirror.*) After forty, each one is responsible for his own face.

MARIA: Marcel Proust, 1913. (*She sighs.*) The end of the Belle Epoque! Who was preparing the obituary of a whole era?

FAN: (*With less enthusiasm.*) *La Belle Otero*, the film you made in 1952?

MARIA: Thanks, young man, thanks for being my cheerleader. But that is not the point. The point is that before, you were only responsible for your little mask in front of your own mirror. There was no other proof that you were you.

FAN: Unless you had the luck of being painted by Rubens or Titian.

MARIA: Oh, that was like winning at the lottery, godfather. But if not, what sort of mug would you leave for posterity, please tell me? I'll tell you: None. Just think of the millions and millions of women who died with no one ever left to remember them again.

FAN: Because they left no trace of their faces.

MARIA: You're catching on. Today you are not only responsible for your own face in front of your own mirror . . .

DOLORES: (*Gazing at her mirror.*) You're also responsible to the public who knows your face better than you do because we have all been photographed . . .

MARIA: But a star has been photographed more than anyone, and photographed in movement, and from ever, and forever.

DOLORES: An eternal phantom and a passing flesh, alas!

MARIA: A bum rap, Lolita, a bum rap. Think about what I'm telling you when both of us go of to push up daisies. (*Uncomfortable silence. It is finally broken by the Fan.*)

FAN: The Arabs say that the face is the portrait of the soul. (*He gulps.*) That's why they never let anyone photograph them.

MARIA: The Yaqui Indians neither, so what?

DOLORES: (*Goes on looking at herself in the rococo mirror. To Maria.*) Diego Rivera once said that we shouldn't worry about age because we had beautiful little skulls, do you remember?

MARIA: (*To Dolores.*) You and I are different. Do you know why? You only love me and love yourself through the public.

DOLORES: (*Without ceasing to look at herself in the mirror.*) Don't tell me that you do not love yourself more only because the public adores you . . . I mean, adored you.

MARIA: (*Without taking notice of the Fan.*) Yes. But I love you only because of yourself, not because of the public. (*Pause.*) I am the only person who has managed to love you for yourself, including yourself.

FAN: (*In an obsequious tone.*) Forgive me . . . it's not that I want to contradict you . . . but I . . . (*Now Maria does concentrate her attention on the Fan.*)

MARIA: You are the public, popcorn eater! You are the pale reflection of what you see in a darkened theater. Look at yourself, paleface! (*She advances in a menacing manner towards the Fan.*) You are like the singular eye where the sun never shines, you asshole! You kill a bullfighter under the true sun, screaming, condemning him with shouts and bottles, you coward, may the bull gore you! A lover you murder wrapped in the true night, with the arms of blood and treason and the tender words and the exhausted dream of the heroes . . . But this love and this crime in an artificial darkness, in the false night of a movie house, the love and the crime of the public against the star, that is the coward's love! And that is the coward's crime, when he forgets us! (*She stops, looking for words she cannot find. Dolores lets her mirror fall as a swordsman lets fall his guard. To Dolores.*) I love you for yourself, little sister, not because you are a star and have a public. (*Dolores is about to get up and embrace Maria. But the Fan quickly intervenes to prevent it.*)

FAN: (*To Dolores.*) Don't listen to the arguments of spite. I . . .

MARIA: (*Furiously, to the Fan.*) You? Who the hell are you? How did you get here? Who gave you our address? (*The Fan is physically attacked by Maria.*)

FAN: (*Warding off Maria's attack with his hands.*) Excuse me, it was an accident.

MARIA: An accident? An accident is to die or to be born. You're not even a quicky fuck.

FAN: I am her fan. You cannot offend me.

MARIA: Listen, inoffensible, I have asked you a polite question. How did you go about . . . unearthing us?

FAN: (*Flattered that once more he is the center of attention.*) This morning, as I proceeded to take my place in front of my desk and my archives so as to initiate my quotidian tasks . . .

MARIA: You were going to work.

FAN: Precisely. Alexander Graham Bell's genial invention rang in my office . . .

MARIA: The telefunken.

DOLORES: Aaah Hollywood, Hollywood, you have invented everything. Spencer Tracy discovered the electric light, Paul Muni pasteurized milk, Greer Garson radium, Edward G. Robinson news agencies, Rodolfo Valentino the tango and Don Ameche the telephone.

FAN: Precisely. The machine rang and I took it. Fortunately, it is the public telephone of the enterprise where I lend my services and anyone could have . . .

MARIA: We get it.

FAN: (*In a sort of very personal access.*) It was she. (*He turns towards Dolores. He approaches her.*) It was she. Saying: "Hello . . ." (*The Fan and Dolores now talk simultaneously, with imaginary receivers in their hands.*)

DOLORES & FAN: "With whom do I have the pleasure? . . . Oh, I see . . . Could I speak to . . . ?" (*Dolores ceases speaking.*)

FAN: A silence. Then she hung up. But how was I not to recognize her voice, the voice of *What Price Glory?* . . .

MARIA: You're nuts. That was a silent movie.

FAN: The voice of *Evangeline* . . .

DOLORES: (*Dizzy.*) My love . . .

MARIA: Watch out. Ask him to tell us where he hangs out.

FAN: (*To Maria.*) I cannot understand your picturesque way of expressing yourself. It is not of my times. (*Maria starts circling around Dolores and the Fan, observing the latter as though he were a strange bug.*)

MARIA: Desk . . . archives . . . a public office . . .

FAN: That's it. A bureaucrat. A public servant.

MARIA: (*Goes on circling.*) Many telephones, did you say?

FAN: (*Getting nervous.*) Oh yes, many, going tilin . . . tilin-tilin?

MARIA: Functioning?

FAN: Perfectly.

MARIA: Then they're not phones in a public office. Those never work. A hospital?

FAN: Colder.

MARIA: The Phone Company? No, nobody would answer. An enterprise, you said? A newspaper enterprise, hot? (*Maria looks at the Fan with curiosity. She picks up the paper. She starts glancing through it. Dolores profits from the pause and tries to prevent Maria from reading the paper.*)

DOLORES: Oh stop it, stop all these unnecessary cruelties. Stop reading that paper. I'm not interested in knowing who died today. I'm not interested in knowing if today's dead are older or younger than I. I don't care if Mother finds out, I don't care if Mother suffers if they are older than she is and is happy if they are younger, I don't . . . (*The following scene should be interpreted in a very stylized manner, practically as an operatic trio. Nevertheless, Dolores's voice shall dominate the ensemble, without obliterating it. This stylization has been prepared for by the previous verbal trios between Dolores, Maria and the Fan. Now it should be extremely evident that the Fan moves his lips in silence while Maria reads the newspaper, repeating exactly, but in a silence, what she reads out loud.*)

MARIA: (*Deliberately reading.*) "Born May 6, 1915 in Kenosha, Wisconsin, U.S.A. . . . "

DOLORES: (*To Maria.*) Do you realize what you're doing? You are making it impossible for us to celebrate today, today when the thing we had so wished for has finally happened, the thing we've been wishing for for so many years, since ever, and you do not stop and celebrate . . .

MARIA: "Son of an inventor and a pianist . . . "

DOLORES: Today I was recognized! I woke up, I had breakfast and no one . . . (*She turns round and violently points toward the public.*) No one . . . not one of you . . . recognized me . . . But lo and behold, noon is hardly passed when an admirer has arrived with a bouquet of flowers in his hand, saying: I admire you. You are she. (*Maria goes on reading the newspaper. The Fan repeats with silent lips Maria's words.*)

MARIA: "He studied painting in the Arts Institute of Chicago." (*She pronounces the word in the French manner: Shicagó.*)

DOLORES: (*To Maria.*) Do you understand me? You are she. He also said it to you. You are she.

MARIA: (*Reads.*) "At age fifteen he made his debut as an actor in Dublin. He directed Shakespeare's *Julius Caesar.*"

FAN: We are all honorable men.

DOLORES: Don't you realize? We don't have to prove we are they anymore!

MARIA: "He creates and directs the negro *Macbeth* for the Federal Theater during the Great Depression of the thirties."

FAN: (*With syncopated rhythm.*) When shall we three meet again, yeah man!

DOLORES: We have a witness!

MARIA: "He directs and interprets *Julius Caesar* in fascist uniforms."

FAN: We are all honorable menschen.

DOLORES: (*Pointing at the Fan with her finger.*) He doesn't lie! He has seen all our pictures! He doesn't lie!

MARIA: "In October 1938, he frightens thousands of listeners with his radio adaptation of H. G. Wells's *The War of the Worlds*."

DOLORES: (*Sadly*.) Wells . . . He doesn't lie . . .

MARIA: "In 1940, he reinvents the art of the cinema with *Citizen Kane*."

FAN: We are all honorable tycoons.

MARIA: "His name enters the Hall of Fame alongside those of Griffith, Chaplin and Eisenstein."

DOLORES: (*Ever more unsure of herself*.) He does not lie . . .

MARIA: "In 1942 he dresses Dolores del Rio as a leopard and employs her in *Voyage au pays de la peur*."

DOLORES: (*In desperation*.) No, *Journey into Fear*, that film is called *Journey into Fear*, you cannot read in English . . .

MARIA: (*Without ceasing to read the paper*.) Tex-Mex.

DOLORES: You envy me Hollywood!

MARIA: Greaser. Pains of the River.

DOLORES: Frog. Marie Joyeuse.

MARIA: Douleurs de la Fleuve.

FAN: We are honorable sub-affluents.

DOLORES: Maria de los Angeles Feliz! Happy Little Mary of the Angels!

FAN: Mary had a little angel, its cock was black as coal, and everywhere that Mary came, the cock was sure to grow . . .

DOLORES: You forced me to come to Los Angeles just because your name is Maria de los Angeles, you conceited bitch, we could have gone to live in Rio, flying down to Rio, oooh, my youth!

MARIA: Or to the village of Dolores Hidalgo, to ring the bell of Mexican Independence. Oh what the hell. (*She goes on reading*.) "And in 1941 he did not film *The Way to Santiago* with . . . "

DOLORES: "Dolores del Rio." (*A certain sadness. The trio breaks up. Maria throws the newspaper far from her*.)

MARIA: (*To Dolores, but looking directly at the Fan*.) Permit me to introduce to you the author of the obituary column in the *Los Angeles Times*. (*Directly to the Fan*.) We have been reading you all these years, honorable sir. Nothing interests us more than finding out who died yesterday. You seem too young to devote yourself entirely to the stiffs.

DOLORES: What are you saying? How do you know?

MARIA: I saw him moving his lips in silence every time I read from the paper. Lip-synching, you know, repeating by heart his memorable phrases about the illustrious dead of yesterday.

FAN: (*Corrects her*.) Today. What you read is the noon five-star final. My newspaper is proud to be the first with the last.

MARIA: In love with what he writes.

FAN: (*Suddenly cynical*.) You really think you've got all the brains, don't you.

MARIA: More than you, you constipated ink-shitter; sure, I've got all the brains, more brains than anyone in the world, I'm Tarzan's mother, and also the mother of all the little chickens that have ever been born, do you see, I am all that and you are the stupidest, shittiest guy who ever put his paws on my rug. Go move somewhere else, little lamb. This is the domain of the Big Fox.

DOLORES: *Madre mia de Guadalupe!* You have offended my fan! (*The Fan makes a gesture as if to leave.*)

FAN: (*To Dolores.*) I'm sorry. I truly am.

MARIA: (*To Dolores.*) Don't be silly. He is just a second-rate newspaperman who got too big for his britches and wanted to know what you thought on the day of the death of Orson Welles.

DOLORES: That's all very fine, but he recognized me, he admitted I am she! You did not, you say you love me yet you don't admit it.

MARIA: Because I love you. Because I love you for yourself, Lola.

DOLORES: (*Heedless, insistent.*) Mummy doesn't, Mummy also says I'm crazy . . . that we're both crazy, both of us: You Maria and I Dolores!

MARIA: Today she shall be happy. Welles was younger than she.

DOLORES: (*Dizzy.*) Welles? No, I remember she cried very much when he died, she said they had been contemporaries, travellers in the same time-machine, she said . . .

MARIA: Orson?

DOLORES: No, he's just a child. How is he going to die? I refer to Herbert George.

MARIA: (*Takes Dolores by the shoulders.*) Wake up, darling. Come out of your trance. Orson died today. Orson. Your contemporary. (*Dolores remains dazed. She looks blindly at the public in front of her. She murmurs.*)

DOLORES: Wells. H. G. Wells. The author of *The Invisible Man.* Mother says she knew him. Once when she went on a vacation to the Caribbean. To the island of Doctor Moreau. A most uncomfortable place, Mummy told us. Very strange service. The maids ate the soap and tore the sheets every morning. The waiters entered through the windows with bananas in their hands.

MARIA: You confuse everything. You are writing history in your own way.

DOLORES: (*Resuming a logical, mundane, serene tone.*) No. Welles adapts Wells to the radio and frightens the good people of the State of New Jersey but also fools the newspapers of the Hearst chain who believe the Martian invasion dramatized by Welles to be true. Welles thus steals the first page from Howard Hughes who is trying to circumnavigate the world in a wooden plane called the *Spruce Goose* but is left without publicity due to Wells, Welles and the Hearst chain which is the reason why Hughes offers Welles Orson all the money in the world to do *Citizen Kane* and Welles Orson doubts between doing the anticipated parody of what shall be the future life of Howard Hughes through a parody of the present life of William Randolph Hearst laughing at both men: that is to say Welles Orson invades the future of Hughes Howard through the past of Hearst William Randolph and Wells Herbert George invades the future of Hearst offering him a Martian grand-daughter who holds up a bank machine gun in hand the same day in which Howard Hughes flees in helicopter from Managua Nicaragua to die of malnutrition, surrounded by cellophane sandwiches and coca-cola bottles, isolated and invisible and with long, rapier-like fingernails, the better to scratch you with! H. G. Wells writes *The Invisible Man* who is Howard Hughes and Welles (who?) adapts Wells (who?) (Pause.) I cry for both of them. (*She sings the Beatles's music "We all live in a yellow time-machine." Now, with anguish again, she addresses Maria.*) Who will cry for us?

MARIA: Who?

DOLORES: Yes, will anyone cry over you and over me?

FAN: (*Clownishly.*) Your grateful public. (*Dolores and Maria go on interpreting the scene in the greatest intimacy, totally indifferent to the music hall clowneries of the Fan.*)

MARIA: Mummy . . .

DOLORES: No, she'll be happy that we went first.

MARIA: The public, our public. Our public will cry for us. Listen to it. (*A sound of growing applause, vivas, bravos, ovations. It grows until it reaches an unbearable pitch. Maria listens without wincing, rather with an air of sadness; Dolores with growing terror, until she feels she has to put her hands over her ears and scream. The Fan, meanwhile, has gone towards the toilet, with his reel under his arm and the projector in his hand. He takes the white telephone off the toilet seat and puts the film projector on the seat. While Maria and Dolores are occupied downstage in the scene that follows, the Fan, upstage, prepares his projection. He takes off his jacket, revealing a sleeveless sweater with a rhomboid design. He carefully takes the reel of film from the can, puts it next to the projector, closes the can and starts rolling the film. From time to time he interjects, it is true, a very dubious pun.*)

DOLORES: (*Screams.*) No! Make them shut up! No applause! Applause pursues us like a ghost! Applause is worse than a shriek, a moan or a murmur of chains! Applause is our Frankenstein: it created us, Maria, and it killed us!

FAN: Citizen Frankenstein. (*Maria holds Dolores so she will not fall. Both sit downstage, on the floor, Dolores's head resting on Maria's shoulder. Maria caresses Dolores's head. Dolores embraces Maria's waist.*)

MARIA: I'll cry for you, little sister, if you go before I do.

DOLORES: Together. Together.

MARIA: Will you cry for me?

DOLORES: No, together, please.

FAN: Kane or Abel?

MARIA: Do you need me?

DOLORES: You know it. My memory . . . is you.

MARIA: You forgive me for not being like you?

DOLORES: The black sheep?

MARIA: (*Nods.*) Ebony.

FAN: Citizeness Cain.

DOLORES: I think I envied you your life a tiny bit.

MARIA: And I yours, honey.

DOLORES: (*With a cute little frown.*) We are different. Don't rub it in anymore.

MARIA: No. I didn't envy you. I'm not complaining. We danced through life. Who can take that away from us?

FAN: An Amerikane in Paris, that's who.

MARIA: Are you sorry for not having done something?

DOLORES: A son of my own?

MARIA: No. No. They would have taken him away from you. I didn't abandon him. They took him away from me.

DOLORES: It was always said that you abandoned him.

MARIA: (*With a harsh voice.*) No. They took him away from me. The public, the producers. All of them. They got together. The sexiest vamp of them all, the woman without a soul could not have a son. It would be against nature. The devourer of men

FAN: Kanibal!

MARIA: (*To Dolores.*) Do you know what I envy you?

DOLORES: What my love, my poor little sister?

MARIA: You never had to lie.

FAN: Hughes lying?

DOLORES: (*With a flash of flirtatiousness.*) Oooooh, if you knew, if you only knew! Once I married at fifty and my husband was forty. He asked me that we both declare before the judge to be forty, you know, so as to be the perfect pair. When the judge asked him his age, he answered very seriously: "Forty years old." When he asked me mine, I flashed a smile and said: "Twenty." (*The two women laugh and hug each other, happy, having recovered their most intimate relation.*)

MARIA: Oooooh, when I was launched, they invented an official biography that was not mine, not my origins, not my husbands, not my son, nothing. I read it with unbelieving eyes. I was another. My life had gone up in smoke.

FAN: Hughes Who: That's Hughes.

MARIA: My husbands, my son, my lovers had been hidden, taken out of the photographs in which I appeared with them.

DOLORES: Jesus! Like poor Trotsky.

FAN: Jaguar Whose? Leon Brainstain, that's whose.

MARIA: (*With a bitter smile.*) Up in smoke. They never existed, you see?

FAN: Jesus! The Cruci Fiction.

DOLORES: Why did you accept it?

MARIA: Why? Because I wanted to be loved. I wanted to be admired. I deserved it. Half of my life was used by other people. The other half I auctioned off so that I would be successful and recover the life that others took away from me.

FAN: You Kane take it with you.

MARIA: Everything I've done is in order to be loved and admired. First admired, I said, then love would come after. (*Pause.*) But all this I'm telling you is not true. The truth then and now is that I want to be loved, Lolita, and in order to get love I was willing and I am willing to pay any price, humiliation first and then glory and oblivion now, do you realize?

DOLORES: Oblivion now . . .

MARIA: Yes, because now we must be forgotten, Lolita, so that our films shall be remembered. Our films are ageless you know, they are eternal.

DOLORES: (*Dreamily.*) They are like the perfume that is left of our lives.

MARIA: Yes, our films are the only thing that mocks and conquers our age. Against the sad childhood, a film.

DOLORES: No, it was a happy childhood, full of ribbons and hoops and carousels.

MARIA: Against the poor, uncertain teen-age, a film.

DOLORES: No, no, balls and beaus and rowing in the moonlight.

MARIA: Yes, against the dirty, sold, humiliated youth, a film.

DOLORES: No, Hollywood, the invitation to Pickfair, the contract with Warner Brothers, the swimming pool, the Afghan hound, the silk parasol and the organdy summer hat.

MARIA: Yes, Guadalajara, the invitation to Lake Chapala, the contract with the producer who demands to test the merchandise before signing, the sleazy little motel, the hungry dogs barking, the mariachis stopped playing.

DOLORES: (*Passionately hugs Maria.*) No more, no more, Maria, now we are both queens, both of us, floating forever in our gondolas down the Grand Canal in Venice, floating towards the palace where the doges await us. (*Pause.*) Two queens of a single domain. We shall be remembered. Nothing has been forgotten.

FAN: Nothing has been forgotten. (*The Fan lights up the projector. The light from the projector must blind the public, physically hurt it as if to take the place of the vision the public is about to be denied. The Fan's projection shall be seen by him, by Maria and by Dolores, and imagined by the public, since one supposes that the screen occupies the place of the public.*)

MARIA: Any price. Humiliation first and then glory and now oblivion.

FAN: Sorry. I warned you that I've got all the films you ever made, gals. I'm sorry. The only film of yours I'm missing, Lolita, is *Carmen*. On the other hand, Maria, I have all your films. Not a single one is missing, not even this one. (*As the projection proceeds, Dolores first looks at the imaginary screen with astonishment, then with shame, finally she puts her hands over her eyes and sobs, denying many times with her head, unbelieving. Maria remains unshakable, neither happy nor sad, rather she looks severe, grave, as if she witnessed a dance of death.*)

FAN: You can't believe what you can find in the old archives of an old news-paper such as the *Los Angeles Times*. These are things that the boys in the deskroom inherit from the executives, you know, executive images, eh?, seen too many times, sort of frayed at the edges and out of fashion. Even the worst pornography bores if it is seen more than twice, sex is something so mechanical, twice is too much, but once is okay, the first time is always a surprise, an excitement. *Madre santisma*, we tell ourselves this time it shall be better, this time it shall be true. Truth? Truth? . . . The cinema, is it perhaps the truth because in the darkness it gives back to us the world of pure gesture before language, when it was not necessary to speak in order to say I love you, I hate you, I'm going to save you, I'm going to kill you, flee, come here? (*Pause.*) But you two did not hear me. You were too busy with your ridiculous lies. Truth? No. Look at that monkey business. He really looks like a monkey, a gorilla, and you know the gorilla is obeyed without second thoughts. He says: we are fleeing because there is danger. And every female of the species flees and follows him without demanding proof. And she. She looks like she's going to rip the sheets and eat the soaps. Such vulgarity, *Dios santo*. Is this what we were created for in the image of you know who et cetera? To behave like this, worse than fierce, brutish beasts and in a bed, ooooh, maybe in the same bed where we were born and where we shall die, the cradle and the tomb of our filthy pleasures, ooooh! (*The Fan lets the film flow by itself and advances, with fierce scorn, towards Maria who is seated downstage, next to Dolores. The play of white, blinding light and the shadows of the bodies must create a sense of hallucination and the struggle between the Fan and Maria shall project itself as a fierce parody of the sexual act. The Fan takes Maria by the wrists and tries to raise her.*) I am sorry to deny you oblivion. Look. Look at yourself, orchid, in your true light . . . (*He takes her roughly by the neck and forces her to see the images.*) Do you remember? Do you remember when you did this? What year was it? Thirty-five, thirty-six? Just look at that primitive technique. They didn't even use sound. They were really filthy. (*Maria's voice, as she tries to free herself from the Fan, has the tone of negative pain, almost a moan. The Fan picks her up by the armpits.*) The reel was forgot-ten in the oldest archives of the *Los Angeles Times*. You fled from Mexico so as to flee from your lost youth, you crossed the desert and you didn't come face-to-face with You Know Who, what appeared before you was your forgotten, putrid, stinking youth: look at it. Who was going to go to the trouble of looking at a porno film from the thirties, with a forgotten little girl who today was surely a stinking old hag? Ughhh. Nobody likes to think that his mother also fucked, that his grandmother opened her legs in Dallas Texas, that his sister sucked the milk of human kindness, that his daughter is also going to go on a vacation to the island of Doctor Moreau, that all of them shrieked with pleasure with another man, said to another man the same they said to you: Stick it in . . .

MARIA: (*Struggling, defensive.*) Macho . . . you repulsive macho . . .

DOLORES: (*With her eyes still covered by her hands.*) No more, enough!

MARIA: Doesn't a man also open his legs, doesn't a man also suck and is sucked, doesn't a man also fuck and is fucked, isn't he fucked when he fucks? (*Dolores, in supreme self-defense, sings in order to transform reality. The lyrics she sings are those from the tango, "Orchids in the Moonlight.")*

MARIA: (*To the Fan.*) Only you can be the owner of your own body, you stinking macho, a woman cannot? (*She screams.*) A woman cannot? (*She throws the Fan to the floor. She kicks him. The film stops; the projector ceases to throw light. The lonely end of the film goes round and round on the reel.*) I'm going to castrate you, you bugger.

FAN: (*From the floor.*) You dike!

MARIA: If all the men in the world were like you, that I would be. (*She gives him a final, spectacular kick.*) I'm a lady but I'm more of a man than you are. I'm an old lady but I still excite you, eunuch.

DOLORES: (*Stands up and puts herself between Maria and the Fan.*) Stop it. Forgive him.

MARIA: (*Shrugs her shoulders.*) You're right. This dwarf isn't good enough to unplug my dirty bathwater.

DOLORES: (*Strangely conciliatory.*) Besides, you know. We owe him something very important.

MARIA: Sure. I know. He recognized us. But at what a price.

DOLORES: What we hoped for all our lives.

MARIA: Since we were little girls. Ever since we went to a double feature in the old Balmori filmhouse in Mexico and saw *Doña Bárbara* and *María Candelaria*. Popcorn, chewing gum, chocolates.

DOLORES: Yes, ever since then.

MARIA: And you think that today we finally triumphed?

DOLORES: (*Forcing her answer.*) Yes. Thanks to him.

MARIA: (*Slightly disconcerted, she prefers to look with scorn at the Fan who lies on the ground.*) What do you want, you worm?

FAN: Can I get up?

MARIA: (*Goes through a mimic of politeness.*) You're in your own home, you little bastard.

FAN: (*Gets up with aching bones, shaking the dust off his knees and shoulders, adjusting his bow tie. He does something unforeseen: he takes Dolores by the hand.*) I want her to come to me. (*Several, conflicting feelings appear on the face of Dolores. Disbelief, revulsion, resignation, the will to sacrifice. She opts for the comical attitude of a young virgin.*)

DOLORES: I?

MARIA: (*To the Fan.*) What do you need, a nanny or a nurse?

FAN: No. I want her for myself.

MARIA: I warn you, she doesn't know how to mend a sock and she doesn't have a dowry.

DOLORES: (*Faking her trance.*) I?

FAN: (*To Maria.*) I want to marry her.

DOLORES: (*Looking enraptured at the Fan.*) You? (*In this moment Dolores seems to have persuaded herself of her own comedy. Maria corrects her with disbelief and mockery.*)

MARIA: (*To the Fan.*) Listen. You don't have to ask for my permission. Madame is quite a grown woman.

FAN: (*To Dolores.*) Yes? Since I saw *The Jungle of Fire* directed by Fernando de Fuentes with Arturo de Córdova?

MARIA: (*Mockingly, but with a defensive humor.*) Go on, Lolita, don't forget he is going to write your obituary. Better be nice to him.

DOLORES: (*With her hands to her head.*) What am I thinking about? This ridiculous puppet has come here to insult you . . . to insult both of us, with his filth . . . his canned filth . . .

MARIA: (*Surer and surer of what is coming.*) Cheers, my Lola. (*Dolores adopts her most melodramatic attitude.*)

DOLORES: (*To the Fan.*) Out! Out of here, sir! Respect our advanced age and our artistic achievements! (*She points towards Maria.*) Madame and I . . . are queens.

FAN: (*Coolly*) Well one of you is going to have to resign the throne as soon as I start circulating the short by Popeye and Olive Oil I've just shown you.

DOLORES: (*With her hands on her waist.*) Bah. It's been sleeping for half a century in an archive and no one has ever been interested . . .

FAN: Because no one knew it was *she*.

DOLORES: No one will recognize her.

FAN: As soon as they know it is she, they'll all say it is she even if they don't recognize her. They'll all want to recognize her, you know, that's the way people are.

DOLORES: Don't you speak to me in that tone!

FAN: Okay. But I have completed the filmography of the lady. They thought it was complete and it wasn't. I am like Champollion. Now they can know what the mummies used to do, when they were little. (*He laughs in a vulgar way.*)

DOLORES: (*With decision.*) All right. How much do you want for the copy?

FAN: What? There are many copies, I warn you.

DOLORES: We'll buy them all. Won't we, Maria?

FAN: No. It's you or nothing.

DOLORES: (*Ever the coquette.*) I?

FAN: You or nothing. As clear as that. Easier than spelling Zbigniew Brzezinski. (*Pause.*) You. (*Dolores is disconcerted. A silence follows. Dolores goes towards her little altar. As in the classical Mexican films, she kneels to ask counsel from the*

Mother of God.)

DOLORES: *Madre mia de Guadalupe.*

MARIA: (*Seriously.*) In sin conceived, all . . .

DOLORES: God save you, full of grace . . .

MARIA: (*Smiles.*) Because if we didn't conceive ourselves in sin, what fun would it be?

DOLORES: Blessed be thou amongst all women . . .

MARIA: The lord is with thee only to conceived in sin the son of the whore . . .

DOLORES: (*With open arms.*) Praised be the Lord, praised be the Lord, praised be the Lord . . .

MARIA: (*With folded arms.*) I am not sorry, do you all understand? I am not sorry for anything. (*Dolores crosses herself. She rises. She takes her piggy bank. She caresses it, with sadness. Maria lights up one of her black cigars.*) Don't torment yourself over me, doll. (*Dolores lifts her chin with a sort of awkward hope.*) I want to tell you something: the decision is yours, only yours. Because for me, a scandal more or less . . . Besides, as I've said, I'll always have a dwarf to unplug my dirty bathwater.

DOLORES: A man for whom I can unplug the bathtub; press the shirts; sew the buttons; cook the beans. I've never done it before. There was always a butler at home.

MARIA: Then this is your chance, my dove.

DOLORES: (*Trembling.*) No, Maria, no, how can you think . . . ?

MARIA: That you might leave me? Listen: in the same way that I could leave you.

DOLORES: You . . . me?

MARIA: Sure. Not for this near-sighted buzzard. But for a musician who is also a poet, a *charro* who knows how to sing, even for a well-developed mariachi, why not?

DOLORES: (*Inquisitive, reflexive.*) Because *she* had them . . . because that was part of *her* life and that way you could complete your life which is an imitation of *her* life? (*Maria doesn't respond.*) But a young author of obituary columns and a blackmailer besides, someone like that doesn't figure in my life . . . I mean, in *her* life.

MARIA: No, not that I know of, no. It would be a novelty. You were too decent.

FAN: (*Intervenes to hurry things up but also trying to hide a certain fear.*) Okay, make up your minds. It's almost three o'clock. I have to go back to the paper. My corpses await me.

MARIA: No one can die without you, you dribbler?

FAN: No. Nobody important that is, no.

MARIA: Ah. (*On an impulse, Dolores kneels in front of Maria, embraces her legs, rests her head against the other woman's knees.*)

DOLORES: You don't care about a scandal, but I do, I do. (*She looks at Maria with imploring eyes, blinded by tears.*) We are queens, the two of us, together, if one falls the other falls, if one is hurt the other dies, don't you realize it?

MARIA: Yes, but only through the public, remember, Lolita, you only love yourself and love me through the public.

DOLORES: (*Naively.*) It was such a cozy arrangement, just the two of us, together . . .

MARIA: Yes, just you and I, darling, plus our two shadows on the screen. Plus the audience to see the shadows and assure them: "You exist."

DOLORES: (*Emotional.*) I would have given them up.

MARIA: Too late. We are two myths. Our biographies don't count. We don't belong to ourselves any more.

DOLORES: Just you and I. Maria. Dolores.

MARIA: And their inevitable Fan. The price, my dear, must be paid, I tell you. (*Maria looks at the Fan. She introduces him with an elegant flourish of her arm as though he were the Prince Charming in a fairy tale. The Fan adjusts his bow tie and picks up his jacket.*) There he is.

DOLORES: Do you love me?

MARIA: No one, not even yourself, loves you so much, because no one, not even yourself, loves you alone, without your public, except me.

DOLORES: Then?

MARIA: Then it's up to you, my little sister.

DOLORES: (*Full of doubts.*) Doña, Doña, Doña . . . (*She covers her head with the rebozo. She caresses the piggy. The Fan puts on his jacket. Dolores speaks with the accent of an Indian girl.*) Ooh, our little piggy, Lorenzo, don't let them take away our piggy, it's the only thing we have. (*She puts the piggy back in its place. She looks at Maria.*) "Don't leave me alone. I won't do anything bad. It's better to kill our little pig. The pig must die." (*She changes her tone. She fakes an attitude of pride. She extends her hand to the Fan, who takes it avidly. Dolores once more addresses Maria.*) It's true, my love. I know you're not going to stop loving me because of all this. (*She shrugs her shoulders.*) After all . . . a man . . . For all other men, I was one less. For him, I shall be one more. (*The Fan has opened the door with a slight noise of creaking hinges. The Fan and Dolores exit quickly, leaving the door open. For a few seconds, Maria gazes fixedly towards the door. Once more she lets the black cigar fall inside the kettle. Then she throws herself against the door and shuts it. We now hear the same metallic, penitentiary noises as during the Fan's entrance. Maria leans against the closed door and suppresses a sob, biting her fist. Then she rushes towards Dolores's altar, picks up the piggy bank and gazes at it with scorn.*)

MARIA: (*Mimicking Dolores.*) "We don't have another thing in the world, Lorenzo." (*She violently hurls the earthenware object to the floor. It is immediately broken. She gasps for breath. She slowly recomposes herself. She goes to the telephone. She nervously dials a number.*) Hello? The *Luz del Dia* Restaurant? This is Lupe Vélez speaking . . . No, not the same as usual, no thank you . . . What? . . . No, I tell you the same as usual is not good enough today, please listen to me. This is a special occasion. I'm going to order . . . Yes, bring your little pencil out . . . No, not that one, don't be such a jerk. You dirty old man, as though somebody could be interested in that old Aztec ruin. Listen, I want to talk to the boss . . . Yes, with don Pancho Cáceres, quick . . . I said quick . . . Hello? . . . Little boss! Listen, this is a very special occasion . . . Sure I know . . . but you know what? I was left alone, don Panchito, and I'm hungry . . . Ay, I know, little boss, you were sent to me by Jesus Christ himself . . . Look: to begin with, a thick Tlalpeño soup with the *epasote* herb and the tiniest young chilies, then the corn mushrooms in cheese, two yes, and two of pumpkin fungus. The *pambazo*, do you still know how to make the *pambazo*, just a little wet, like they used to do it in Guadalajara years ago? (*She laughs.*) . . . No, wait for me, I'm only beginning. Then the eggs in the Yucatan style, you know, very well-seasoned, and with almond sauce, very very light the almond sauce please, I'm not trying to die of indigestion . . . Now this is the most important chapter, let's go to the tacos, those very fine, soft, little tacos where the tortilla is only slightly heated but without frying please, you know I cannot tolerate anything that is fried . . . The stuffed chiles, sure, if the pomegranates are good, but I want them to really crack between my teeth, eh?, the last time they were wet, aaah, you weren't nice to me that time, my nice little merchant, aren't I your very best client? . . . The enchiladas, the green ones, only the green ones, I want the guacamole to be very, very fresh. And now the main course. For the main course, what can you offer me? . . . No, *mole* no, not *mole* . . . or who knows, maybe after all, yes . . . but I want it in the pickled oriental style, do you have the pickled oriental sauce, you know, with its onions and its pimentos, so that I can feel that my tongue is about to evaporate, that the sauce doesn't even touch my palate, oh my little boss, do you know what nostalgia of the country is, the nostalgia of the land, you should know better than anyone, you who came here to California twenty-five years ago, to pick lemons and stayed here to feed all of us, all of the Chicanos, look at yourself my dainty little man! . . . No, no, no, don't exaggerate, a big Oaxaca *tamal* after all this . . . You really want to kill me with love . . . what I want is to wash down the banquet. Tell me: is the *pulque* fresh? (*She laughs.*) Oh my land of the sun, how I pine to see you again . . . And a lot of fruit, my little boss, many colors for my banquet, all the holy Mexican Republic in the colors of its fruits for my banquet, yellow mangos and rose-colored papayas and ocher mamey and dark *zapote* and white *guanabanas* and green *tunas* and red pomegranates and tequila, little boss of my soul, lots of tequila, lots of salt, lots of lemon and blood of the widow, the blood of Jalisco, that is what we need, ever since the parish priest don Miguel Hidalgo sat up and lit the flame of liberty, no son of his fucking mother has been capable of putting it out. Amen! . . . What? No, it's not a fiesta, it's for me, my little boss, it's for me because I'm alone, I was left alone but now I'm free. A mariachi, my boss, a really good, trumpet-playing mariachi, one that knows all the songs, please don't fail me, don Panchito, at eight o'clock sharp, if you fail me today you've failed me forever, I swear it on your holy mother's head! (*Sweet and resigned.*) Thank you, don Panchito . . . thank you, good man. (*She hangs up the telephone. She doesn't move for an instant. Then she stretches her arms as though she were waking up. She walks quickly to her personal altar. She opens a drawer. She takes out a medicine bottle. It should be understood clearly, because of the size and color of the bottle and the pills, that it is precisely that. Maria takes a pill out of the bottle, then another and another and another, until she has a dozen pills in her hand, then she puts them in her mouth as though they were candies. She swallows them. Then she stops. She looks astonished for an instant. Then she attempts to listen or to feel something. Nothing happens. She walks to the closet. She takes out the Cleopatra gown. She goes with the gown in her arms to the down center of the stage. A white curtain closes behind her to disguise the very slight change of scenery which is taking place upstage. We hear the music of the tango "Orchids in the Moonlight." On the white curtain, we see the projection of a montage of films consisting of nothing but alternating close-ups of Maria Félix and Dolores del Rio: films from all the eras, with all the dresses, but always with the alternating faces of the two women: two eternal faces, in effect two faces that in some way are the same. Slowly, Maria puts on the grand ceremonial robe of Cleopatra. When she finishes doing it, the music and the film stops as well. We hear the first trumpet blare of the mariachi song "La Negra." The curtain that served as a screen opens. The original stage setting, without losing any of the details we already know—it continues to be the apartment in Venice, California—now has a harmony because of the absence of the closet and the accumulation of clothes in the center. Instead, the central space is now occupied by a banquet table heaped with Mexican dishes, little pulque earthenware jugs and plates flowing over with tropical fruits. There is a great pharaonic throne at the center of the table and behind it, the Mariachi Band is playing. Enter the Nubian Slaves, two beautiful girls dressed as Aida in the Verdi opera, with great fans in their hands, half-dressed, barefoot, singing in Spanish the lyrics of the absurd Spanish operetta La Corte de Faraón in counterpart with the Mariachis who go on blaring out "La Negra.*)

NUBIAN SLAVES: (*Singing.*)
Ay Ba, ay Ba, ay Babilonia que marea,
Ay Va, ay Va, ay Vámanos para Judea . . .

(*Maria walks serenely towards her throne, followed by the Slave Girls who fan her and then leave their fans in order to help Maria take her place on the throne. Immediately one of the Slaves crowns Maria with the extraordinary-looking headpiece of the Egyptian queen and the other one offers her the Ptolemaic insignia which Maria crosses over her bosom. The Slave Girls start to serve Maria her food. They give it to her in her mouth, as if to a little girl, they stain her lips with mole, her chin with* beans, but Maria does not lose her hieratic, imperial attitude. In her eyes, nevertheless, a mortal turbulence appears. She slowly sits up with an air of desperation.)

MARIA: Thank you, my people. Thank you for accompanying me in my solitude. You have understood our sacrifice. (*The Slave Girls, acting as though they were cybernetically synchronized automatons, hum the aria from La Traviata, "Conosca il Sacrifizio." Maria raises her little jug of pulque.*) If they had only seen us, defending them against blackmail, if they had only seen when Dolores told the pig, how much, how much for the copies?! In their name, clinging to them, to their films, because without them we have no way of going back there, to the land we lost, Dolores . . . (*The Mariachis play and the Slaves sing the nostalgic Mexican song, "México, lindo y querido, si muero lejos de ti."*) Oh my land of the sun, how I pine to see you, now that I live far from you, without light, without love, and when I see myself so sad and lonely like a leaf in the storm, I would like to cry, I would like to die from sheer longing! (*She lets the jug fall and she herself falls sitting, heavily, sickly.*) We left the land of the sun and came to live in the dark cave of the north, ay Dolores and the condition was that we should never separate, the two beasts never leave each other, when one devourer goes out to look for her nourishment the other goes with her, it is impossible to separate . . . It is the condition for living, do you understand?, alone each one of us goes back to the jungle of fire, not to God but to the jungle. All the dead in the world are younger than God, don't forget it, don't forget me, oh my land of the sun, how I pine to see you . . . (*Maria loses the movement of her head. She lets fall her scepters in a plate full of mole. Her head gyrates without any control. She takes her hands to her temples. The headpiece falls. Maria rises. The Mariachi stops playing.*) No! I don't want to die! Not yet! (*All those present make way for Maria. She walks lurching the length of the banquet table. When she reaches the far end, she hangs on to the cloth, drags it with her and makes everything on the table crash to the floor. The Nubian Slave Girls try to run to her aid. One of the Mariachis stops them. Maria advances alone, in silence. The white telephone rings. It is, as usual, on top of the toilet seat. Maria turns around, supports herself on the table, falls on her knees and advances on all fours toward the telephone and the toilet. She tries to reach the phone. She makes it fall. We hear Dolores's voice from the receiver.*)

DOLORES: (*Voice over.*) Hello? Hello? Maria? Maria? Answer me! (*Maria tries to say something, but she cannot. The sleeping pills are taking effect.*) Maria . . . what's wrong with you, my love? Listen to me. I've something to tell you.

MARIA: Tell him . . . tell your sweetheart . . . that he has a job to do tomorrow . . .

DOLORES: (*Voice over.*) Beautiful Maria, Maria of my soul . . .

MARIA: Tell him to prepare a nice farewell for me, tell him . . .

DOLORES: (*Voice over.*) Maria! I'm coming, Maria, Maria of the Angels!

MARIA: See that they take me to the land of the sun and bury me there. Let them say that I'm only sleeping and then they . . .

DOLORES: (*Voice over.*) I'm going to hang up . . . I'm coming . . .

MARIA: Pain . . . Dolor . . . Dolores . . . I don't want to die, my love . . . (*A click when Dolores hangs up. Maria continues with the receiver in her hand.*) I love you too. I am you, didn't you know it? We both have to be Dolores and Maria if we are to be ourselves . . . I'm . . . I'm going to throw up, Lolita . . . maybe that way it'll go away . . . maybe that way . . . ayayay . . . Now you are going to see who Doña Diabla is! (*During this scene, the Nubian Slave Girls have left the stage and the Mariachis first have turned their backs on the public and then leave playing the sad, Mexican farewell song "Las Golondrinas." When Maria lifts the toilet seat in order to vomit, she is alone on a stage of extinguished lights, with the exception of the one that sharply outlines her on her knees, prostrate over the white toilet, trying to vomit, until, exhausted, her head plunges into the toilet and we hear the hideous noises of suffocation, a mortal spasm, an irrevocable asphyxia. The Mariachis, off, play and sing their farewell song. But their music also little by little is extinguished. We hear the sound of feet hastily coming up a staircase. The jingling of a set of keys nervously used. Finally, the door opens and Dolores appears, now dressed in a sober manner, with a black coat, modern shoes and stockings, but with a tiny hat from the forties. She screams when she sees Maria prostrate with her head inside the toilet and runs towards her, brings the wet head out, screams, cries, cradles the head, looking directly at it, until she lets the head fall on her lap.*)

DOLORES: Maria, beautiful Maria, you should have trusted me. That bastard will never again write a line or menace anyone ever again, do you understand me, Mariquita? Why didn't you understand me? Why didn't you trust me? I told you when I left, I'm going to kill the pig, we're going to kill the pig. I did it for you, my little sister, the love of my life, ayayay. Why didn't you wait for me? Ayayayayayay . . . (*Suddenly as if she remembered something, she puts her hand over her mouth. She looks suspiciously around her. She has left the door open. She looks at the open door with panic.*) But don't make a noise, Maria of the Angels, because Mummy can hear us. You know? She would be so happy to know that you died younger than she . . . She mustn't find out. How nice . . . how nice to think that that . . . gentleman . . . won't be able to tell the world . . . about your death . . . because no one must find out . . . Mummy less than anyone . . . No one must find out . . . They must all believe that you have never died, that you are the immortal beauty . . . There won't be any funeral ceremonies, beautiful Maria . . . Nobody shall visit your grave . . . except myself . . . your funeral is now . . . You're back in Mexico . . . in the land of the sun . . . You are no longer in Venice or in Venezia . . . Let them say that you are asleep and bring you here . . . Your funeral is today . . . this is the ceremony . . . no one must know. (*Maria and*

Dolores compose a female Pieta.) What did you tell me this morning? I'm trying to remember, Maria. Something we must remember now, I know. You must have faith in me, you said. Mother *is* going to care if you and I die. You trust me. (*She vacillates for a moment.*) Have faith in me? You didn't . . . You thought that I . . . I and that . . . that . . . (*Dolores again puts her hand over her mouth, repressing the feeling of nausea. Speaking through her fingers:*) You should have seen him. He invited me to a bottle of champagne, third class, California champagne to me! I broke the bottle, he laughed, with the broken neck of the bottle of his undrinkable bottle of champagne I slashed his throat so that he might only drink his own blood . . . (*She represses her nausea, lets her hand fall.*) He won't laugh anymore. (*She interrupts herself. She looks around her.*) Trust me, you said. Mother is going to mind if we die. Mother is going to mind? How? How? (*She looks with terror towards the door, towards the altars.*) Your altar. My altar. We called them that since we were children. We would keep our memories, our illusions and our prayers in the drawers. Is the secret there? (*Her attention turns to the film projector used by the Fan, which is placed on top of the water closet. Dolores sweetly raises Maria's head, then lets it rest on the ground and she herself rises little by little. Pause. Then she adds precipitately:*) The camera, Maria? The camera is our salvation? In the movie camera do our horizons come together, is the camera our common altar, my love? (*She goes to the film projector and lights it. As in the former scene, the light blinds the public.*) Oh, look at yourself, look at yourself so beautiful, so much in love, following Pedro Armendáriz towards the revolution, in love, Enamorada, imitating death in life, wild Mexican flower, look at me following Pedro Armendáriz towards the execution wall, Enamorada, Flor Silvestre, feigning death in life, feigning life in death. (*She turns the projector around towards the back of the stage so that there in the space liberated behind the banquet table, the alternating images of the two stars project themselves again. She walks away from the projector.*) I'm going to let it run, Maria. Now I understand you. Oh yes, by God but I've understood you, here lie the elegance and grace and loveliness . . . Let our films run forever, without interruption, let Mother hear us from the upper floor, let her hear our voices and let her die little by little, in her wheelchair, the atrocious old lady, believing she can take our life because she gave us our life, the hypocritical whore older than all the dead, let her die of fury and spite hearing us and believing that we are still alive, imitating life in death, with elegance and grace and loveliness, Maria of the Angels, loving, cold, disdainful, feigning so well that even Death is unresolved if you simulate death as one dead or submit to death as one alive. (*She stops for an instant with a triumphant air. She exclaims:*) "Here lies the purple sleeping/And here lie elegance and grace and loveliness." (*Little by little, without ever turning her back on the film projector, she reaches the door. Her words, all of them titles from Felix and del Rio films, are smothered by the dia-dialogues of the films. The dialogues grow and grow in volume from the voices on the screen as Dolores's voice shrinks and shrinks. The voice enunciates the following titles:*) Resurrection . . . Rio Escondido . . . Wonder Bar . . . Mare Nostrum . . . Evangeline . . . Juana Gallo . . . The Loves of Carmen . . . La Escondida . . . In Caliente . . . Ash Wednesday . . . La Casa Chica . . . Vertigo . . . Flor de Mayo . . . La Malquerida . . . La Paloma . . . French Can Can . . . The Power and the Glory . . . Amok . . . La Otra . . . Lancer Spy . . . Corona Negra . . . Madame DuBarry . . . Mesalina . . . Doña Diabla . . . Les Héros sont fatigués . . . El Monje Blanco . . . (*Dolores rests against the door.*) Resurrection. (*Dolores hangs her head sadly and then, as if by habit, walks to the same place that she occupied at the beginning of the play. She takes her place next to the colonia table and gazes intensely at the audience while the music of* Orchids in the Moonlight *slowly insinuates itself until it drowns the dialogues of the films. Maria, slowly, as if she were a ghost, rises, arranges her hair-do, adjusts her dress and walks to the hall of mirrors. She too freezes facing the audience, her gaze as intense as that of Dolores.*

Then everything comes to an abrupt end. The music. The films. The voices. The lights go out.)

END

ON THE EDITORS

George W. Woodyard is professor of Spanish at the University of Kansas and editor of *Latin American Theatre Review*. He has traveled extensively to observe first-hand the work of groups most active in creating new theatrical modes in Latin America. His publications include *Dramatists in Revolt: The New Latin American Theatre*, edited with Leon Lyday, and *The Modern Stage in Latin America: Six Plays*.

Marion Peter Holt teaches in the Ph.D program in Theatre of the City University of New York and at the College of Staten Island. His translations of contemporary Spanish plays have been staged in New York and in leading regional theatres. He is the editor of *DramaContemporary: Spain* and his articles and reviews have appeared in *Modern Drama, Theatre Journal, Performing Arts Journal*, and *Estreno*.

AAP-9884